HOW TO STAY AHEAD FINANCIALLY

HOW TO STAY AHEAD FINANCIALLY

The Complete Guide to Financial Security in a Changing World

Philip Gordis

W · W · NORTON & COMPANY · INC · NEW YORK

DESIGNER: MARJORIE J. FLOCK

Library of Congress Cataloging in Publication Data
Gordis, Philip, 1911–
How to stay ahead financially.
Includes bibliographical references and index.
1. Insurance, Life—Handbooks, manuals, etc.
2. Insurance, Disability—Handbooks, manuals, etc.
3. Insurance, Health—Handbooks, manuals, etc.
I. Title.
HG8871.G58 1977 368.3'002'02 77-9334

ISBN 0 393 08794 8

2 3 4 5 6 7 8 9 0

TO SAR A. LEVITAN

Contents

III MEDICAL EXPENSE INSURANCE

Acknowledgments

MY THINKING on the subject of this book has matured over some forty years in discussion with colleagues, clients, students, and experts in the several branches of the field of financial planning. To these men and women, too numerous to sort out or enumerate, this book owes a debt. I do wish to single out several individuals who have been involved more directly in the writing of the book. Sar Levitan, economist, and Philip Siller, attorney, read most of the manuscript in course of its preparation. I am deeply indebted to them for many trenchant criticisms and valuable suggestions. Philip Siller and my son, Kent, spent many hours developing and checking the figures in several of the more involved tables cited in the chapters on life insurance and investments. Leonard M. Gold of Bear, Stearns and Co. made an exhaustive study of several life insurance stocks, the result of which is set forth in a rather terse footnote in the Introduction. My daughters, Elizabeth and Susan, typed and retyped the manuscript.

Introduction

Only three out of 10 people who buy life insurance think they know what they are doing . . . Four out of 10 feel uneasy because they are not sure they are getting the right kind of policy . . . Only one out of four people thinks that agents present their products understandably, accurately and honestly . . . Only three out of 10 people think that life insurance companies give them their money's worth.

DOES THIS jaundiced view of the life insurance industry and its sales force emanate from a special interest group? Or from an over-zealous consumer movement that might be suspected of slanting the views of its constituents? Quite the contrary. These opinions were gathered in surveys conducted by the industry's own Institute of Life Insurance, an organization comprised of 212 member companies which account for over 80 percent of the life insurance in force in the United States.

Can the average individual obtain informed and impartial advice on this important element of his financial life? Even the industry's own leaders hold out little promise of this. "Until now," said Richard E. Sauder, president of Kemper Life Insurance Co., the life insurance arm of one of the country's largest insurance conglomerates, "the products and services delivered to the buyer have been dictated by the whims, ineptness, attitude and avarice of the people doing the so-called selling rather than by the desires and needs of the consumer." In a similar vein, Donald S. MacNaughton, president of the Prudential, the nation's largest company, linked what he termed "the most commonplace consumer complaint about the insurance industry, high early lapses" with "high pressure selling tactics." High early lapses may be a "commonplace complaint'' but they cost the American public hundreds of millions of dollars annually.

In the wake of the consumer movement that surfaced in the late 1960s, it was inevitable that the spotlight should be turned on life insurance, a product for which the public laid out over $29 billion in premiums in 1975 alone. The Antitrust and Monopoly Subcommittee of the Committee of the Judiciary of the United States under the vigorous chairmanship of the late Sen. Philip A. Hart gathered comprehensive data on pricing, policy benefits, and other relevant information from 198 companies which were responsible for about 95 percent of the individual ordinary life insurance business of the United States. The results shocked even those who had never held too rosy a view of the industry.

Among other findings, the Subcommittee discovered that ''the cost ranges among similar policies were even greater than we had thought, the rate of return on most policies was very low . . .'' Even more startling was the number of policies consumers had bought and allowed to lapse before paying the second premium.

Extensive hearings were held by the Subcommittee and testimony taken from experts within and outside the industry. In all, the printed record runs to over 3,000 pages. Out of the hearings and data, Sen. Hart developed and introduced a bill ''to protect consumers against unfair or deceptive advertising, promotion, or sales practices.'' The bill would have the Federal Trade Commission establish national standards for ''full, accurate, and clear disclosure of price and other information needed for consumers . . .'' The ability of the consumer to make an informed choice, the Senator felt, is an essential ingredient of the free enterprise system.

The main thrust of the proposed legislation is toward price disclosure. It would mandate the furnishing of yearly information to applicants buying a new policy as well as those paying renewal premiums. The traditional cost figures used in sales presentations for over a century would be replaced or at least supplemented by a more sophisticated cost disclosure system.

That the pricing system being advocated is far from definitive is admitted even by its proponents. While it promises a more realistic approach to the cost question, it opens up a nest of new problems, not least of which is its complexity. The mass of figures to be supplied to a buyer of life insurance is more than likely to leave him as confused as ever. The National Association of Insurance Commissioners, the official organization of the top insurance officials of every state in the country, which had conducted a survey of its own, expressed the fear that "when an index cannot easily be explained, rather than helping consumers locate the best buy, it may cause them not to buy."

Only time will tell whether this verdict is unduly pessimistic. One thing, however, is eminently clear. The Senate Subcommittee, which Ralph Nader termed "the first comprehensive investigation into the life insurance industry in the history of the United States Congress," has done much to highlight the fact that the accepted method of illustrating the cost of a life insurance policy is always misleading, and often deliberately deceptive. Also punctured is the myth that similar policies in different companies cost about the same.

More important than its failure to properly disclose cost is the industry's tragic failure to protect the very widows and orphans over whose fate it purports to be concerned. Thus, the Subcommittee called attention to a "Widow's Study" *done by the life insurance industry itself* which revealed that for middle-income Americans life insurance provided only 5 percent of the average per capita monthly income survivor benefits of $155. This woefully inadequate amount of insurance protection could have been multiplied several times, and for the same premium outlay, by any policyholder armed with an understanding of the true function of life insurance. A buyer so informed would have been less easily deflected from buying maximum protection for his premium dollar by a finely honed and often sincerely misguided sales force which complicates this essentially simple and effective tool with extraneous considerations.

The study also brought to light acutely disturbing facts about the perilously brief life span of much of the life insurance being bought by the public as part of its long-range planning for the future. Thus, in 64 of the 148 companies surveyed, one out of four policyholders who bought the company's best selling cash value policy dropped it within 13 months; in other words, they never paid the second premium. Fifteen of these companies reported lapse rate of 40 to 50 percent. All these policies, lapsed before their second premium was paid, developed no cash values. The policyholders had protection while the policies were in force, but nothing else. Since the same protection was available to them *from the same companies* at one-third or less of the premiums they had paid for the policies they had bought and allowed to lapse, this represented an out-of-pocket loss of hundreds of millions of dollars. According to Sen. Hart, in 1971 policyholders who had bought and lapsed cash value policies from just four of the large New York companies alone lost $25 million in this procedure. And this sad charade is repeated every year. Again as in the matter of inadequate protection touched on in the preceding paragraph, an understanding of life insurance would have made it possible to avoid much of this tragic waste.

There is no question but that the Subcommittee has focused attention on a matter of great importance in the lives of most American families. That the public regards insurance as a serious matter was made clear in the surveys. Sixty percent of the people polled agreed that life insurance is as much a necessity as food, clothing, and shelter.

Senator Hart's bill (S. 2065) was referred to the Senate Commerce Committee but never reached the floor of Congress. If it is reintroduced, and passed, it may indeed furnish an alert consumer with a better tool for comparing different company costs, although its very complexity is likely to dilute its utility. While it must be admitted that one is better off paying less rather than more for a wrong policy, it cannot be denied that even a cheaper wrong policy is still a bad buy. The basic problem is likely to remain virtually unchanged. Unless the consumer gets to understand the fundamental concept of life insurance, he will continue to founder, buffeted about by each new wind that issues forth from the marketing departments of the companies and their energetic sales forces.

Section I of the book addresses itself to the entire question of how to protect one's dependents. In the early chapters, the fundamental concept on which all life policies are based is spelled out in a step-by-step, nontheoretical way. It is only when the "mystery" in which this subject has long been enshrouded is dispelled that a buyer can hope to steer a steady course through the bewildering claims of a highly vocal sales force which comes armed with a hundred different policies and riders.

Section I also discusses the place of group insurance in a total insurance program. Analyzed too are the important optional features offered by companies: double indemnity, triple indemnity, waiver of premium disability, disability income, options to purchase additional insurance, and so forth. The extra premium for these "extras" is comparatively small, and they are usually tacked on with little or no thought, often at the expense of more real insurance needs. Each of these widely sold riders is discussed so that it may be assigned its proper place, if any, in an insurance program.

Five options on the use of dividends are made available to policyholders. Several are completely unacceptable, while some may be useful in individual circumstances. These are analyzed in this section with suggestions on their proper use.

Policyholders are urged by the insurance companies to arrange their life insurance so that the proceeds will be paid to their beneficiaries in installments over a period of years. This administrative service is provided by the companies free of charge and is recommended as a wise step in safeguarding against dissipation by an improvident beneficiary of the funds so prudently set up by a thoughtful Insured during his lifetime. It will be shown that this attempt to "rule with a dead hand" may be fraught with serious consequences.

Protection against death is only one of the many virtues attributed to life insurance by its partisans. The industry has long celebrated its product as the ideal instrument to protect against "living too long" or "dying too soon." These two distinct risks against whose sting insurance is being offered are in fact two of the basic hazards which almost all of us face. For many persons, "dying too soon" will mean leaving loved ones in straitened circumstances. Living long past retirement, on the other hand, unless adequate resources are available to provide a minimum level of comfort, may in fact mean "living too long"—economically at least.

In the course of explicating life insurance it is shown that failure to dissect and analyze each of these hazards separately only leads to confusion and to an unsatisfactory resolution of both contingencies. Prying these two discrete problems apart makes it possible not only to properly evaluate one's individual situation but also to provide an effective answer to both needs.

Also explored in the analysis of the true cost of all policies is the place of cash values in life insurance. It is to these cash values, "living benefits" as they are called, that the companies proudly call attention, pointing out that more than 50 percent of their disbursements are made to the fortunate living. These cash values are the investment factor of life insurance and are championed as the perfect instrument to protect against "living too long."

With the protection element lifted out of the "package," it becomes possible for the first time to take a hard look at the investment side of life insurance. Senator Hart's Subcommittee found that "typically most of the policies had from ½ of 1 percent to 3½ percent rates of return on their savings element." In assessing the worth of any investment, it is important to take into account the factor of liquidity. The already low yields which develop under life insurance policies are available only when the contract is maintained in force for a minimum number of years. The yield on a policy terminated in its early stages is even poorer, often disastrous.

If life insurance was always less than desirable as an investment for the short term, the current scene has rendered it totally unacceptable for any long-range accumulation such as is envisioned in plans for retirement. To the already formidable problems of providing adequate resources against all the hazards that threaten financial security, the recent period has added a new dimension—the spectre of a galloping inflation that eats away at the purchasing power of our dollars. Any long-range planning that fails to come to grips with this sinister force is doomed to founder. The security it promises is certain to prove illusory.

In the steep inflation that followed World War II, the low-keyed murmur of discontent with the investment side of life insurance began to mount. The solidity of life insurance was unquestioned but could one continue to entrust his long-range financial plans to this medium? What kind of dollars could he expect to receive at the end of the line in return for the monies he had so diligently set aside over the years? Safety of principal—unquestionably. But what will the principal buy?

Furthermore, it was becoming obvious that the return which a policyholder could anticipate on his life insurance was most unattractive when measured against the surge in the stock market. Some uncharitable commentators pointed out that a buyer could have entered the life insurance edifice through one of two doors. If he had come in the "front" door and bought a life insurance policy, he could have earned as much as 3½ percent on his investment. On the other hand, had he opted for the "side" door and bought the same company's stock, his investment would have compounded three, four, or five times as rapidly, or even more.*

In this climate, the controversy between "pure protection" policies and "investment" life insurance which had surfaced briefly from time to time over the past century was now again clamoring for an answer. How formidable the impediments can be in the path of one seeking impartial advice on this all-important question may be gleaned from a comparison of the commissions paid to agents on the sale of these two kinds of policies. A $25,000 Whole Life policy sold to a male age 40 in a typical company will produce a first year agent's commission of some $260.00 to $310.00 (depending on the company and the state in which the sale is being made), with an additional $212.00 to $255.00 in renewals over the succeeding nine years, as the premiums are paid—a total of between $472 and $565. On a Term insurance policy of the same face amount, the agent's commission at the point of sale is $55.00 to $78.00 followed by $75.00 to $92.00 in renewals, about one-fourth as much as he would receive for selling the Whole Life policy. Moreover, it must be understood that the problem is much more complex than merely resisting a sales talk by an agent seeking to earn a living. As Ralph Nader, one of the most perceptive consumer advocates, puts it,

* One could, of course, come up with fabulous stock profits if one were to pick the best performers in the life insurance field. But even in the largest stock company in the country, the Aetna Life, an investor reaped a growth averaging 16 percent per year from 1946 to the end or 1965. One did not have to reach too far down in the barrel to come up with much more spectacular results. Thus, over the same period of time, the stock of giant Continental Assurance Company grew at an annual rate of just under 21 percent. Not far behind was the Lincoln National Life. The "poorest" performer among the large companies was the Travelers, but even in this stock, an investor would not have fared too badly, with an annual growth rate of over 14 percent.

"The industry's contrived complexity, secrecy and public relations have fulfilled a strongly supplementary and camouflage function." *

In an effort to absorb the impact of inflation millions of Americans who had never before considered the stock market as within their province moved into securities and were doing quite nicely. Inflation may have begun its sickening upward spiral, but one could face up to it with some equanimity if his stocks were showing a growth rate of 10 percent a year, or better.

This relatively benign state, we now know, was not destined to continue. The market went into a tailspin from which it has only just begun to recover at the time of this writing. Disquieting signs of a serious recession made their appearance. In the face of this downturn in the business cycle, and mounting unemployment, inflation not only failed to abate, but obdurately rose to a staggering double-digit level.

To millions of Americans who had cherished certain truths about thrift and orderly planning for the future, the financial picture has become completely fogged over. Disoriented and confused, they continue to search for some anchor to hold them firm in a stormy sea.

Despite these formidable obstacles, making provisions for one's retirement remains a problem of genuine concern for most of us. Whatever defects life insurance may have as a medium for accumulation over the long term, it does offer an important plus—its thrift-enforcing discipline. If an alternative is to be proposed, it too must permit and encourage the setting aside of relatively small sums on a regular basis, such as is offered by the life insurance policy. The pros and cons of several viable competing candidates for the role of retirement vehicle are set forth with recommendations on the most economical way in which these may be utilized.

While the risk of premature death and an insecure old age are two of the larger hazards that threaten family security, they are by no means the only contingencies that must be faced. The possibility of a long-term disability is seven times as high as that of immediate death for an individual age 22. The ratio declines steadily with advancing age, but even at age 62, disability is still twice as likely as death. A protracted disabil-

* Hearings Before the Subcommittee on Antitrust and Monopoly of the Committee of the Judiciary, U.S. Senate, 93rd Congress, 1st Session, Part 1, p. 6, February 20, 1973.

ity can make a shambles out of almost any plan for financial peace of mind just as certainly as the death of a family head.

Section II of the book, "The Risk of Disability," takes up the question of income loss arising out of disability. It seeks to put the problem into perspective so that premium dollars can be directed toward the most pressing areas of the hazard. As in Section I, it shows how to select the proper coverage at the most economical rates from out of the confusing array of contracts being offered by hundreds of life insurance companies, casualty insurers, and accident and health insurance organizations.

The economic consequences of a disabling accident or illness basically affect only gainfully employed individuals, although they can be severely dislocating in the case of a housewife-mother of a family. By contrast, crippling expenditures for medical, surgical, and hospital care can develop for any family member, not excluding dependent children. The recent period has thrown this problem into sharper relief than any of the others with which most Americans have been struggling. Since 1959, medical costs have risen more rapidly than the Consumer Price Index in every year but two. In 1973, over 50 percent of all personal bankruptcies were the result of bills incurred for medical care. It is undeniable therefore that over the most carefully structured program of financial security is poised the threat of a catastrophic illness or accident.

Section III, "Medical Expense Insurance," takes up this most serious hazard of modern life, the staggering costs of severe illness or accident. No major category of personal expense has risen as sharply as the cost of medical attention, and only the wealthiest can out of their own resources hope to meet the medical, hospital, surgical, and related costs of any but the most routine illness. Hundreds of companies offer insurance against some of the medical expenses attending illness or accident, but these range from those that leave the Insured virtually *un*insured for the most catastrophic situations to those that offer fairly comprehensive coverage.

In Section III, the entire medical expense exposure is studied and the central problem is separated from the lesser issues which becloud the quest for a sound and economical insurance program.

Each section of the book includes a chapter, "How Much and from Whom?" Here are established guidelines with which to measure our needs in the particular area under discussion. Also discussed is the all-important matter of utilizing premium and investment dollars in the most economical way. Until recently, most consumers were convinced that "all insurance was about the same." Some criticism of the product so universally bought did surface from time to time and occasional misgivings were heard about company practices and the more strident selling techniques. But such demurrers were generally confined to sectors of the economic community that were competing for the public's savings dollar or from alert (some said overzealous) consumer advocates who found the companies and their agents somewhat less than devoted to the public welfare. By and large, however, these minority opinions did little to weaken confidence in the stability and efficacy of the life insurance product. For the most part, the public continued to see itself "in good hands."

The consumer "revolution" of the 1970s, the acerb criticisms issuing from a scrappy Commissioner of Insurance in the State of Pennsylvania, and the exhaustive surveys and hearing of the Senate Subcommittee already cited did much to puncture the apparent calm that had reigned so long. Elaborate cost comparisons were undertaken which threw into public view tremendous differences in costs among the hundreds of companies proffering their wares. While these ratings cannot give full weight to all the differences between policies, they do point the way to intelligent choice among the numerous products clamoring for the public's dollars.

"In this world," Benjamin Franklin once wrote in a letter to a friend, "nothing is certain except death and taxes." In all plans for the future, an element of uncertainty inheres. Alert and informed individuals can nevertheless take steps to minimize uncertainty. To have any chance for success in this undertaking, they must first be able to correctly evaluate the several hazards of their economic life, separating those that threaten large-scale loss from those of lesser scope. They must then penetrate the claims and counterclaims that assail them from every side, for only then can they cull the "remedies" that promise genuine security from the nostrums being hawked so skillfully. Finally, to make most effective use of their available dollars, they must be able to call on some objective yardstick of costs.

It is only then that they can make the informed decisions that can build a wall of protection around their economic futures. It is the aim of this book to help persons with no special expertise in these areas to attain this worthwhile objective.

I

THE RISKS OF "LIVING TOO LONG" OR "DYING TOO SOON"

1 · The Risk of Dying Too Soon

FOR WELL OVER a century, life insurance companies have been distributing a product which they recommend as ideal to protect against "living too long or dying too soon." So successfully have they marketed this commodity that these two distinct risks are usually thought of together, although it is reasonably clear that no one can succeed in both living too long and dying too soon. It is important that these hazards be analyzed separately, for only when each one is properly understood and weighed can we see how they are related, if at all.

More for the Living. "Living too long" comes up first in the company slogan. We shall begin, however, by addressing ourselves to the second of the risks enumerated, the more unpalatable one of "dying too soon," because financial protection against death is still the unique commodity which life insurance offers, even though the companies take great pride in the "living benefits" they dispense. In 1975, the American life insurance business disbursed a staggering $22.5 billion. $9.2 billion of this amount, or 41 percent, constituted death benefits; the other 59 percent went to living policyholders.* In Canada, in 1975, the ratio in favor of living policyholders was even higher, with almost two out of every three dollars paid out by Canadian life insurance companies going to this fortunate group.†

Life Insurance Creates an "Immediate Estate." Life insurance is the only way to "create an immediate estate," the industry states, and

* *Life Insurance Fact Book,* American Council of Life Insurance, 1976, p. 44.
† *Canadian Statistical Review,* September 1976 (Statistics Canada, Pub. No. L1-003).

this statement is fundamentally true. Life insurance, like any form of insurance, makes it possible for you to put up a small sum in return for which an insurance carrier forthwith commits itself to pay a comparatively large amount of money if disaster strikes. No substitute for this financial cushion has yet been found, and if one were developed, it would, under some name or other, be life insurance.

Of course, no insurance company could long continue to pay out money it was not in a position to collect from the people it insures. All insurance companies are essentially conduits for passing funds they collect from all their policyholders to the unfortunate few who suffer the risk insured against. They merely pool the resources of the many to provide indemnity to the few who suffer loss.

The Policyholders Pay the Claims. A company could possibly endeavor to pay claims out of its capital, but such "altruism" would necessarily be short-lived. An insurance company's capital is always relatively small in relation to its insurance in force.* The companies are basically solvent because their actuaries can predict with depressing accuracy the number of deaths they will sustain each year. They promulgate adequate premium rates, that is, they collect sufficient money from the insured public to meet these contingencies.

Now if you think of life insurance as you do of your fire or automobile insurance as a pool into which you make annual contributions, and to which you look to be reimbursed in the event of a fire or accident, it should be a relatively simple matter to decide on how much life insurance you need.

Do I Need Life Insurance at All? The question, "How much life insurance do I need?" really leaps over a more basic question: "Do I need life insurance at all?" Much like, "When did you stop beating your wife?" which presumes you to have been guilty of this practice, the

* In the life insurance field, as a matter of fact, most of the larger carriers are mutual companies with no stockholders or invested capital. But even the largest stock company, the Aetna Life Insurance Co., which has over $84 billion of insurance in force, has a capital of just under $63 million. Even if its several comfortable surplus accounts are added, the total amounts to some $370 million.

question presupposes that you do need *some* life insurance. While the question does strictly permit the answer "None," it somehow manages to imply a universal need to which all must respond. "Do I need life insurance?" "Why, doesn't everybody?"

Does Everybody? Life insurance is so firmly entrenched in the American way of life that only a subversive or an irresponsible person, it seems, would be caught without it. This article of faith is so widely accepted that it is almost never held up to scrutiny, and very sizable amounts of life insurance are sold merely by an appeal to one's sense of status. Thus, one of the most successful agents in the country who sells many millions of dollars of this product each year boasts a sales presentation which is disarmingly simple. Basically, he says little more than, "Don't tell me, Mr. X, that a man of your financial standing (or position in the community) only carries $300,000?" (Or $500,000, or $750,000, or whatever figure the shamefaced prospect has supplied.)

Life Insurance as a Status Symbol. Few of us are impervious to the pressure of status. And you alone must decide whether you would lose face if you had to admit to not being heavily insured, or as it's put in the drawing room with a wistful look at the "little woman," being "worth more dead than alive." It is the thesis of this book that the question of carrying life insurance is best viewed as a purely practical one, to be answered primarily by appeal to financial considerations. If you agree with this more mundane approach, you may be in a position to profit from further reading of this book.

Warding off the "Evil Eye." Before we get to the matter at hand, I cannot resist a second "psychological" note which may further help us to consider this question on the basis of its merits alone. I have long felt (although I realize that there is almost no way to prove the point) that one of the motives impelling us to buy insurance of any kind is the desire to ward off the evil being insured against, to "protect" ourselves against its happening. On the rational level, we do not believe, of course, that buying a fire insurance policy will expunge the peril of fire any more than we count on the efficacy of knocking on wood. But subconsciously the insurance premium is felt to be a "tithe" we pay to exorcise the threatening calamity. Some compulsion of this kind, albeit unrealized, operate I believe in our buying of any form of insurance—life insurance, burglary, automobile, credit, and so on. But I think we can agree that this is a talisman of dubious potency and that we would therefore be well advised to put out money for insurance only if there is a possibility of a large-scale loss that we could not absorb out of our own resources.*

When a Risk Needs to Be Transferred. This view of insurance—an expense to be undertaken only when one is exposed to a financial loss which needs to be shifted to a risk-bearing institution—seems clear and unequivocal enough when we think of fire, theft, liability claims, or any of the other risks which fall within the province of fire and casualty insurance. We would certainly give no consideration to a suggestion that we buy insurance on a home we do not own (even if such were possible) or cover ourselves against being sued for accidents arising out of the use of an automobile we do not own, and so on.

If I Had Died Yesterday. If, then, we look upon life insurance in this same way—solely as a device to indemnify those who are dependent on

* In a more real sense, insurance does sometimes serve to soften the impact of casualties. The medical examination required of most prospective buyers of life insurance frequently alerts the applicant to a previously undetected medical problem.

Before issuing some forms of property and liability insurance, companies will inspect the risk being submitted and recommend, and sometimes insist on, steps to reduce the frequency and severity of losses. (In some forms of insurance, as in Boiler and Machinery, for example, a substantial portion of the premiums received is expended on such safety engineering activities.)

Whether the companies are playing as important a role in such loss prevention activities as they should is another matter. Thoughtful observers like Ralph Nader have taken the industry to task for its failure to take a more aggressive role in this important area. Thus he considers job casualties and job diseases to be "A problem at least three times more serious than street crime" and points out that "some countries in Eastern Europe have better health and worker safety standards than we do." The "primary justification for a private insurance system, is [a] systematic dedication to loss prevention, pushing for safety, pushing for health, pushing for pollution control throughout the nation . . ." All quotations excerpted from "Insurance and the Consumer," an address by Ralph Nader at a Conference for the Life Insurance Executive held in Chicago on September 20–21, 1972, sponsored by the Continental Assurance Company, Reinsurance Division.

us for financial support—we could quite readily determine our need for this unique product. Clearly, we would consider ourselves in the market for it if, and only if, we were supporting others, in whole or in part. And even if we did in fact have dependents, we would not consider laying out any money for life insurance unless our assets were not adequate to provide for those who were the objects of our bounty during our lifetime. In short, if life insurance functions solely to create "an immediate estate," as the industry puts it, deciding on the extent of our need for its protection would narrow itself down to answering one basic question: "How would my dependents be fixed if I had died yesterday?" (The well-trained insurance salesman always uses the "if you had died *yesterday*" gambit in preference to "If you were to die *tomorrow*, Mr. Prospect," for the latter is still an open and unpleasant possibility while against having "died yesterday" you feel quite secure.)

Life Insurance vs. Other Forms of Coverage. We find, however, that when we approach our life insurance, the picture becomes vastly more complicated than in the case of other forms of insurance. While our need for fire insurance is a relatively simple matter to pinpoint, our life insurance picture is much more elusive. For the latter lays claim to many virtues over and above its promise to pay our families in the event of our premature death. It is prescribed for a host of other "conditions."

It Takes Arms against a "Sea of Troubles." Thus, it is advocated as an ideal way to provide for a secure old age, a superb medium for our savings and investment dollars, and a very effective tool in establishing a "trust" for our unsophisticated dependents. It can serve to minimize estate and income taxes, we are assured, and is an essential ingredient of any plan to assure the orderly continuance of a partnership or closely held corporation. It can be used to assure the loyalty of employees through pension and profit-sharing programs. Young people who have no one looking to them for support, and may actually themselves be dependent on others, are exhorted to buy life insurance because it is cheaper now "than it will ever be again." Millions of policies are purchased by parents on the lives of infants for the sole purpose of accumulating a "college fund" or to give the youngster a "start in life" when he reaches maturity. The protean life insurance product, it appears, emerges in ever new guises to "take arms against a sea of troubles."

In this book, I hope to exfoliate this luxuriant tree and examine each of its layers separately. In the interest of an orderly analysis of this many-sided question, however, we shall first address ourselves to the "death protection" features of the product, bearing in mind that this severely oversimplified approach is tolerated only for purposes of discussion.

Now if the need to provide some continuance of support to those who are dependent on us is the primary motive for buying life insurance, we will consider its purchase only to the extent that any assets we possess plus any provisions made by the Government for our dependents would leave a void in our family's economic picture.

"Scientific" Programming of Your Needs. As soon as we focus on the amount of life insurance our situation warrants, we are urged to "program" or plan our estate *scientifically*. The life insurance agent, or underwriter, as he may prefer to be called, is ready to help in this somewhat elaborate rite. On a set of impressive forms furnished him by the company he asks you to project your family's economic needs for many years in the future after you are deceased. With a nod in the direction of the electronic revolution, many companies now feed the data into their computer. The solution to the prospect's problem then appears in very impressive "printout" form, which of course tends to allay any lingering doubts about its "scientific" character.

Think in Terms of Monthly Income. In any event, the cornerstone of estate planning, we are given to understand, is "thinking in terms of monthly income" rather than lump sums. The agent will point out to you, and not without justice, that $25,000, which is an impressive sum of money to most people, will provide an income of $880 a month for less than three years. He will propose that you first decide on a fixed sum to take care of last expenses, which goes by the somewhat grisly name of "clean-up fund." After this contingency has been covered, your family's security plan should be laid out in terms of monthly income for the fatherless family. Once you have structured these monthly incomes, your attention will be directed toward the college expenses of your children, and then possibly to giving them "a start in life." When all your long-ago-orphaned children have been firmly set on their life's path, a relatively small income should suffice to carry your aging widow through a serene, grandmotherly old age.

The estate planner will usually "credit" you with any survivors' benefits to which you may be entitled under Social Security and any liquid assets which you may possess, although he generally tends to downgrade the latter unless they consist of cash or high-grade bonds, or possibly top-grade blue chip stocks. If you own all or part of a small business, he will usually emphasize the ephemeral nature of this interest, particularly if the continued prosperity of the business is dependent in large part on your own services. If you own your own home, he will recommend a policy to "pay off the mortgage" and leave your bereaved family to mourn in a free-and-clear dwelling.

A Whopper of a Figure. The family's financial "map," even after all these credits have been tolled, almost always produces a surprisingly high figure for the life insurance required by the average family head (which helps to explain the zeal which life insurance agents frequently display in the pursuit of this technique). But this should not serve to denigrate the value of this form of planning, which does help to concretize the gap between what we now have and what our family would need if we were removed from their midst. A full discussion of this device, together with a set of charts to work with, will be found in Chapter 13.

Choosing from among 100 Different Policies. For the purposes of our discussion, let us assume that you have made the necessary calculations and have settled on the amount of life insurance you feel you should carry to provide some measure of financial security to those you leave behind. Or that you have postponed the chore, important though you realize it to be, and have settled somewhat arbitrarily on an amount of life insurance to provide an economic "cushion" to your dependents. A loose rule of thumb sometimes invoked calls for insurance equivalent to at least five years' earnings.* But this "guideline" is obviously subject to important variations, depending on the number and ages of your dependents, the skills of your wife and her earning potential, and numerous unpredictable vagaries of the future.

In any event, you have in one way or another settled on an amount and are ready to make application to a life insurance company. But at this point, you find yourself facing a decision you didn't have to make when you set out to buy any other form of insurance. For there is now spread out in front of you a bewildering array of different policies which offer protection for premiums ranging from approximately $4 to over $100 per 1,000.

It is not unusual to find over 100 different policies in a company's portfolio plus an awe-inspiring collection of riders, special features, benefits, and options which permit almost endless permutations and combinations. In the face of such a spectacular galaxy of products (surely a tribute to the fecundity of the companies' merchandising talents), you may understandably lose confidence in your ability to make a decision. You are ready to surrender yourself completely to the "good hands" of initiates in this arcane lore.

A Consoling Note. Be reassured that the picture is not as dark as it might appear. One relatively simple idea underlies all the myriad forms of life insurance now being offered and any that will issue from the drawing boards of the companies in the future. Once you have mastered this concept, you can make it work for you most effectively.

"Pure" Protection against Death. You will recall we agreed, purely for didactic purposes, to assume that the sole function of life insurance is to create "an immediate estate," that is, to provide some economic security for dependents. In this light, you would then look for a policy which takes into account only the actual risk of death (the mortality hazard) and bases its premiums on this hazard, plus a charge to cover company overhead.

This is of course precisely the way you handle your fire insurance,

* In actuality, the total amount of life insurance in force is closer to only two years' income.

automobile insurance, as well as insurance on your business and all other property and liabilities you wish to cover. It would also appear to be a sensible approach to your personal coverages—accident and health, hospital and medical care—*and* your life insurance.

Enter Term Insurance. Such life insurance, with premiums limited to the actual cost of insuring against death plus a factor to cover the company's operating expenses is, in fact, available to everyone except persons in certain hazardous occupations. This form of insurance which carries the lowest premium per $1,000 of protection is usually known as *Term* insurance although it sometimes carries other more appealing names such as Family Security, Income Protector, and so on. Practically every company offers several Term insurance policies, which differ only as to the period for which each is written. Term insurance is also very commonly sold as a rider on other "permanent" policies. In a later chapter, we will deal with the relative merits of different Term policies; here, we are concerned only with the basic question of Term insurance as it compares with other more commonly purchased plans.

Why the Premium Must Go Up. At this point we digress briefly to comment on a feature of Term insurance which we should understand if we are to make any real progress in planning our financial future. As indicated, the Term insurance premium is calculated to cover the cost of insurance against death. Since the percentage of death, we all know, increases with advancing years, it is evident that the premium for any Term policy must of necessity go up steadily to reflect the increasing mortality. Thus, Annual Renewable Term insurance increases in premium each year; a 5-year Term policy every five years, a 10-year policy every ten years, and so on.

Or the Amount of Insurance Comes Down. It is possible, however, to write a Term insurance policy which does *not* increase in premium with the passing years. But since the inexorable rise in mortality is still to be contended with, such a policy can maintain a level premium only by *decreasing the amount of insurance,* for the same premium will buy less insurance each year as the age of the Insured advances. There are then *two* forms of Term insurance—level *amount* Term insurance with increasing premiums, or level *premium* Term insurance which decreases in amount. A moment's reflection will show that these two forms of Term insurance are really only mirror images of each other. Each in its own way—the level *amount* policy with its steadily increasing premium or the level *premium* policy with its steadily decreasing amount—reflects the fact that the cost of providing insurance protection against death must increase as the policyholder gets older.

Does Everybody Buy the Lowest Premium Policy? To return now to our original theme, if life insurance sought to provide protection only against death, we would expect it to materialize in one or another form of Term insurance. Or that in any event, regardless of the staggering variety of policies put forth to attract the consumer's dollar, the public would respond only to Term insurance since it offers the lowest possible outlay per $1,000. The facts, however, are quite different—almost directly the opposite. Term insurance makes up only a relatively small, albeit a constantly increasing percentage of the total insurance sold by most companies.

Term Insurance Suitable Only for Temporary Purposes? Almost universally, life insurers indoctrinate their agents to consider Term insurance as suitable only for certain limited purposes. It is characterized as "temporary insurance" or as "designed to meet the need for protection covering a limited period of years at low cost" or as "not suitable for normal purposes of life insurance protection." It is put forth as generally suitable only to cover special needs, like the mortgage on a home or other financial obligations in the process of being paid off.

That Term insurance is not "permanent" insurance is only one of the objections that are brought to bear on a prospect who evinces an interest in this low-premium protection. An even more shattering argument against its purchase is the charge that it is actually the most *expensive* of all plans, *"when properly understood."*

Is Cheap Really Dear? "You mean that a policy which costs $4 per $1,000 is more expensive than one which develops a premium of $20 or $30 or $45 for the same amount of protection?" you ask incredulously.

"Exactly, and there are figures to prove it!" you are assured. "The apparently low premium of Term insurance is only the tip of the iceberg," you are warned, "hiding the bitter truth that this form of insurance is the most expensive of all, and by far." In the face of such a charge, all other discussion of the pros and cons of Term insurance would appear irrelevant.

In the next chapter, we shall seek to unravel this tantalizing paradox. We have not forgotten our pact—that it is only for purposes of discussion that we consider insurance solely as "death protection." And we shall in good time explore the other ends which this polymorphous commodity promises to serve.

First, however, we must see what we can make of this apparent self-contradiction, that is, low premiums result in higher cost. This unraveling of the contradiction will give us an understanding of the one essentially simple principle on which *all* life insurance is based. And this insight, I hope to show, will give us the power to dissolve all the dilemmas that seem to hover over the question.

What Does Term Really Cost? Although it is lowest in premium Term insurance is actually the most expensive, it is maintained, when you "really figure it out." How much something costs, you are reminded gravely, is a function not alone of what you put down for it, but also of what you can get back. This seems irrefutable, and a set of coldly impartial figures is at hand to back up this sage observation.

A period of time over which this question is to be studied is decided upon, usually 20 years. The premiums you will pay out are totaled and the *guaranteed* cash value of your policy at the end of this period is subtracted from your total premiums. (If the policy is on a participating plan, which returns a part of the premium each year in what is euphemistically known as a dividend, these refunds are deducted from the premiums as well.) The resulting figure is your true out-of-pocket cost for insurance, and no right-minded person would question it. This computation is generally called a "net cost analysis" and is employed to compare the costs of different policies in any one company, or to check out how different companies stack up against each other.

Enter Net Cost. So that you may see how this works out in practice, we reproduce, in Table I, a typical "net cost analysis" commonly invoked to compare the cost of a Whole Life policy with a 5-Year Renew-

TABLE I. FACE AMOUNT OF INSURANCE: $25,000.
MALE, AGE 40

Whole life policy annual premium	*Year*	*5-Year term policy annual premium*
$471.75	1	$139.75
471.75	2	139.75
471.75	3	139.75
471.75	4	139.75
471.75	5	139.75
471.75	6	198.25
471.75	7	198.25
471.75	8	198.25
471.75	9	198.25
471.75	10	198.25
471.75	11	303.00
471.75	12	303.00
471.75	13	303.00
471.75	14	303.00
471.75	15	303.00
471.75	16	512.50
471.75	17	512.50
471.75	18	512.50
471.75	19	512.50
471.75	20	512.50
$9,435.00	Total Premiums Paid—20 years	$5,767.50
− 8,700.00	Less Cash Surrender Available	− 000.00
$735.00	Net Cost—20 years	$5,767.50
$36.75	Average Annual Cost for $25,000 of Insurance	$288.37
$1.47	Average Annual Cost per $1,000 of Insurance	$11.53

able Term policy. The figures, for a male age 40, are those of the Aetna Life Insurance Company. Its nonparticipating (no dividend) policies make our calculations simpler than they would be in the case of dividend-paying companies, and it is for this reason alone that this company is being used. No comparison, invidious or otherwise, of the Aetna with its competitors is intended.

The 5-Year Renewable Term policy, you will note, increases in premium every five years; the premium for the Whole Life policy remains level throughout the period.

You Pay More but You Get More Back. Over the 20-year period, the outlay for Term insurance is $5,767.50. The policy has *no* cash value. So all your money is "down the drain" as it is put. For the Whole Life policy, a total of $9,435.00 has been paid in premiums. This is almost twice as much as for Term insurance, it is true. But under the Whole Life policy, the policyholder has amassed a *guaranteed* cash value of $8,700.00. And this is a pretty big "but," you are cautioned to remember.

When the cash value of the Whole Life policy to which the Insured is entitled is deducted from the premiums he prudently paid out over the years, his out-of-pocket cost for the $25,000 of protection is only $735.00—$9,435.00 in premiums *less* his cash surrender value of $8,700.00. This comes to $36.75 per year for the $25,000 of insurance protection, or only $1.47 per $1,000. Contrast this situation with that of the individual who bought Term insurance. He has no cash value at all. The entire $5,767.50 which he paid in premiums must be chalked up to out-of-pocket costs. This comes to $11.53 per $1,000.00 of insurance per annum. The "net cost" of the Term policy is almost *eight times* as high as for Whole Life. "Cheap is dear" is the triumphant but apparently inescapable conclusion.

More Bargains. Even more exciting "bargains" can be turned up in the grab-bag of policies offered by the average company through this kind of "net cost" analysis. Incredible though it may seem, this numbers game can conjure up policies which cost nothing! Thus, applying the same "net cost" yardstick to another policy of the Aetna Life, the 20-Payment Life, we come up with a *minus* "net cost." The premium for $25,000.00 of this plan is $752.50 (as compared with $471.75 for Whole Life). Over 20 years, you pay out a total of $15,050.00 but your guaranteed cash value at the end of this period is $15,450.00—$400 *more* than all your premiums. And you have been insured all through the years "for free." The policy develops a "return over cost" as it is called, of 80¢ per $1,000 per year. And if a "profit" of 80¢ per $1,000 doesn't tempt you, there are even more irresistible goodies available. For example, at this same age, an annual premium of $1,089 will buy $25,000 of 20-Year Endowment. This particular policy for which the policyholder will pay out $21,780 over 20 years has a guaranteed cash value of $25,000, leaving him with a "profit" of $3,220, or $161 per year—an annual "return over cost" of a whopping $6.44 for *each $1,000 of insurance*. Not only do you get insurance protection for free, but you end with a handsome "profit" in your pocket, if you live. And obviously, the more you buy, the more money you make. Surely, a "wondrous strange phenomenon."

I wish fervently I could leave you this vision of an alluring oasis in a world where everything costs, but sad to say, the "rude truth" is that it is only a mirage. The facts of the case are very different, as shall be demonstrated to your satisfaction, I hope, in the next chapter.

2 What Does Term Insurance Really Cost?

THE "NET COST" analysis in the preceding chapter, you will recall, proposed to compare the costs of two policies—Whole Life and Term. It took for granted that when two different individuals of the same age set out to establish identical estates of $25,000, each needs $25,000 of insurance, *regardless of the type of policy selected.* At first, this certainly seems the only way to correctly relate the cost of different policies, that is, to compare the policies of like amount. And yet, strange as it may seem, this would *not* be comparing *equal* things, but rather *unequal* things—apples and oranges, so to speak.

"How can this be?" you ask in understandable confusion. The answer, which may seem somewhat elusive at first, is really quite simple. And as it is a point of the widest import to our entire understanding of life insurance, I would ask that you pay most careful attention to it.

You and Your Neighbor—Creating Equal Estates. Assume that you and your neighbor are both 40 years old and that you both decide to set up "estates" of $25,000 for your families in the event of your death. You elect to buy a $25,000 Whole Life policy while your neighbor opts for Term insurance.

Your $25,000 Whole Life policy carries an annual premium of $471.75. (We are again using the rates of the Aetna Life Insurance Company for the reasons already stated.) To match the $25,000 estate you have just set up in your Whole Life policy, your neighbor, who is buying Term insurance, does not need to buy *$25,000* of insurance. If he buys only $24,666.34 of Term insurance, his premium will be $138.09—$333.66 less than the $471.75 you are paying for your

$25,000 of Whole Life insurance. And if he now sets this difference of $333.66 aside in a bank (or hides it under the mattess or a floor board of his home), his "estate" in the event of his death will be equal to yours, for the insurance company will pay the face amount of his Term policy, $24,666.34, which when added to the $333.45 in the bank (or other depository) will equal $25,000. Obviously then you will both have laid out the same amount of money, and in the event of your deaths, each beneficiary would have $25,000.

To carry on with our study of the true cost of Term insurance, we will have your neighbor prudently deposit the money he "saves" each year on his insurance (the difference between his premium and yours) in a bank or other savings institution, and we will credit him with 6 percent interest per annum on his money. As this fund grows, your neighbor will reduce his insurance, carrying only enough to make up the *difference* between his cash in the bank and the $25,000 he wishes to leave behind in the event of his death.

The End of the Line. Let's assume you both go merrily on your respective ways for 20 years. How would you then emerge at the end of the line?

Table II charts the results of this somewhat involved transaction over a 20-year period. Because this table is central to any real understanding of the life insurance principle, we will have occasion to refer to it again on several occasions.

Let us look at the situation as it really is. Your cash value in the Whole Life policy at the end of the Twentieth year is $8,700. Your neighbor who has been insured under a Term policy and has been stashing away the money he saved each year in premiums has $10,666.81—$1,966.81 *more* than you (over 22 percent more).

True Cost vs. "Net Cost"—Piercing the Veil. Quite clearly, our analysis produces results very different from the "net cost" analysis which is hallowed by usage in the industry. Far from having paid seven times as much as you paid under your Whole Life insurance (as the so-called "net cost" analysis purports to show), your neighbor is actually substantially ahead of you. You have both paid out exactly the same sums each year during the 20-year period. The cash available to you in the Whole Life policy is $8,700; your neighbor has accumulated $10,666.81.

TABLE II. AN ALL-IMPORTANT COMPARISON.
TERM INSURANCE AND SEPARATE SAVINGS FUND
ACCUMULATED AT 6 PERCENT

Year	*B/F fund*[a]	*Prem. rate*[b]	*AMT. of insurance*	*Premium*	*Prem. savings*[c]	*Savings fund*	*Total estate*[d]
1	0.00	4.99	24,666.34	138.09	333.66	333.66	25,000.00
2	333.66	4.99	24,310.88	136.31	335.44	689.12	25,000.00
3	689.12	4.99	23,932.20	134.42	337.33	1,067.80	25,000.00
4	1,067.80	4.99	23,528.79	132.41	339.34	1,471.21	25,000.00
5	1,471.21	4.99	23,099.03	130.26	341.49	1,900.97	25,000.00
6	1,900.97	7.33	22,694.58	181.35	290.40	2,305.42	25,000.00
7	2,305.42	7.33	22,262.69	178.19	293.56	2,737.31	25,000.00
8	2,737.31	7.33	21,801.50	174.81	296.94	3,198.50	25,000.00
9	3,198.50	7.33	21,309.04	171.20	300.55	3,690.96	25,000.00
10	3,690.96	7.33	20,783.17	167.34	304.41	4,216.83	25,000.00
11	4,216.83	11.52	20,307.35	248.94	222.81	4,692.65	25,000.00
12	4,692.65	11.52	19,797.11	243.06	228.69	5,202.89	25,000.00
13	5,202.89	11.52	19,249.94	236.76	234.99	5,750.06	25,000.00
14	5,750.06	11.52	18,663.19	230.00	241.75	6,336.81	25,000.00
15	6,336.81	11.52	18,033.98	222.75	249.00	6,966.02	25,000.00
16	6,966.02	19.90	17,507.67	363.40	108.35	7,492.33	25,000.00
17	7,492.33	19.90	16,938.46	352.08	119.67	8,061.54	25,000.00
18	8,061.54	19.90	16,322.84	339.82	131.93	8,677.16	25,000.00
19	8,677.16	19.90	15,657.03	326.57	145.18	9,342.97	25,000.00
20	9,342.97	19.90	14,936.95	312.25	159.50	10,063.05	25,000.00
21	10,666.81						

[a] Fund at beginning of year.
[b] Based on 5-Year Renewable and Convertible Term; Premium per $1000 (plus $15 policy fee) Age 40 through 44: $4.99; Age 45 through 49: $7.33; Age 50 through 54: $11.52; Age 55 through 59: $19.90.
[c] Between Whole Life premium of $471.75 and premium for Term insurance.
[d] Amount of Term insurance plus amount of savings fund. This is the minimum that will be available at the beginning of any policy year. The total estate will actually be higher if death occurs at any other point than the beginning of the policy year, since the savings fund will have increased by the interest earned to the date of death.

A Few Minor Caveats—For the Record. Before proceeding, we would note here a certain arbitrariness in the "You and Your Neighbor" figures on which our case is posited. First, it should be pointed out that the cost relationship of the two policies could differ in companies other than the one used in our model. Second, the edge which one policy enjoys might shift if our hypothetical purchasers were older or younger than the age we used. A further change in the balance would develop if policy amounts other than $25,000 were tested, due to the almost universal practice of scaling down premium rates as the size of the policy is increased. Then again there are different methods of computing reserves and other policies might show slight variations in the cash available. Policies issued on a participating (dividend-paying) basis could show up differently, too.

While any of these factors may cause a shift in favor of one or the other type of policy, none is of sufficient substance to affect the basic point being made. The protection purchased in a Term policy does not cost eight times as much as Whole Life insurance, or three times as much, or twice as much. Term insurance protection is certainly no more expensive than any other form of life insurance as might be expected in a business which prides itself on its scientifically calculated rate structure. After all, it should come as no surprise that individuals insured under Term policies do not exhibit higher mortality than their contemporaries insured under higher premium forms of life insurance.* It is of the utmost importance that this point be clearly understood and remembered. We must keep the spotlight trained on the usual "net cost" analysis in order to expose its fundamental hollowness, that is, to show that one need not avoid buying Term insurance because of its alleged expensiveness.

Possible Tax Consequences—A More Important Consideration. A more important demurrer can be entered by those who point out that the cash savings fund accumulated by your neighbor in a bank or other de-

* There is a fairly impressive amount of discussion in life insurance circles as to the effect of "adverse selection" by Term policyholders. It is held by some that persons insured under Term policies tend to discontinue their insurance as the premiums increase unless they have become uninsurable in which case they "hang on for dear life," despite the mounting burden of the accelerating premiums. As a consequence, this group of policyholders, it is contended, show higher than average mortality. This somewhat technical question should not obscure the basic thrust of our analysis, as any "adverse selection" is already reflected in the figures adduced above.

pository would generally be subject to income taxes, while the cash surrender value of the Whole Life policy is free of such impost. Obviously, the extent to which this difference in tax treatment may alter the picture will depend on an individual's tax bracket, but its importance should not be exaggerated. To show that our point remains entirely sound, we have set forth in the Appendix a revised set of figures which reflect the attrition in the outside savings fund for a taxpayer in a 33 percent tax bracket.* Under these circumstances, the Term policy holder is no longer ahead at the end of 20 years, but even after taxes, he is still almost even with his Whole Life carrying "competitor," actually $727.83 behind, or about 8 percent. And as will be shown later, to look only at the comparative results at the end of a 20-year period is to overlook the exposure to severe losses in earlier years. In any event, the study is not intended to counter the meaningless net cost analysis which alleges that Term insurance is the most expensive form of life insurance with the equally jejeune statement that it is a "hot bargain." The involved computations are invoked to show that there is no warrant for the allegation that Term insurance is the most expensive way to protect against the economic consequences of death—that it is actually no more costly than other forms. The decision as to the proper way to insure oneself can now be made on the basis of facts, not chimeras.

Your neighbor's method of insuring his life, actually cutting down on the size of his policy each year was not spelled out as a recommended method of buying life insurance, but merely to expose the hollowness of the widely used "net cost" analysis which seeks to damn Term insurance on the grounds of its high cost.

A Bugaboo Dispelled. The Term policy much maligned at least with respect to its cost, can now be readmitted "separate but equal" alongside its formerly more respectable rivals. Released from the paralyzing

* A married taxpayer with two children will have to earn $30,000 in order to be in a 33 percent tax bracket. An individual in a lower tax bracket will of course suffer less attrition in the outside savings fund. By the same token, any return on the fund in excess of 6 percent will tip the balance further in favor of the Term/separate savings technique. Thus, a taxpayer who earns 5 percent after taxes on the fund will accumulate $9,223.08 or $523.08 more than his Whole Life carrying neighbor. A 7 percent yield would produce $12,332.59; 8 percent would produce $14,253.77, and so on.

fear that Term insurance costs eight times as much as Whole Life, or 20 times as much as 20-payment, we can continue unfettered in our quest for a sound financial security plan.

At the risk of appearing to be beating a dead dog, we shall return to this concept in the next chapter where we turn the spotlight on the central core of all insurance policies. There, it is hoped, any lingering ambiguity that may still appear to plague the question will finally be dispelled.

3 The Common Core of All Life Insurance

One picture may be worth a thousand words, but although they serve to illustrate a point, charts and tables do not partake of this magic, and most people tend to be put off by severe columns of figures. Nevertheless, the "You and Your Neighbor" figures of the preceding chapter (Table II) and another set soon to appear are so crucial to an understanding of life insurance that we will have to refer to them again and again. We can only hope that repeated contact will soon serve to make them feel like an old friend.

Let us look back now at Table II. A glance at the Amount of Insurance column shows that the Term coverage being maintained is reducing each year; the Whole Life policy, by contrast, seems to remain level. But what is actually at work is a very interesting process.

The Overpayment in Whole Life Policies. The Term insurance policy is "death protection" only. Thus, the premium for a Term policy is no more than is needed to cover the mortality risk. Obviously, then, under any higher premium form, some payment in *excess* of the actual mortality cost is being collected. It is this extra money that accumulates as a reserve similar to the fund your neighbor is setting aside in his savings account. It makes up the cash value available to the policyholder while he is living. If the policyholder dies before he has withdrawn his cash value and the Company is called upon to pay a death claim, the Company has this cash reserve available to it. It needs to add to this sum only the *difference* between this fund and the face amount of the policy.

Cash Values Reduce Real Risk of Company. The cash reserve, it can be seen, actually reduces the Company's risk, the "net amount at risk," as it is known. Each year the policy holder lives, the cash reserve of his policy *increases,* the amount of true risk *decreases.* Thus, in the example we have been using, if death occurs in the twentieth year, under a Whole Life policy, the Company's risk is not $25,000, but $16,300, since the Company already has on hand a reserve of $8,700. This same mechanism is at work in every cash value policy from the moment it is purchased. Thus, at the end of the tenth year, the policyholder could surrender his policy and receive his surrender value of $3,575. If now he does not ask for the cash and the policy matures as a death claim (he dies) the Company needs to add only $21,425 to the cash fund to make up the face amount of $25,000 for which it is liable. If he had been insured for 15 years, his cash surrender value would be $5,500 and the Company's "net amount at risk" would have been reduced to $19,450, the difference between the cash reserve and the face amount.*

Common Core of All Cash Value Policies. In all cash value policies, as opposed to Term, only a portion of each premium is needed to cover the Company's mortality expense, the mortuary fund as it is known technically, and the balance is invested for the policyholder. It is this excess over the mortality expense which becomes the basis of the cash and loan values of the insurance policy.

If we appear to belabor this point it is because we have found this apparently simple fact to be more elusive than it seems, and all too frequently misunderstood or overlooked. The combination in *all* life insurance policies (other than Term) of two distinct elements—protection and savings—lies at the heart of the life insurance mechanism, and no informed decision on the place of life insurance in one's financial planning is possible without a firm grasp of this concept.†

* We are deliberately glossing over the difference between cash surrender values and reserves, although the latter are frequently higher than the former, particularly in the early years of a contract. The "net amount at risk" is technically reduced even more sharply than shown in our tables. For our purposes, this lack of rigor is of little consequence.

† This critical point is misunderstood and therefore misrepresented not only by those who deprecate Term insurance in favor of cash value policies. Consumer-minded "termites"

From Theory to Practice. Because an understanding of this piquant amalgam in most life insurance policies of savings and protection is central to our entire thesis, we shall offer in evidence an example of how this works out in a "real life" situation.

Assume you have been inspired by an advertisement of a bank in your locality to embark on a "Programmed Thrift Plan." You set yourself a goal of accumulating $25,000 in 20 years to take yourself and your wife on an extended trip around the world (or for some other purpose which savings institutions and insurance companies consider worthy objectives for your "sunset years").

The bank employee consults his charts and informs you that an annual deposit of $762 at a rate of interest which he projects for the coming 20 years will produce the desired result.

What If You Don't Live? You are ready to leave the bank, proud of your far-sightedness and quietly aglow with a sense of accomplishment when the banker brings you back to earth with this sobering question, "Mr. Saver, you've just taken an important first step on the road to financial security for yourself and your wife. That's all very good, if you make it through the next 20 years. But what if you don't?" he asks gravely. "Where would this leave your wife (and children)?"

Your complacency is deflated as you admit the trenchancy of the question. Mercifully, the banker does not allow you to long wallow in despair. With a smile, he explains to you that you can take care of this contingency very easily by going across the street to the XYZ Life Insurance Company office where you can purchase a special policy that has been designed to take care of this very problem. Known as "The Programmed Thrift Special Protector Policy" this marvelous policy is most sensitively attuned to your newly opened savings account. The amount of insurance in the policy will decrease each year by the precise amount by which your savings account is increased. The savings account together with the amount of insurance in the Decreasing Term

---

(as they have been dubbed) all too often mire down in the same bog of confusion and impute sinister practices to the insurance industry. These charges are in the main unwarranted and frequently impel life insurance buyers to precipitous and unwise actions with respect to their existing insurance, as will be shown in a later chapter.

policy *at each and every point during the next 20 years* will always total $25,000, never more and never less.

A Brilliant Solution. You gratefully seize upon this brilliant device to insure against your dying before the completion of your thrift program. You now have two documents in hand—a regular savings account and a Decreasing Term policy. (If you work or live in Connecticut, Massachusetts, or New York whose savings banks sell regular life insurance in a separate department, you could accomplish both ends under the same roof, but the net result would be quite the same.)

Known to you or not, a program of the kind we have projected would be the equivalent of a 20-Year Endowment policy. The traditional 20-Year Endowment Policy does in *one* document what the two pieces of paper do for you, that is, guarantees to pay your beneficiary the face amount of the policy should you die within the 20-year period, and assures you of this amount in cash if you survive to the end of this time.

Varying the Ingredients. The "Programmed Thrift Plan" alluded to above sets $25,000 as the goal for both your savings *and* your life insurance protection. But since you are buying the life insurance protection separate and apart from your savings plan, you could quite easily vary either of the amounts in almost any proportion you desire. Thus, you might set yourself a more modest savings goal—to accumulate only $12,500 at the end of 20 years, but *without decreasing the protection* in the event of your death during that period. In other words, you could start a savings program aimed at reaching only $12,500 at the end of the 20 years but still buy enough Decreasing Term insurance to make up the difference between the sum on hand at any point and *$25,000*. This latter program would understandably require *more* life insurance protection all along the line, since you would be saving at a slower rate and as a consequence the Term insurance would need to come down more gradually. You might even elect a $25,000 protection figure for your beneficiary with a still smaller savings goal, say $7,000, and so on.

By way of illustration, the three above programs can be charted as follows:

PLAN A	PLAN B	PLAN C
$25,000 death protection	*$25,000 death protection*	*$25,000 death protection*
$25,000 cash accumulation	*$12,500 cash accumulation*	*$ 7,000 cash accumulation*

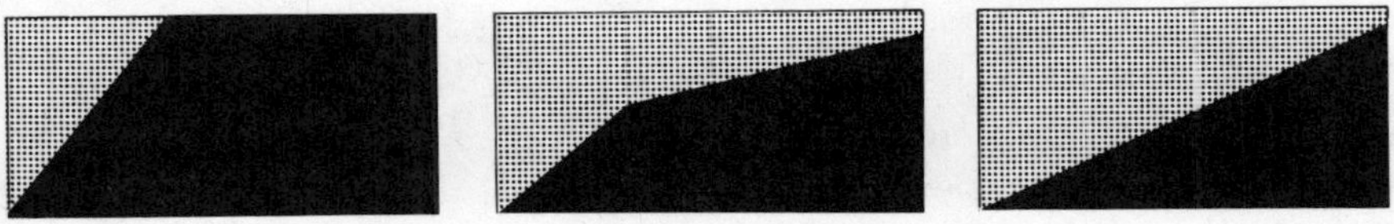

The shaded areas in each instance represent the annually increasing cash fund, the unshaded portion is the amount of decreasing Term insurance. Under all three programs, and at any point during the 20-year period, the two funds equal $25,000, payable to the beneficiary. Note that under Plan A, the cash is growing more rapidly than under either of the other two plans, and as a consequence, the decreasing Term insurance (the unshaded portion) is reducing most rapidly. Under Plan B, the rate of cash growth is less than under Plan A and the Term insurance protection is decreasing less sharply, while under Plan C, with the slowest rate of cash accumulation, the death protection ("the net amount at risk") is declining at the slowest rate of all.

The three programs touched on above, which vary only in the proportion of savings to insurance, are actually rough equivalents of three of the stalwarts in insurance companies' rate books. The package which combined a $25,000 savings goal with $25,000 of life insurance if the saver dies before completing his program is the 20-Year Endowment. The combination of a $12,500 savings goal with $25,000 of life insurance protection in the event of death during the 20-year period is fairly close to a 20-Payment Life policy which is urged on loving fathers who would introduce their young sons to the virtues of thrift. The $25,000 insurance with $7,000 available in cash if the Insured survives for 20 years is much akin to the Whole Life policy, the single most popular policy being sold today. Actually, an almost endless variety of policies can be created by changing the "mix" of savings and death protection.

Variations on a Theme. All life insurance policies (other than Term insurance) are merely variations on this basic theme, combinations of savings and protection; they differ only in the proportion in which these ingredients are mixed. Term insurance consists entirely of one of these ingredients, protection against death, and makes no provision for the accumulation of a cash fund; all other policies without exception combine *both* elements. This is true of every one of the over 100 policies that many companies offer and will be true of any "new" product that issues from the drawing boards. "Life insurance policies may be regarded as combinations of pure protection (indemnity at death) and investment (accumulated savings), the proportions of these ingredients varying with different types of contracts" is the way one standard text on insurance puts it.*

A Hard Fact of Actuarial Science. In any policy which accumulates a cash reserve, the amount of protection decreases constantly. It is important to understand that this rather simple but crucial concept is not a matter of opinion, held by some and disputed by others. It is a hard fact of actuarial science. In his widely used book on life insurance, the vice-president and actuary of one of America's leading life companies states, "When a policy becomes a death claim, the accumulated excess payments, i.e., the reserve in respect of that policy, makes up part of the amount payable. Thus, the actual 'insurance' or 'risk' is constantly being reduced."†

After you have grasped this concept and made it part of your thinking, you will be insulated against chasing mirages. You may feel somewhat deprived at first at having to give up such delectable products as "cheap insurance" or "free insurance" or insurance policies that promise you free insurance plus a "handsome profit." The cold air of reality when it is first admitted may be a bit harsh but it will prove bracing in the long run, and you will be deaf to siren songs that would beguile you from a sensible quest for a genuine solution to your economic problems.

* Robert Riegel and Jerome S. Miller, *Insurance Principles and Practices.* Englewood Cliffs, N.J.: Prentice-Hall, Inc., 1959, p. 137.

A standard work on insurance law characterizes life insurance as "principally a contract of investment." Endowment insurance with its relatively high mix of cash values in relation to insurance protection is "primarily one of investment and only incidentally insurance." William R. Vance, *Handbook of Insurance Law,* 3rd Ed., by Buist M. Anderson, St. Paul, Minn., West Publishing Co., 1951, p. 160.

† Joseph B. Maclean, *Life Insurance,* 6th Ed., New York: McGraw-Hill Book Co., Inc., 1945, p. 126.

"But If I Get Most of My Money Back?" Let us return to the "net cost" analysis which is so frequently conjured up to prove how much cheaper it will be for you to buy Whole Life rather than Term insurance. It may be that even in the face of the patiently worked out "You and Your Neighbor" charts which were submitted for your consideration earlier in the book you cannot entirely suppress an insidiously nagging voice which whispers over and over, "But if you get most of your money back under Whole Life and nothing under Term . . . ?"

Let us then try to overcome your uncomfortable feeling by submitting a rewritten version of the "You and Your Neighbor" charts, calling on our new-found insight into the nature of the life insurance mechanism (Table III).

TABLE III. $25,000 DEATH PROTECTION—MALE, AGE 40

YOU WHOLE LIFE POLICY				YOUR NEIGHBOR 5-YEAR RENEWABLE TERM
(1) Your cash value	*(2) Net amount at risk*	*(3) Total estate*	*Year*	*(4) Total estate*
0	$25,000	$25,000	1	$25,000
0	25,000	25,000	2	25,000
400	24,600	25,000	3	25,000
825	24,175	25,000	4	25,000
1,275	23,725	25,000	5	25,000
1,700	23,300	25,000	6	25,000
2,150	22,850	25,000	7	25,000
2,625	22,375	25,000	8	25,000
3,100	21,900	25,000	9	25,000
3,575	21,425	25,000	10	25,000
4,050	20,950	25,000	11	25,000
4,550	20,450	25,000	12	25,000
5,050	19,950	25,000	13	25,000
5,550	19,450	25,000	14	25,000
6,050	18,950	25,000	15	25,000
6,575	18,425	25,000	16	25,000
7,100	17,900	25,000	17	25,000
7,625	17,375	25,000	18	25,000
8,175	16,825	25,000	19	25,000
8,700	16,300	25,000	20	25,000

Dissolving the "Mystery." If you compare the Net Amount at Risk in the Whole Life policy (column 2) with the figures for the Term policy (column 4) the "mystery" should dissolve forthwith. Note that the true protection under your neighbor's Term insurance remains *constant throughout the 20-year period,* while your insurance in the Whole Life policy decreases steadily. Thus, at the end of the tenth year, the "net amount at risk" in your Whole Life policy is already reduced by 14 percent to $21,425; at the end of the twentieth year, to $16,300. Throughout this time, your neighbor's protection stands at $25,000. You are actually insured under a *Decreasing* Term insurance policy in your Whole Life; your neighbor has *Level* Term coverage.

The Hand Is Quicker than the Eye. And so, as might be expected, the premium outlay for $25,000 of *level* protection from age 40 to age 60 is higher than for *decreasing* Term over these same years. And when you are next shown a "net cost" analysis which purports to compare the cost of Term with Whole Life, or with 20-Payment Life or any other non-Term contract of the same face amount, you will understand that despite the apparent identity of the numbers, it is comparing not equal things, but profoundly unequal things. And no amount of sleight of hand should serve to confuse the issue, or you.

Now you may feel that the difference in cost between level Term insurance and the decreasing variety, which is part of any other policy (like Whole Life), is high. Remember then that the cost of protection increases *sharply* at higher ages. As a consequence, keeping insurance unchanged in the face of advancing years must inevitably result in steeply increased premiums because the rate of mortality increases "geometrically." Thus at age 30, 2.13 men out of 1,000 die; by age 40, there has been only a relatively small increase to 3.53, but at age 50 the rate is 8.32 and shoots up to 20.34 for age 60, and so on.

Life Insurance Always Costs—No Matter What. What we hope has been demonstrated conclusively is that life insurance protection costs money, at *any* age, and must continue to cost more as the years go by. There is no way to avoid the inevitable increase except through some form of legerdemain which purports to make unequal things appear interchangeable.

The meaninglessness of the familiar "net cost" analysis is clear not only to "consumer-minded" students of life insurance but also to the more perceptive executives in the business itself. Thus, Valentine Howell, Vice-President and Actuary of the Prudential Insurance Company, the largest in the world, characterizes this concept in unequivocal terms, as follows: "The practice of showing net cost as the difference between the net payments and the cash surrender value, by the way, is a usual one in life insurance circles, in spite of its theoretical incorrectness and absurd results. By it, the net cost of endowment contracts can often be shown to be less than nothing . . ."*

Term insurance, then, at least as far as its cost is concerned, need hold no terror for us. We can use it in our planning alongside any of the other forms of insurance which are made available to us in such profusion.

Unfortunately, the opposition to Term insurance is a many-sided adversary which like the mythical monster of old sprouts two heads in place of the one lopped off. After we have dealt with its expensiveness, we find other evils attributed to this simple product. And these roadblocks in the way of an orderly and economical planning of our financial affairs must also be faced. In the next chapter we shall address ourselves to the remaining obstacles which hopefully should dissolve without too much resistance in the face of our newly acquired understanding of the life insurance mechanism.

*"Comparative Net Cost Factors in Ordinary, Group and Industrial Insurance," an essay in *Life Insurance—Trends and Problems,* edited by David McCahan, Ph.D., (CLU), Executive Director, S. S. Huebner Foundation for Insurance Education. Philadelphia, Pa.: University of Pennsylvania Press, 1943, p. 133.

4 Other "Objections" to Term Insurance

THAT Term insurance is the most expensive of all forms of life insurance is only one of the frequently voiced charges made against this low-premium protection. Another popular inference is that while it may be all well and good for you to embrace this policy when you are young, you would be well advised to look ahead to your later years. If you try to maintain this insurance *for life,* you are reminded, the premiums increase constantly and become ''prohibitive'' at older ages. ''After all,'' it will be pointed out to you somewhat archly, ''you might live to a ripe old age.''

In a burst of selling zeal, if not of rigorous logic, the agent may show you that your chances of living to 60 (if you are 30) are better than 4 out of 5. (This last point, pleasant though it may be to contemplate, would appear to be a bit dangerous as a sales pitch since it might lead you to the intolerable conclusion that with your chances of survival so high, you don't need life insurance at all.)

At any rate, you are urged to look ahead to age 60 when the premium per $1,000 will have soared to $26.53. At age 65, you will be able to continue your insurance but only if you convert to Whole Life at a premium of $65.82 per $1,000. $1,645.50 for $25,000 of insurance—a far cry indeed from the $5.00 per $1,000 with which you started out when you were a 40-year-old innocent.

You Can't Beat the Actuaries—Really! Truly a sobering thought, but we know now that nothing can be done to avoid the rising costs of mortality. The Whole Life policy can promise a serenely level premium only because the amount of true protection, *the net amount at risk,* is reduced steadily. Thus, if you buy $25,000 of Whole Life at age 30, the cash value of your policy when you reach age 40 will be $2,875, and the Company's net liability is thereby reduced to $22,125—the difference between the cash value and the face amount of the policy. By age 50, the true protection will be reduced further, to $17,550—and at age 60 to $13,325. The only reason the premium under the Whole Life policy does not increase is because the protection is *decreasing* steadily, exactly as it does under a Decreasing Term policy, which also maintains a level premium.

Given the inexorable rise in the mortality rate, no policy, *but none,* can circumvent the inevitable increase in the cost of keeping life insurance in force as one gets older. And the quest for insurance that will somehow redeem us from this implacable fate is doomed to founder.

Another Bugaboo Dissolved. This alleged weakness of any long-range program of Term insurance—that it is doomed to collapse because of the "prohibitive" premiums—dissolves as did the charge that it is more expensive than other forms of insurance. And for the same reason. The entire case is posited on the same quicksand of comparing *level* Term insurance with *decreasing* Term. If one is prepared to overlook this fatal flaw in the original premise, one can of course come up with all kinds of magic potions. But "nonesense only leads to nonesense" as someone once said.

Term Insurance Is Temporary—Like Life. Those who oppose Term insurance are not easily daunted, however. Even if the cost of this form of low-premium policy does not become prohibitive at older ages, or no more so, when properly understood, than any other form of insurance, it is indicated as unsuitable for "permanent" protection because it cannot be carried throughout life.

Most companies do offer some form of *renewable* Term insurance, and such policies may be renewed by the Insured for successive periods without *evidence of insurability,* that is, without being required to submit to another medical examination or furnish proof of moral and financial probity. But this option is almost always restricted. Thus, the 5-Year Renewable Term of the Aetna Life, which we used in our "You and Your Neighbor'' charts, is only renewable through age 64. Five- and ten-year policies are commonly available from most companies, and these are generally renewable for successive periods, but only to age 65, or age 70.

It is true then that Term insurance cannot be carried throughout life. It is not too difficult then to indoctrinate agents to consider this form of protection as suitable only for temporary purposes, like paying off a mortgage or other waning obligations. Some companies concede rather grudgingly that Term insurance may be indicated for a young father who is just embarking on his career and cannot yet afford the premiums for ''permanent protection,'' but the purchaser of Term insurance is admonished to regard the policy as a temporary expedient to be disposed of as soon as possible, as though it were a kind of time bomb.*

The Lure of ''Permanent'' Protection. To encourage the holder of a Term insurance policy to get on to the firm soil of ''permanent'' protection, the companies have elaborated a follow-up procedure which often includes direct sales material from the Home Office. The policyholder's attention is again directed to the transient nature of his policy, which, it is suggested, may have been suitable for a time, when it was bought. In addition to urging conversion to a plan like Whole Life for its ''permanence,'' the sales presentation usually dangles attractive economies in cost. As might be expected, the meaningless ''net cost'' on which we have dwelt so affectionately in earlier chapters looms large in such argumentation.†

* The ''nonpermanence'' of Term insurance permeates insurance company philosophy on all levels. Thus, in a bulletin to ''all members of the sales force'' announcing reduced Term rates which are trumpeted as enhancing ''the agent's competitive position,'' the ''sales significance'' of this move is stated in the following terms: ''Net opportunities are created for sales to prospects interested in the lowest possible premium outlay. The opportunities for future *permanent* insurance sales through conversion of Term, are enhanced.'' Information Bulletin, Issue No. 750, Equitable Life Assurance Society of the United States, December 11, 1972, p. 1. (Editor's emphasis)

† By and large, the message would appear to be getting across. ''A study of over twenty thousand term policies issued by five life insurance companies showed that over 50% were converted.'' This study appeared in the June 1964 issue of the *Journal of Risk and Insurance,* quoted in his essay, ''Contracts—Term Insurance,'' by Professor William T. Beadles, CLU, Professor of Insurance, Illinois Wesleyan University, Bloomington, Illinois.

To inspire the agent to help in this "missionary" work the companies pay full first-year commission on the replacing policy. This practice contrasts sharply with the strong impediments which companies seek to place in the way of replacing any policy *other* than Term.

A Stalwart Stand against Replacement. Every life insurance application asks whether the policy being applied for is intended to replace any other, in the same or other company. Where the policy to be replaced is in force in another company, most companies put their competitor on notice and hold up the issuance of their own policy until the original company has had an opportunity to "conserve" its business. If the policy being applied for is to replace an existing policy in the same company, or is being applied for within a short time after another policy has been lapsed, the agent is charged back with the commission paid on the older policy. By contrast, the replacing of a Term policy with a "permanent" policy, which is called conversion, is not considered a replacement and suffers from none of the disabilities that surround this practice when other forms of insurance are involved.

The essay appears in *Life and Health Insurance Handbook,* 2nd Ed., edited by Davis E. Gregg. Homewood, Ill.: Richard D. Irwin, Inc., 1964, p. 41.

In this same essay, the author, in a section titled "Sales Suggestions for Conversion," says, "Perhaps the most powerful way to present the advantages of conversion is to compare the additional annual premium (assuming conversion at the attained age) with the additional values which result from that larger premium." The statement is followed by an example which deducts the cash value available to the Whole Life policyholder from his premiums to arrive at his cost. The entire case is posited on comparing the two policies, that is, Whole Life and *level* Term insurance, as though they were equivalents, a technique which we have dealt with on several occasions and whose hollowness should now be apparent. Later on in this same essay, Professor Beadles allows that Term insurance "is low in cost only, if the insured dies during the term of the policy protection. If the Insured survives, then the Term insurance will prove to have been the most expensive form of life insurance which could have been purchased—expensive, that is, in regard to total cost." The writer concludes on a somewhat equivocal note, "This makes Term insurance both the cheapest and the most expensive form of insurance." This "dilemma" would appear to be insuperable, at least for those of us who do not know when we will die. Fortunately, we need not remain impaled on its horns, for we now know that a more precise comparison of Term insurance with cash value life insurance recognizes that the former provides *level* protection while the latter is equivalent to *decreasing* net amount at risk. In the more rigorous light, it turns out that under all life insurance policies, although their number be legion, protection must be paid for, and at more or less the same cost.

It is interesting to note too that the state regulatory bodies concur in this view of the conversion of Term policies. In a number of states, when a policy is intended to replace another, the agent is required to make a complete comparison in writing of the pros and cons of the entire transaction and submit a copy of the analysis to his Home Office which is mandated by law to keep it on file for a prescribed number of years. Replacing a Term policy is not interdicted in any such way.*

Now it might seem a little indelicate for the industry to place limitations on the renewability of its Term policies and then discover that as a consequence, such insurance is not suitable for "permanent" protection. It is a little reminiscent of the young man, being tried for the murder of his parents, who threw himself on the mercy of the court on the grounds of his being an orphan.

The companies contend that Term insurance renewable throughout life would invite "adverse selection," that is, only those who had become medically impaired risks would continue to hang on to their Term policies in their advanced years when the premiums were soaring.†

* It is important to underscore the fact that dropping an existing policy to buy a new one can prove quite costly to the policyholder. Since the largest part of the commission expense and one-time costs like medical examinations, inspections, policy issue, and so on, are incurred when the policy is first written, there is a severe drain on reserves which necessarily reflects itself in a loss of cash values during the early years. The policyholder's interest in continuing his insurance runs counter to those of the agent who would fare best if he could write a new policy each year. (This is not to imply that all agents would necessarily adopt so antisocial a course, as would be involved in encouraging policyholders to discontinue older policies to buy new ones.) The efforts of the State regulatory bodies and the companies to discourage policyholders from such actions or to put the would-be replacer on notice as to the possible adverse effects of such a course are therefore essentially in the public interest.

† Term insurance renewable throughout life was offered by one company at the turn of the century—The Provident Savings Life Assurance Society. The company withdrew from business in 1905, and ever since its demise has been pointed to as the proof of the impracticality of writing lifetime Term policies. The memory of this relatively small company has been kept green by its more long-lived competitors while the other eight New York domiciled companies which withdrew or were taken over by other carriers during the first decade of this century have sunk into a merciful limbo. Parenthetically, an impartial study of this unique company's brief history would probably prove quite rewarding for an understanding of the development of life insurance, and would also afford decent burial for a much-abused corpse.

The question of "adverse selection" is a most intriguing one, but is outside the scope of this book which seeks to provide answers to the problem of financial security within the present structure of the insurance business. With a few exceptions, so small as to be negligible, there is *no* Term insurance which grants the policyholder the right to renew as long as he sees fit. How then can one secure himself against being without the insurance protections he might still need in later life?

Will You Need Life Insurance after Age 65? Champions of Term insurance commonly point out that most people will not need life insurance much beyond age 60 or 65, or that the need for protection at these ages is usually sharply reduced, with children grown to maturity and accumulated assets (including Social Security benefits) usually sufficient to take care of a wife's remaining years.

This contention is hotly disputed by others who adduce human interest stories of families with a handicapped child requiring support into maturity, or of men who, with wives much younger than themselves, require insurance at fairly advanced ages.

It is important to understand that even the situations cited do not *necessarily* justify the expense of carrying life insurance. And expense it is at any age we now understand. Not every dependent creates an insurance exposure. For if our older father or husband has accumulated sufficient assets to provide for his dependents, there is no warrant for the expense of life insurance protection. Then again, retired persons, unless their sole source of support is a pension which would cease at their death, do not generally require life insurance, even if they have dependents.

Will You Live to Regret Your Early Decision? But what if you are still gainfully employed at 65 and have not been provident enough to set aside assets of any substance and still have dependents? Will you now be forced to repent in your indigent old age the decision to buy Term insurance which you made in unseemly haste when you were young? It is good to be able to report that no such dire consequences will follow from your having bought Term insurance during your productive years.

You will recall we spoke of *renewable* Term insurance earlier in this chapter. Renewable Term policies are almost always *convertible*. It is important to be clear on the difference of these two features. Renewability is the right of the insured at his sole option to renew the policy *as Term insurance* for successive periods—one year, five years, ten years, as the case may be. Convertibility gives the Insured the right, again without having evidence of insurability, to convert the policy to *Whole Life or any other higher-premium form* which the company offers. A policyholder carrying Term insurance who finds that he still needs insurance at age 60 or 65, can *convert* his Term policy at that time to Whole Life and carry it indefinitely.

Conversion—But at What Premium? The classic objection to this procedure is that the premium will be "astronomical" as indeed it will be ($65.82 per $1,000 in the Aetna Life, for example). This is of course the "prohibitive" cost gambit we discussed previously. We have faced up to the fact that there is no way to avoid meeting the cost of insurance at any age, regardless of the form of policy or when it is taken out; the $65.82 per $1,000 rate at age 65 is therefore neither high nor low. It is merely an unavoidable if grim fact of insurance at age 65. Before we leave this question, let us look at it "practically."

Suppose that when you set out on your insurance program at age 35 you were warned against Term on the grounds that you would not be able to carry it for life, and that if you should still need protection past age 65, you would have to convert to Whole Life at the burdensome sum of $65.82 per $1,000. To avoid this "tragic" denouement, you prudently bought Whole Life. Now at age 65, you can continue your policy for as long as you deem necessary, at the comfortable rate of $16.89 you have been paying since you were 35 years old.

On the other hand, if you had been insured under a renewable Term policy from age 35 onwards, and found yourself still in need of life insurance at age 65, your only course would be to convert to Whole Life. This option is available to you, but at what rate?

The True Cost of Protection. "A new Whole Life policy entered into at age 65 develops a premium of $65.82 per $1,000 whereas the rate under the policy you could have brought along from age 35 is a mere

$16.89," you are reminded sadly. "The rate at age 65 is almost four times as high as it is at age 35." Surely a shattering consummation to a saga that started so hopefully. But what are the facts? What is an individual insured for 30 years under a Whole Life policy really paying for life insurance protection at 65?

His cash value in his $25,000 policy is $13,050. He could surrender his policy, deposit this sum in a bank and receive over 5 percent in a completely liquid account, insured by the U.S. Government. His interest would come to $652.50. To leave an estate of $25,000, he needs to buy only $11,950 of insurance, for when this amount is added to the savings account which he could leave to his beneficiary, he would be providing $25,000. $11,950 of Whole Life at the "astronomical" rate for age 65 would cost $811.47. If he applied the savings bank interest toward his premium, his out-of-pocket cost would be $158.97. This figure, you will agree, compares favorably with the $422.25 premium for the Whole Life being carried from age 35.

Admittedly, the preceding illustration is a bit redundant, for it is really only a rehash of the "prohibitive cost" gambit treated earlier. But it is a point used so often to blunt the determination of a would-be buyer of Term insurance that it bears repeating. It also serves, we hope, to strip away the last vestige of any bugaboo of "nonpermanence." One can quite confidently buy Term insurance policies under which the premium is computed on a pay-as-you-go basis to reflect the rising curve of mortality, and still be in a position to maintain insurance protection as long as necessary.

Uncle Sam Joins the Chorus. Warnings on "prohibitive cost," it is interesting to note, do not issue only from commercial insurance companies. The United States Government joins in this same chorus, counseling the veteran in much the same terms: "IS YOUR NATIONAL SERVICE LIFE INSURANCE TERM POLICY ALL OR A LARGE PART OF YOUR INSURANCE PROTECTION? DO YOU INTEND TO KEEP THIS INSURANCE FOR THE REST OF YOUR LIFE, EVEN IF YOU LIVE TO BE 70 OR 80, AS MANY PEOPLE DO? If your answer to these questions is yes, then you probably should not carry term insurance indefinitely. WHY NOT? Because for one thing you may not be able to afford it when you approach or pass 70. You can see what it will cost at that time on the accompanying renewal certificate and the longer you live the higher the premium gets.'' Further on in this Veterans Administration bulletin, the veteran is alerted to another ''problem'' of term insurance: ''REMEMBER NO MATTER HOW LONG YOU CARRY IT AND NO MATTER HOW MUCH YOU PAY OR HAVE PAID IN PREMIUMS YOUR TERM INSURANCE HAS NO CASH VALUE EVEN IF THE PREMIUM PAID EXCEEDS THE CASH VALUE.'' Veterans Administration VA form 20–35 8b, April 1970, p. 1. (emphasis in original)

The Veterans Administration does not tire in its efforts to convert the ''heathen'' who may still be carrying his Term insurance. Almost 30 years after the end of World War II, he is still receiving ''Conversion Information'' (VA Form 29–35 8b—August 1973) which alerts him to the ''dangers'' of continuing his Term policy. ''While this insurance has its uses,'' the Administration experts advise, ''it is not designed for lifetime protection. The increase in premiums required each five years can become burdensome, if not prohibitive, in the later ages of life.'' And if the veteran nurses any doubts about how burdensome the future costs can be, the form letters include a schedule of renewal premiums. Thus, he is warned that at age 86 (sic!) the premium will be $1,803.65. A chilling prospect indeed which is calculated to weaken the resolve of all but the hardiest, it is clear.

Veterans of the Korean and Vietnam wars were mercifully spared the dilemma of choosing between Term insurance and cash value policies. The Congress of the United States in 1965 enacted a life insurance program which gave $15,000 of coverage to in-service personnel (instead of the $10,000 under the earlier Government programs), but this coverage could not be continued by a veteran beyond 120 days after he left the service, unless he was disabled. The only way a discharged veteran could continue his insurance was by converting to a cash value policy sold by one of some 600 companies which were on a list supplied by the V.A. The Government solicitously presented each departing serviceman with a booklet which set forth the options available to him, ''Strongly suggesting that the only intelligent option is to convert to cash value insurance.'' (Statement of Ralph Nader before the U.S. Senate, Subcommittee on Antitrust and Monopoly of the Committee on the Judiciary, February 20, 1973.)

Renewability and Convertibility. A caveat on renewability and convertibility is in order at this point. The difference between these features has already been touched on. It should not be assumed, however, that all Term policies incorporate one or both of these options. There are *non*renewable Term policies and others which severely limit the number of renewals one is permitted to make without evidence of insurability. It is important to make certain that the policy is renewable until a fairly advanced age, and that it is also convertible.

It must also be stressed that the two privileges are not necessarily co-terminous, that is, the privilege of renewal may run out at a different point in time than the conversion might. Thus, as a case in point, the Aetna's Annual Renewable policy is *renewable* to age 70, but convertible only to age 60. In other words, if a man of age 30 buys this policy, he can renew it every year without evidence of insurability until he is 70. The conversion privilege however, terminates at 60, so that while the policyholder can continue to renew to age 70, he no longer retains the option to convert. If he should still need life insurance at age 70, when his Term policy will expire, he will need to apply for a new policy. The objection to this procedure is *not* that the premiums will be "prohibitive," as is so often intoned, but that this applicant will be required to submit to a new physical examination and otherwise stand up to scrutiny on his moral and financial standing.

Under these circumstances, an individual insured under a policy of this kind will need to take stock *at age 60*. If he has reason to believe that his need for life insurance will continue beyond age 60, he should give serious consideration to *converting* the policy while he still can, before he passes age 60. He will then be in a position to maintain his protection for as long as is indicated.

Needless to say, maximum flexibility is provided in policies which are renewable *and* convertible to the highest possible age, and in choosing among Term policies, these features should be kept firmly in mind.

With the phantom of "nonpermanence" expunged, we are left with a few lesser spectres, and these will make up the subject of the next chapter.

5 The Remaining Objections to Term Insurance

We have examined the more important weaknesses that are attributed to Term insurance and found that they are essentially phantoms that vanish when the facts are presented. The "pure" protection policy is not more expensive than other forms of life insurance. It does not, if properly bought, labor under the stigma of "nonpermanence"; and even if carried into the older ages, it is not more prohibitive in cost than other policies with which it shares a company's rate book. Even with these impediments removed, the obstacle course which confronts a would-be buyer of Term insurance is still studded with a last few hurdles which need leaping over.

But Term Insurance Never Develops Any Cash Values! First among the remaining deficiencies alleged to Term insurance is the fact that it never develops any cash values. Every other form of life insurance, it is pointed out, offers some security to its owner, at least after a period of time, in the form of immediately available loans without any ifs, ands, or buts. The interest rate is fixed in the policy. And these loans are available without co-makers or any questions as to the borrower's financial standing.

Cash Values Do Not Materialize Ex Nihilo. Now there is certainly no denying the comfort in a liquid cash reserve with an insurance company or other similarly secure depository. But loan values in a life insurance policy, we have learned, do not come into being *ex nihilo;* they materialize out of the portion of the premium which is *over and above the cost of protection* (the difference between the cost of Term and

Whole Life, for example, which were dealt with in the "You and Your Neighbor" tables).

We do not call attention to this by now obvious truth to disparage the value of a regular savings program, a factor which is certainly of central importance in financial planning. Nor is there anything intrinsically wrong with a policy which combines protection and savings, although some "consumer" zealots condemn such a union on the grounds that life insurance companies should confine themselves to providing protection against death, while the savings and investment dollars of the American public should be handled by banks, savings and loan associations and similar thrift institutions.

At this point, we are merely pointing up the fact that the absence of loan values in Term insurance is in and of itself no reason to rule out its valid place in any life insurance program.

An Investment Question—Not an Insurance Question. Whether you are well advised to buy a life insurance policy with a premium several times as high as that for Term insurance in order to accumulate a nest egg for emergencies is not, it turns out, an insurance question at all, but an *investment* consideration. Or put another way, whether you should buy one of the numerous policies which combines in the one contract life insurance protection and systematic investment program, or buy pure protection against death in a Term policy and entrust your savings dollars to some other institution must depend on what alternatives are available to you, and how these compare with the investment opportunities in the life insurance "combination" product. This is the vital question that needs to be faced. It will in fact form the subject of a later section of this book.

At this point, we need merely agree that loan values do not appear out of the blue, and that their absence in Term insurance need give us no cause for concern if Term insurance appears warranted in our situation.

What about Retirement Values? "Term insurance never builds any retirement values" is another of the accusations directed at this low-cost protection. Lest we be accused of insensitivity to the problems of the senior citizen, we hasten to endorse the importance of financial planning for retirement. But as in the case of loan values, we know that retirement values do not emerge from nothing. Retirement values in a policy build up only from the payments made *over and above* the cost of protection. These payments are a *discretionary* investment made by the policyholder, and can be saved in a variety of ways. As in the matter of loan values, the best way to save for retirement needs to be discussed *on its own merits*. On one thing, however, all can agree—that a life insurance policy is not the *only* vehicle for retirement funds. And the absence of a retirement fund in Term insurance should not on that score alone bar it from a place in any insurance program.

The "Miracle" of Paid-up Insurance. A third weakness of Term insurance, we are given to understand, is: "It never becomes paid up; you have to go on paying forever." Every other policy, we are asked to note, develops some paid-up insurance after a period of years. The 20-Payment Life is fully paid up after 20 premiums have been paid; even the Whole Life policy on which premiums are payable throughout life can be surrendered after a time for a reduced amount of paid-up insurance. And surely it's a wonderful thing to be free of the burden of premium in one's later years!

This mirage of insurance without premiums, you may remember, was dealt with in Chapter 3 where we saw how the increasing cash value in any policy steadily reduces the "net amount at risk." All fixed premium policies, you will recall, combine decreasing Term and savings. A paid-up policy, it was shown, requires no further premiums only because the interest earned on the cash value is sufficient to pay for the decreased amount of protection still left in the policy.

Variations on Same Old Tired Theme. I believe it is sufficiently clear that the triad of laments about Term insurance—the absence of loan values, retirement values, and paid-up insurance—are all variations on the inadvisability of using Term insurance to protect our families against our premature demise. If they prove anything, it is that if one never sets aside any money, one will never accumulate any, which should come as no surprise even to the most naive.*

But the Only Way I Ever Save a Buck! We come now to what I believe is the last ditch defense against the rapidly gaining Term insurance concept. ''All the things you say about term versus cash value life insurance may be so, but the only way I ever save a buck is in my insurance. If I didn't have to meet the premium, I'd sure as hell blow the money on something or other. . . .'' Now this contention, being basically a subjective one, is difficult to counter on an objective basis. You alone are the best judge of how well this profile of the profligate fits you. If it is in fact true that you would forthwith make a beeline to the races every payday with every dollar that wasn't being weaned from you by the insurance company, then a life insurance policy with cash values may indeed be the one thing that will stand between you and the poorhouse. But even then, I think you will agree that it might be well to have a hard look at the kind of savings package your insurance policy offers, and before you opt for its rather unique features to devote a few minutes to checking out how it stacks up against competing thrift and investment media. Certainly if it compares favorably in safety, yield, and liquidity, it will stand high as a medium for protecting against *both* ''living too long'' and ''dying too soon.'' And there is no denying its positive value as a ''thrift enforcer.''

* The combination of insurance protection and savings frequently stimulates the advertising departments of insurance companies to flights of hyperbole. Thus one of the larger carriers recently erupted in a full-page advertisement which spoke of the ''miracle'' of its policy which ''creates cash values at the same time as it provides protection.'' The age of miracles is dead, alas, and once again a little understanding goes far in dispelling mist.

6 A Hard Look at the Savings Element in Life Insurance

THE "YOU AND YOUR NEIGHBOR" charts dwelt on in earlier chapters compare the savings results in your Whole Life policy with those of your neighbor's who bought Term and set aside in a 6 percent interest his annual premium savings. Your neighbor is ahead of you at each and every step of the way, it can be seen at a glance. Even at the end of 20 years, his $10,666.81 fund was $1,966.81 better than your cash value of $8,700. If all other elements of the two programs were basically the same, we would prefer to err on the side of conservatism and overlook the not inconsequential difference of some 22 percent in light of several factors previously mentioned which might modify the results.

A Look at the Early Years. To take stock of your fund and your neighbor's only at the end of the twentieth year, however, is to overlook some extremely important differences between these funds *during the course of the years*. In Table IV we have set down the sums available to you and your neighbor at the end of each of the 20 years, if you both live. Of course, if death should overtake you during this period, his estate will always be as large as yours.

It can be seen at a glance that your neighbor is out in front at every point along the way. Even after five years, he has available to him $2,015.02 compared with your cash value of $1,275.00, an advantage of some 58 percent. At the end of the third year, he has almost three times as much as you—$1,131.87 to your $400.00. In the second year, when he can lay his hands on $730.47, your cash value is $0.00. At the end of the first year, he has $353.68, while you have nothing.

TABLE IV. CASH AVAILABLE, AGE 40

YOUR PROGRAM $25,000 WHOLE LIFE POLICY		YOUR NEIGHBOR'S PROGRAM DECREASING TERM INSURANCE AND 6% SAVINGS ACCOUNT
Policy cash value	*End of year*	*Amount accumulated in savings*
$ 0.00	1	$ 353.68
0.00	2	730.47
400.00	3	1,131.87
825.00	4	1,559.48
1,275.00	5	2,015.02
1,700.00	6	2,443.74
2,150.00	7	2,901.54
2,625.00	8	3,390.39
3,100.00	9	3,912.40
3,575.00	10	4,469.82
4,050.00	11	4,974.19
4,550.00	12	5,515.05
5,050.00	13	6,095.04
5,550.00	14	6,717.00
6,050.00	15	7,383.96
6,575.00	16	7,941.85
7,100.00	17	8,545.22
7,625.00	18	9,197.77
8,175.00	19	9,903.52
8,700.00	20	10,666.81

Granted that you don't buy a life insurance policy expecting to drop it after a few years. But there is always the real possibility that your circumstances may change and you may wish to, or have to discontinue your insurance or reduce its amount. Even if your financial situation does not change materially, you might become eligible on your present job or in a new position for substantial amounts of group insurance which is not only low in cost but has the added bonus of being paid for in whole or in part by a benevolent employer. Or a promotion at your present place of employment may put you in line for additional insurance of this kind. Affiliation with a labor union or trade association, a membership in a professional society or fraternal organization—any of these may bring you the opportunity to obtain group insurance which is clearly preferable to the individual policy you bought some time ago.

One cannot then rule out the possibility that a policy being purchased today with an eye toward its long-range savings and retirement features will be discontinued early in its life cycle.

A Sober Note on the "Life Expectancy" of Many Policies. Do many policyholders in fact drop policies in their early years? The rate at which policies are discontinued, the lapse rate, is a matter of considerable importance to actuaries constructing rate tables for life insurance. The most widely used figures in the industry are derived from tables first developed almost 50 years ago by an eminent actuary, M. Albert Linton. Termination rates are understandably influenced by factors which vary with the individual company, but these tables, which are still known as *Linton Tables,* establish several broad categories.* According to the Linton B Tables (medium range), 20 percent of all newly purchased life insurance policies are discontinued *in their first year*. An additional 12 percent do not go beyond their second year; 10 percent terminate in their third year; 8.8 and 8 percent, in the fourth and fifth years, respectively. In other words, *over 46 percent of all policies do not survive their fifth year* (when your neighbor is still about 60 percent better off than you are).

The Linton A Table does not yield as dark a picture but even under this, the most favorable set of statistics, only 75.1 percent of all policies are paid for five years. (Linton C gives 59.7 percent as having gone off the books by the end of the fifth year.) Thus, a substantial percentage of savings programs undertaken through life insurance as a hedge against "living too long" are abandoned within five years. Surely a chastening thought to anyone considering the investment opportunities of a life insurance policy!†

* Three basic sets of figures are published: Linton A (lowest lapse rate); Linton B (medium), and Linton C (highest lapse rate). There is also a Linton BA Table but it does not develop significant variation in the early years of policy history and is therefore of virtually no effect during the period we are discussing.

† These figures are borne out by other data. "In the recent Variable Life Insurance Proceeding before the SEC, the Equitable Life Assurance Society, number three in the industry, revealed that 25 percent of its ordinary life policies (sold to 25- and 35-year-old customers) lapsed in the first year, another 10 percent in the second year. The first year lapse rates for New York Life and Aetna were 19 and 15 percent respectively." Statement of Ralph Nader before the Subcommittee on Antitrust and Monopoly. Op. cit. p. 9.

Such drastic loss of liquidity in the early years of an investment program might be palatable if the long-range returns were sufficiently high. But as we have seen, the policy cash values do not, even after 20 years, equal the sums available to your neighbor in a 5 percent interest account. Certainly so unexciting a final result gives little warrant for exposing one's funds to risk of even more serious loss in the early years.

But I'm Not a Statistic! The sobering lapse figures cited above may give an accurate picture of the depressingly brief life span of so much life insurance but you may nevertheless feel that they do not apply to you. After all, you are an individual and not a statistic making up part of an "average." In your own situation, you may be prepared to gamble on your ability to carry through on any program of annual premium payments you contract for. In that light, the long-range results of the Whole Life program will approximate, if not equal, what you could expect from any program of savings of comparable safety. And furthermore you feel there is merit in the premium notice as a "thrift enforcer." After all, who can deny that it takes more will power to make regular deposits into a voluntary savings account than to meet an insurance premium when it falls due? And isn't it true that even the strongest-willed individual will more readily invade his savings than his life insurance to buy that new car or those home improvements or any of the myriad delights that beckon from the TV screen or the pages of newspapers and magazines?

These arguments, it must be allowed, have much merit, at least for those of us who can, in Oscar Wilde's phrase, "resist everything but temptation." The periodicity of the premium and the fact that the cash values of the policy are tied to the insurance protection undoubtedly lend more certainty and permanence to this form of savings.*

* Definitive figures on how effectively the insurance-savings combination defends against extravagance are of course almost impossible to come by. Some light on the question may perhaps be gathered from a survey of *mutual fund* investors conducted by the Securities and Exchange Commission.

Under most contractual plans for the systematic purchase of mutual fund shares, life insurance is offered to the investor on an optional basis. The combination is therefore much akin to a high cash value policy like the Endowment form.

"The Special Study, while being highly critical of the contractual plan, did conclude that a comparison of planholders who purchased group credit life with those who did not, indicates insurance is a 'stimulant to regular investing.' The study focused on contractual

A "Plague on Both Houses." It would appear then that if one is prepared to overlook the loss of liquidity in a life insurance policy's early years, he is left with a set of pros and cons in the rivalry between cash value life insurance and separate savings. In our opinion, however, this is one dilemma that need not be resolved in favor of either of these competing savings devices. For we submit that *both* are inadequate as a repository for the long-term investment which is contemplated in planning for retirement.

Savings banks, Government or high-grade corporate bonds, cash values in life insurance—all proffer guarantees of the principal plus a return on the investment. The risk of loss of initial capital is minimal. But sad to say, security of principal is not enough. There is still another risk which must be faced—the constant erosion of the dollar's value, its steady decline in purchasing power which goes by the name of inflation.

In the next chapter which addresses itself to this much discussed but little understood subject, we hope to show how important it is in any long-range financial planning to come to grips with this elusive problem.

---

plans opened in February 1959. By August 1962, 16.3% of insured planholders made payments in every month, compared with 9.2% of uninsured planholders. Of the uninsured planholders, 48.1% had missed payments in 21 or more months, compared with 29.3% of insured planholders." Quoted in Herbert S. Denenberg and Robert J. Ferrari, *Life Insurance And/Or Mutual Funds, A Comparative Analysis of Endowment Life Insurance and the Insured Contractual.* New York: Pageant Press, Inc., 1967, p. 13.

7 Inflation and Long-Term Financial Planning

INFLATION, like most of the larger problems in economics, is a very thorny subject. Endless debate, usually distinguished by more heat than light, swirls about such questions as to what inflation *really* is, steps that might be taken to eliminate it or at least slow its ravages, whether controlled dosages of the drug can be absorbed without damage to the organism, or even with beneficial results, what factors encourage or stunt its growth, and so forth. The more one studies the pronouncements of the experts, the more inexorably is one led to conclude that forecasting developments and suggesting methods of offsetting disastrous declines in the purchasing power of the dollar must be considered highly problematic.

"Economics—Not an Exact Science." "Economics is not an exact science," Nobel prize-winning economist, Paul Samuelson, has observed with admirable terseness. "Here is another one of those cases," he continues, "where the plot is being acted out in front of us. As in any thriller, we won't know until the third act who is responsible for the killing of price stability. And unlike the land of fiction or the laboratory of the experimental scientist, the real world of economics may never reveal to us just what caused our inflation or just what would be the potency of conventional fiscal and monetary policies to affect the rate at which inflation proceeds."*

The period during which this book is being written has underlined the trenchancy of Professor Samuelson's remarks. The upward spiral in

* Paul A. Samuelson, *Economics, An Introductory Analysis,* 4th Ed. New York: McGraw-Hill Book Company, Inc., 1958, pp. 339–340.

the cost of living became front page news early in 1973 and remained fairly secure in its prominence until it was elbowed aside by more piquant events like the resignations of a vice-president and then a president, Watergate, and so on.

Prophet without Honor. Early in 1973, we read "Nixon Sees Food Prices Easing After A Brief Rise" (*New York Times,* February 20, 1973). This prophecy, we now know, like so many others, proved to be a pious hope, all too soon to be ground into dust by the harsh facts of reality. If the President's statement prepared us for the February Consumer Price Index which "posted its largest one month increase in 22 years" (*New York Times,* March 22, 1973), it gave no warrant for the depressing dirges which followed during succeeding months. In August of the same year, after there was some slight glimmer of hope that the beast may have been brought to bay, prices picked up steam again and took off with renewed vigor. Farm and food prices set an all-time record with a 19.3 percent increase.

These dreary facts are not dredged up out of any desire to join the Monday morning quarterback chorus which is always on hand to tell anyone who will listen how the Government has gone about the whole thing in a manner guaranteed to produce results directly the opposite of those intended, "as any child could have been expected to know." What becomes reasonably clear, we believe, from any reading of the savants in the field, is that we are dealing with an area which regrettably does not lend itself to scientific forecasting.

Whether "economics today is in crisis because it lacks the concepts, methods and philosophy that would enable it to come to grips with social and political reality," as is contended by one of the most prestigious members of the profession, Professor Oskar Morgenstern of Princeton and New York Universities, or whether the reality which economics seeks to encompass is too complex and replete with variables to be reduced to manageable proportions is a highly technical question on which this writer claims no competence to discourse.

The Experts Disagree—Violently. One thing at least is certain—there is not even a firm consensus among economists on what inflation really is. It is not surprising therefore that little agreement can be found on proposed methods of cure for the condition. Or as it is put more formally by another economist, "The frustrations of our inflationary depression with its dilemmas, and the difficulties of escaping from them, grow out of faulty diagnoses of what is wrong."* As might be expected, the treatment prescribed as appropriate for one disease can do little to help a patient suffering from a different malady. "The persistence of this treatment of Inflation II—administered inflation—by the appropriate cure for Inflation I—overspending inflation—can be explained, in part, by a couple of misunderstandings and distractions."†

Enter the Unexpected. When faced with the failure of the real world to correspond to the models of it on which the professionals rely as a basis for prognostication, it is fairly standard procedure to point to hitherto unprecedented phenomena which have knocked hallowed classical theories into a cocked hat. "In the usual inflation the sellers find it easy to sell and buyers find it hard to buy (even if they have the money to pay the price for the goods). In this inflation it was the other way around. Buyers (if they had the money to pay the price) found it very easy to buy and sellers found it very difficult to sell. There was a *deficiency* of demand. As a result of this perverse relationship, policy was paralyzed."‡

This was written in 1972, and as is the case with so much literature in the field, the situation is found to be "perverse" in refusing to behave as the laws of economics would appear to dictate. But as far back as 1958, in Paul A. Samuelson's classic work on economics (which may well have set an all-time high for a text's sales on economics), we read "*A New Inflation?* These are fine examples of our aggregate demand tools. But what about recent years? Some economists have testified before Congress that we may now have a 'new inflation.' For years after 1955, prices were rising: wholesale prices, farm prices, cost-of-living prices—in fact, all but a few metal prices.

"Every one was disturbed about the month-to-month announce-

* Abba P. Lerner, *Flation*. New York: Quadrangle Books, 1972, p. 23.

† Abba P. Lerner, ibid., p. 61.

‡ Ibid., p. 11.

ments of higher prices. But what was it due to? To excessive demand?

"Turning to look at each industry, it was hard to perceive excessive demand. . . ."*

The Mirage of the "Good Old Days." And so we find, when we close in on those "good old days" when economic life was supposed to have behaved according to orderly laws, that in this sector of human activity, as in most others, the nostalgically remembered golden age continue to recede even further back into the dim past.

Theories about the etiology of the disease may be diverse; agreement on its treatment is almost nonexistent. The reality of the condition, however, is universally accepted. A constant increase in the cost of living is seen as "normal" and it is only when this insidious eroder of our dollars gets "out of hand" that we deem it worthy of comment.

It is all too easy, therefore, to lose sight of the cumulative impact of even relatively small annual increases in the cost of living. Thus, during 1973, when the Government planners were toiling mightily to curb the galloping inflation which was churning our cost of living, even the rosiest forecasts which issued from high places did not look to getting the rate down much below 3 percent (and cynics were heard in numerous quarters to dub such predictions more political than realistic).

Every Little Bit Hurts. Let us look then at the real effect of even a "modest" inflation of just 3 percent. Thirty years from today—and many programs for accumulating a retirement fund and then spreading income over a retiree's years encompass periods much longer than this—it will take $2.43 to buy what $1.00 buys today (based on an annual increase in living costs which never exceeds 3 percent). Even in only 20 years, this relatively "benign" 3 percent inflation will have shrunk the dollar's purchasing power by almost half.

One can, of course, envisage protracted periods of stable prices (or even of reductions in the cost of living), but most of us will agree that the prospects for such developments are very dim. Some inflation, it is now conceded almost universally, is endemic to our social system. And any orderly planning of one's economic future must as a consequence

*Paul A. Samuelson, op. cit., p. 339.

come to grips with this contingency. "Do you really think you should put *all* your old-age savings in the form of bonds and money?"* is the question with which Professor Samuelson closes his chapter on "Synthesis of Monetary Analysis and Income Analysis."

Life Insurance and the Fixed Dollar. As long as life insurance promises to deliver a specific number of dollars at specified dates in the future, it must of necessity invest its policyholders' funds primarily in fixed-dollar investments. In this light, government bonds, high-grade corporate bonds, mortgages, and direct loans which guarantee a fixed rate yield comprise the bulk of the companies' portfolios. This was, and still is, in the main the path followed by the industry.†

As inflationary pressures continued to build up, cracks began to appear in the otherwise self-confident posture of the insurance industry. Most policymakers held out for "business as usual," but some more forward-looking executives began to suspect that the spectre of inflation could not be exorcised by paeans to the virtues of thrift and American enterprise. The insurance business, this latter group felt, could not fulfill its obligations to the buying public unless it faced up to inflation as a "fact of life."

Life Insurance Guarantees—of What? According to these "dissidents," the industry could fulfill its obligations to the dollar but this was a hollow promise. The real issue, it was contended, was "what will these guaranteed dollars buy?" It was misleading to guarantee a client a fixed pension which buys less and less of the necessities of life each month as the cost of living climbs (as one executive of a mutual fund sales organization put it, "Life insurance does offer guarantees—guaranteed losses").

While there was some dispute as to the exact nature of the new product that was called for, all agreed that the answer to the knotty problem of inflation would have to be sought in some form of *variable* dollar product. Freed from the contractual obligation to pay a fixed income,

* Paul A. Samuelson, op. cit., p. 341. (Emphasis in original)

† The industry's holdings of common stocks have trebled during the past decade, it is true, but at the end of 1973, this form of investment made up only some 9.7 percent of its portfolio.

the industry could seek out investments which might better keep pace with inflation.

Starting as a low-keyed debate within the inner circles of the business, the dispute soon gathered momentum and ultimately engulfed the entire industry and large sectors of the general financial community.

The Industry's Broken Field Running. Over the years, the stance of the life insurance industry on this most basic question has undergone some fascinating turns which add up to an absorbing chapter in American financial history. It is instructive to follow the broken field running within the various sectors of the business for the light it sheds on the problems of financial planning.

In the 1920s and 1930s, the business saw itself called on to stand at the bridge, like Horatio, the legendary Roman hero, and turn the enemy back single-handed. Company executives took every opportunity to make proper obeisance before the altar of the gold standard which was invested by them (as by most respectable economic thinkers of the time) with a mystical power to stabilize the value of the dollar.

An Undercurrent of Uneasiness—Even at the Top. As the cost of living, despite a few temporary retreats, continued its obdurate climb in the face of all litanies and recommended nostrums, an undercurrent of uneasiness began to manifest itself even in high places. Adherents to the virtues of a stable dollar continued to be heard but there was less confidence in the ability of the dollar to regain the substantial ground it had lost or even to hold firm at the new levels.

Thus, in May/June 1955 the president of the giant Mutual Life Insurance Company of New York, in his address to the Annual Field Club Meetings of MONY Field Underwriters* discussed inflation and its possible impact on the insurance business. He called attention to the fact that during or after each of the five major wars that this country had fought, inflation had soared and noted that following the first *three* of these wars, a later deflation of prices had ultimately brought the cost of living back to prewar levels. "But after World War I," he admitted,

* One of several euphemisms for the somewhat tarnished word "agent."

"despite some marked fluctuations, the cost of living never fully returned to former figures but moved toward a new plateau. And since the end of World War II, the price level has declined only slightly as of today from the postwar peak. The cost of living today is still 90 percent above the 1940 level."

Deflation Possible but Not Likely. "It is entirely possible that we may again have price deflation in the future," he continued, "but there are a number of good reasons for believing that this new 'plateau of prices' may last a good deal longer than others have." (Mr. Dawson's address was titled "The New Plateau").

The speaker then took note of a question that was being raised in some quarters as to "whether it is wise for people to buy more life insurance, in the light of possible future inflation." (The criticism was being considered even in the face of the executive's belief that inflation "was now under control . . .").*

Toward the end of his address, Mr. Dawson again referred to the possibility of deflation. "It follows that the man who puts 'cheap' dollars into life insurance premiums today, may very well be paid out in more 'valuable' dollars later, when the insurance is payable. It has happened before." The overall conclusion to be drawn was that life insurance was basically sound, "better than ever" as Mr. Dawson put it. "Our whole economy has moved up to a new pleateau," he indicated, "and personal insurance must move up there too, if we are to play our proper role in the new economy." He saw the insurance industry poised on the brink of expanding opportunities to substantially increase the amount of life insurance being carried by the American people. If this "real revolution in American life" could not be accomodated by busi-

*The rise in the cost of living was in fact almost negligible in 1955, after having posted almost steady increases since 1943, but the respite was woefully temporary. The cumulative percent increases in the cost of living as recorded by the Bureau of Labor Statistics took off almost at once as can be seen from the following figures:

1956—63.43 (change as related to 1943)
1957—68.38
1958—71.34
1959—73.91
1960—76.48

(By 1972, this same index stood at 151.19.)

ness as usual, it could be met by *more* business as usual, it would seem.*

Meanwhile down at the Farm. But if the gathering winds of change did not always reach up to the high-level executive suites of the companies, rumblings could be felt in other quarters. In the face of a constantly shrinking dollar, a growing plaint was making itself heard from retirees under conventional plans whose fixed incomes were proving inadequate to maintain the standard of living they had been led to expect during their working years.

As early as 1958, an executive of one of America's largest insurance brokerage firms, specialists in pension and profit-sharing plans for corporations was quoted as saying, "The greatest problem in the pension field is inflation . . . ⅔ of the work is taking down pension plans and resetting them." This step, he pointed out, would not have been necessary if there had been the flexibility which the variable annuity could give (quoted in the November 29, 1955 edition of the *Journal of Commerce*).

Some Rumblings in the Ivory Towers. The usually staid world of academe also ventured an occasional note of dissidence. In 1956, Professor Wilford J. Eitmean of the University of Michigan's School of Business Administration advocated the sale by life insurance companies

* If in retrospect this position seems conservative, it should be remembered that it was for its time relatively forward-looking. As a matter of fact, less than six months later, Mr. Dawson issued a statement to his company's agency managers titled "A Calm View of Variable Annuities" (although it is not quite clear who was being calmed). For the most part throughout this period, the larger carriers with the notable exception of the Prudential, were giving short shrift to any inference that their tried and true product was in need of re-evaluation in light of the changed economic climate.

It should also be remembered that almost any stance can be structured to appear middle of the road, for there are almost always positions at either end of the spectrum that are more extreme. Thus while some of the more thoughtful leaders of the industry were seeking ways to adjust to the changing realities of American life in the fifties, the chairman of the board of one of the country's largest casualty insurers and recipient of the "Insurance Man of the Year" award for 1957 took occasion to remind the annual convention of the Federation of Insurance Counsel of his oft-repeated warning that the Federal Security plan was "probably the greatest fraud ever perpetrated on the American public." (Quoted in the *Insurance Advocate,* issue of August 30, 1958.)

of variable annuities based on common stock investments to protect the purchasing power of those who buy annuities. Reviewing the past 75 years, he found that "Not once in this period has the person who accumulated funds for retirement over a 20-year period and lived out a life expectancy of 20 years been able to enjoy as much purchasing power as he paid for in annuities."

The same Federation of Insurance Counsel, which had been alerted by James S. Kemper to the fraud being perpetrated on the American public by the Federal Social Security system, heard a prominent Washington insurance lawyer characterize the variable annuity as "the best hedge against inflation" and prophesy that these equity-based annuities would receive the recognition from government and public that they deserve.

Some Bankers Join In. Banks, understandably concerned about the trust funds they were administering, began to join the mounting chorus favoring this radical departure from the fixed-dollar annuity. The assistant trust officer of the National Bank of Detroit closed his article on the variable annuity with these words, "Essentially, the variable annuity is a manifestation of the growing acceptance of common stocks for conservative investment purposes. A trustman, believing the preservation of purchasing power is the goal of conservative investment, finds it difficult to take other than a constructive view of the variable annuity. . . ."*

Examples of the change in thinking among individuals concerned with inflation and the insurance business' ability to keep its place in the financial scheme of things could be multiplied many times over, but the concern was soon to leave the realm of the conceptual and translate itself into more practical terms.

While at the Grass Roots. Inside the industry, warning signals were sounding about the growth of Term (no cash value) insurance which had risen from 8 percent of the business in 1946 to 25 percent—largely because of people's fear of inflation. This was pointed out by a vice-

* John F. Fralick, "The Variable Annuity," in *Trusts and Estates,* July 1958, p. 67.

president of one of the major companies, The Bankers Life Company of Des Moines, Iowa. The Life Insurance Association of America, one of the leading industry organizations in the field, reported that in 1956, for the first time in any year, total income received by insurance companies for group annuity plans failed to show an increase.

As might be expected, if the public was having misgivings about the standard product being offered by life insurance companies, there were ardent suitors in the wings. One such upstart was the still infant mutual fund business whose gross sales in any single year since 1945 had never exceeded $300 million. In 1950, five years later, volume exceeded $500 million, and from then on it rose every year to top $1 billion in 1955 and $2 billion by 1960. (This growth curve was to continue for some time before it took a downward turn—by 1965, it was over $4 billion.)

And so at the grass roots, where it's at, as modern parlance would have it, the conventional life insurance was encountering considerable resistance. It might be interesting in this connection to cite a sales presentation developed by some enterprising mutual fund salesmen who gleefully seized on the erosion going on in the cash values nestling inside life insurance policies to push their own wares.

How I Retired on $100 ($200) ($300) a Month. They would archly spread before their prospect a series of full-page advertisements which had been placed in national magazines by one of the life insurance companies. Each of these displayed a serenely happy elderly couple (whose only concession to the passage of years showed in their silvery white hair) enjoying one of the several pursuits which insurance companies assume are universally coveted by all of us, to wit, strolling arm in arm in the shadow of the Eiffel Tower, fishing, lolling about on a gleaming white beach, and so on. The earliest in this series of advertisements carried the caption "How I Retired on $100 a Month." A few years later, the head of the family was trumpeting the fruits of his far-sightedness in a similar ad which now featured the legend "How I Retired on $200 a Month"; the last in the series had raised the ante to $300 a month. (Incidentally, no candidate for a more current version in the sequence of ads has been seen in these parts.)

I am told that these advertisements trotted out in succession often helped incline a prospect toward the mutual fund being proposed by the salesman in place of the high premium life insurance policy which was to protect not only "dying too soon" but also against "living too long."

Let's Not Panic! Competition from other investment mediums may have begun to make waves, but these were still only ripples on the surface of a giant and thriving business. Gross sales of mutual funds, it was indicated, had increased from a little over $2 billion in 1960 to some $4.3 billion by 1965 (net sales after redemptions from $1.2 billion to $2.3 billion). In this same period, the policy reserves of the life insurance industry had increased by just under $30 billion. It was not too difficult then to dub as alarmist the occasional demurrers that surfaced about the ability of the life insurance product to hold its place in the hearts of the American public. As a case in point, a scholarly article titled "Life Insurance, Variable Annuities and Mutual Funds: A Critical Study" concluded in 1968 that there was "no discernible evidence that life insurers are losing their share of personal savings . . ." and even if they were, "they were not losing it to mutual funds. . . ."*

While the theory of the variable annuity versus the fixed dollar was being agonized over inside and outside the industry, isolated but noteworthy sectors of the "practical" world were taking steps to provide for fluctuations in the dollar through equity-connected savings plans. In 1956, the Legislature of the State of Wisconsin, without a single dissenting vote, sent to the governor for his certain approval, a carefully worked out variable annuity program on an optional basis for up to 50,000 State and local government employees and teachers in the public school system "who desire to have a hedge against the erosion of their retirement funds through inflation." In the same year, a variable annuity feature was added to the General Mills retirement plan for their salaried employees.

Industry Takes Steps to Hedge against Inflation. In 1958, the life insurance industry was still unable to offer variable annuities on any-

* William R. Sloane, Ph. D., Professor of Insurance in the College of Business Administration at Drake University, *Journal of Risk and Insurance,* vol. 37, 1970, pp. 87–104.

thing resembling a national scale, but large company employers were developing other methods of financing their pension plans on at least a partial equity basis. Among such concerns were to be found giants like Aero-jet-General, Boeing Airplane Co., Bristol-Myers Co., Chemstrand, General Utilities Corp., General Tire and Rubber, Jersey Central Power and Light, Kidder, Peabody & Co., Long Island Lighting Co., National Airlines, Smith, Barney & Co., Vitro Corp., and Warner-Lambert.

This radical change in the concept of savings and retirement plans also manifested itself in countries outside the United States, most of which had lived through inflations far more severe than those which assailed the American dollar. "Dutch Firm Plans Equity Annuity Sales," "Israel Links Life Cover to Cost of Living," "Norwich Union Life Insurance Society, Toronto broke—or at least bent—the 'club rule' that says a life insurance company should deal only in guaranteed payments," "Policies based on variable index numbers are being written in France for fire and certain other lines of casualty insurance (in 1955)"—these were straws that reflected a basic shift in the direction of the wind which was being registered only sporadically in this country.

Defending the Faith. Throughout the fifties, however, with certain isolated but important exceptions, the life insurance carriers concentrated on their established course of offering the fixed-dollar product. Any deviation from the concept was seen as a threat to the very bedrock of life insurance and of the economy in general. "If the variable annuity becomes generally accepted, it may kick back on life insurance companies and the economy" warned H. E. Luedicke, editor of the *Journal of Commerce* (December 9, 1955). A few days later, M. Albert Linton, the prestigious Chairman of the Board of the Provident Mutual Life Insurance Company and one of the country's leading actuaries told the American Finance Association that "the institution of life insurance has too much at stake after long years of outstanding service to its policyholders to allow its position to be undermined by what at best would be considered a side issue. Its paramount business is life insurance and annuity services on a fixed-dollar basis—a field in which it stands unrivaled.''*

Only a few months earlier, the *Commercial and Financial Chronicle* (August 25, 1955) published an article by A. M. Sakolski whose purpose it was "to point out that the term 'variable annuity' is a misnomer, being neither an annuity in the proper sense of the word, nor a form of scientific insurance, based on an actuarial concept. It is a mongrel—a hybrid which contains in itself forces destructive to the principles of insurance protection and to the proper basis for safeguarding investors.''

The Battle of the Giants. While most of the larger carriers were holding fast to the sanctity of the fixed dollar, the Prudential, then second only to the Metropolitan Life among the world's life insurance companies, came out foursquare on the side of the variable annuity. Under the leadership of Carroll M. Shanks, one of the most farsighted executives at the head of any large life company, the battle to legalize the variable annuity was vigorously prosecuted on state and national levels. The company's opposite number, the Metropolitan, picked up the gauntlet of defending the chastity of the life insurance product, and there was set into motion a dispute which was dubbed "The Battle of the Giants.''

The address of Arnold R. LaForce, second vice-president of the Metropolitan Life before the New York City chapter of the Chartered Life Underwriters was reported in the *Journal of Commerce* (January 20, 1956) under the headline "Metropolitan Hits Variable Annuity.'' Mr. LaForce's boss, company president, Frederick W. Ecker, wrote to State Senator Malcolm S. Forbes, chairman of the Senate Committee on Financial Reports of the New Jersey Legislature, which was scheduled to vote on the variable annuity, that "variable annuities were not in the public interest.''

A Clarion Call to Man the Barricades. Another of the company's vice-presidents, Charles C. Dougherty, testifying at a hearing of the

* As quoted in the *Insurance Advocate,* December 31, 1955.

Massachusetts Joint Legislative Committee in connection with a bill that would authorize life insurance companies to sell the variable annuity, issued a clarion call to his fellow Americans. In rather grandiloquent words, reminiscent of an earlier Paul Revere he said, "America today is at the crossroads. We can go down the easy path of inflation, or we can show the fortitude to make a stand, here and now, before it is too late. All these plans for variable annuities, in one form or another, are merely trimming our sails to the inflationary wind. I trust that all of us appreciate this danger and that you and other legislative bodies will make those decisions that will aid in the fight before we reap the whirlwind."

A well-documented article in the January 23, 1956 issue of *Barron's* on this controversial question was titled "'Met.' vs. 'Pru.,' The Variable Annuity Touches Off a Free for All." It was pointed out that "the question of the variable annuity, academic sounding though it might seem, had already engendered one of the bitterest disputes to erupt in the staid life insurance business in years." The writer went on to point out that the issue "goes straight to the heart of how the industry can best meet the challenge of persistent inflation and mounting competition from the outside. Lining up on one side or the other in the fray are agents, actuaries, accountants, attorneys, economists, tax and investment experts, and top-echelon executives. Symptomatic of the deep-seated schism in the insurance world is the fact that the two biggest insurance companies have taken contrary stands on the variable annuity. Prudential, as noted, is for it. Metropolitan is just as fervently opposed."

Breakthrough in the Popular Press. The battle which raged quite furiously at times was conducted for the most part outside the notice of the average American whose financial future was being debated so solicitously. Only periodically did the clang of clashing armor make its way into the popular press, as in the June 1957 issue of *Good Housekeeping* which carried an article on "A Retirement Income that Changes with the Stock Market." The piece was featured with the following introduction: "It's an insurance plan so startlingly different that not even the insurance industry itself can agree on whether it's good or bad. If you haven't heard about it yet, you probably will soon. Here's what the talk is all about.''*

Everybody on the Side of the Angels. As is standard practice in such matters, all the contesting gladiators leapt into the arena draped in the mantle of the public interest. The principle being debated so hotly was only the tip of the iceberg which hid some fairly frenetic jockeying for position by the various sectors of the insurance and financial communities. The question of the soundness of the variable dollar product for the average American was all but obscured under such issues as whether the commodity was insurance or a security.

To the industry, this question was of more than academic interest. If the variable annuity was a security, and the controversy was ultimately carried to the United States Supreme Court which held that it was, a Pandora's box of problems would be opened. The product would have to be marketed under S.E.C. regulations which among other things restricted selling practices and commission payouts, a situation which the insurance business eyed with something less than enthusiasm.

Many executives who were not against the variable annuity per se were deeply apprehensive of opening the door to further ''intrusion'' of the Federal Government into the business of insurance and saw it as the better part of wisdom to oppose the whole idea.†

* More specialized publications like *Kiplinger Changing Times, The Kiplinger Magazine* had published articles on ''inflation-proof annuities.'' One such article ended with the rather neuter suggestion, ''Perhaps the best position to take is to try and figure out whether a variable annuity is a good deal for you personally or for your pension.'' The article closed with the wry comment that ''the insurance companies and securities salesmen are well-equipped to look out for themselves.'' (December 1955).

† The threat of Federal regulation has long occupied a prominent place in the industry's demonology. With only a few weak dissenters, mostly in the casualty field, the industry has maintained a consistent and highly vocal campaign against the danger of a single Federal bureaucracy which it considers much more subversive of the free enterprise system than fifty separate State regulatory bodies. Typical of the tocsins warning against this threat is the news story in the November 14, 1973 *Journal of Commerce* which was headlined ''Government Intervention Blasted by NAII's Clendenen'' and opened as follows: ''Los Angeles, Nov. 13: Practicing a time-honored tradition among insurance men, Howard E. Clendenen, the outgoing chairman of the National Association of Insurers (NAII) today denounced Federal regulation of the insurance industry on several fronts.''

The Calm after the Storm. The question of the variable dollar product and its place in the financial planning of the American public is no longer debated with much fervor, leastwise on a *theoretical* level. Voices looking forward to deflation or to any protracted respite from continued inflation are all but muted.* And in this light, to one degree or another, practically every sector of the life insurance community is prepared to accord to this once heretical idea some place in the array of products they market. Despite orotund pronouncements on the sanctity of the American dollar and heroic resolves to dig in and defend its chastity even if it meant going down to defeat, the fight over principle is all but over. Now mercifully forgotten are statements like this one, which was issued not too many years ago from the Metropolitan: "The life insurance contract has been the one outstandingly safe financial medium on which Americans and Canadians have come to depend with confidence. We at the Metropolitan do not want that confidence shaken or impaired."

The formidable legal obstacles in the path of this struggling infant have been resolved and it is now possible to buy a variable annuity on an individual basis as well as under group plans in every state of the Union. But the impact of this product, it must be admitted, has been only minimal.

There were over 50 companies offering variable annuities to individuals at the end of 1975. The reserves for such annuities reached $7.5 billion. In that same year, life insurance policy reserves climbed by just under $19 billion to reach $228.7 billion.

Withering on the Vine. Can one draw any conclusions from these statistics as to the response of the general public to this departure from the traditional fixed-dollar guarantees which the companies had dealt in so long and so successfully? We think not. There has been almost no concerted effort among the carriers to vigorously promote the variable

* Prudential's Annual Economic Forecast for 1974 projected "some slowing in the rate of inflation during 1974, especially in the second half but in the face of this moderation, the conventional year-to-year comparison of the GNP price index will show a 5½ percent increase for 1974," (Sic)

dollar annuity. As a result, in our opinion, neither the basic idea nor any refinement or development of it, such as might have resulted from its active promotion and competition among the carriers, has been put to any real test.

The industry as a whole has devoted very little energy to the care and feeding of this infant. By way of an unofficial sampling, I tabulated the amount of space devoted to life insurance company advertising in *Time* magazine during the first six months of 1976. Of the approximately 19 pages placed by the carriers and industry organizations not one heralded the arrival of this newcomer to the American scene.

The Light Hidden beneath the Bushel. Even more revealing are the figures for this period of the *National Underwriter,* the leading life insurance trade periodical. The companies advertise in its pages to attract business from agents (as well as to preen before their competitors) and can therefore be expected to display what they consider their most exciting and freshest wares. During this six-month period, some 120 pages of company advertising graced the pages of this journal. Much of the copy did not address itself specifically to the policies and annuities offered by the particular company. The company instead blazoned forth its record of growth in assets and insurance in force, invoking the hallowed credo that "nothing succeeds like success," or even more succinctly pointed to its longevity as proof of its being embarked on a proper course. The implication throughout these advertisements was that the standard products which had provided the agents with the ammunition to meet the public's needs were still completely viable. Only some *five* pages of the total 120-page lineage even mentioned the variable dollar. All of this space was bought by one small carrier incorporated in 1967 which specializes in annuity products for the pension, profit-sharing, and tax-sheltered annuity markets. While this company, which is licensed in all 50 states (and has recently been purchased by one of the major life insurance companies) has been chalking up a respectable record in this new field, its assets of $73 million represent some 0.00025 of the life insurance industry's total. It is more than likely then that this medium for retirement planning has never appeared on your horizon, even if you have met with your insurance agent in the recent period.*

We have tracked the controversy that swirled about this upstart in the barest outline because of the light it sheds on the question of saving through life insurance in an inflationary era. As *Changing Times, The Kiplinger Magazine* (which we previously quoted) urged, we have "to try and figure out whether a variable annuity is a good deal" in our personal financial plans as well as under any pension for which we may be eligible.

The question raised its head, you will recall, because of the danger that continuing inflation poses to long-range financial planning. But are there in fact any reliable ways to counter the ravages of inflation? This knotty question will be considered in the following chapter where it will be shown that while there are no sure-fire panaceas, one must nevertheless make a choice from among alternatives of differing degrees of certainty, or uncertainty if you prefer.

* Prophecy is a highly risky activity. Nevertheless, this writer would venture a guess that there will be relatively little expansion of the variable annuity, leastwise in the individually purchased (nonpension) field. The recent approval of variable *life insurance* will give the companies an opening into the as yet untapped variable dollar without many of the marketing problems that hover over the sale of variable annuities.

8 Investing in Common Stocks

THE PRECEDING CHAPTER gave a bird's-eye view of the agonizing within the insurance industry over inflation and its effect on the insurance product. As was indicated, for over a century, the life insurance industry had marketed products that were *guaranteed*. The conventional annuity promised an income that was not only assured for life but also guaranteed as to the amount of each benefit payment. Similarly, the life insurance policy undertook not only to pay a stated amount at the policyholder's death but also to make available to him on demand during his lifetime stipulated sums at any point.

In this light, it can readily be seen, an insurance company would have to place its clients' money in undertakings which promised a fixed yield and return of the principal at some point in the future. Such fixed-dollar obligations account for the bulk of companies' portfolios—bonds of the Federal Government or its political subdivisions or agencies, high-grade corporate bonds, mortgages, direct loans to industry, and so on. The companies lend money rather than invest it directly as one does who buys common stock and thereby acquires part ownership of a business enterprise. This was, and still is in the main, the path followed by the insurance industry.*

Is the Traditional Approach Archaic? In determined opposition to this philosophy is the view that the fixed-dollar annuity has been ren-

* Although the past decade has witnessed a 70 percent increase in the industry's common stock holdings, by the end of 1976 this form of investment still accounted for only 9.7 percent of its portfolio (as reported in the 1976 *Fact Book* of the American Council of Life Insurance). This figure represented a decline from the preceding year's 10.3 percent.

dered obsolete. A pervasive inflation is seen as having dug in for a permanent stay and rendered the probability of any *de*flation in prices virtually nonexistent. Advocates of this position point out that the formerly cyclical pattern of price rises followed by declines has all but ceased. During the past 40 years, prices have risen in every year except 1949 and 1955. Furthermore, we are asked to note that the *rate* of the increases has been accelerating steadily during the past 16 years. Thus, in the period 1959–1963, prices rose 5.5 percent; from 1964–1968, they rose 13 percent; during the period 1969–1974, they rose 21 percent. In 1974 alone, prices rose 12 percent.

The industry could pride itself on its ability to fulfill its obligations to the letter by paying a fixed income exactly as promised. "Guaranteed dollars, indeed! But what will these dollars buy?" What a predicament could be more depressing, they asked, than that of a person retired on a fixed income which buys him less and less of the necessities of life each month as the cost of living rises?

Inflation—The Meanest Thief. It cannot be emphasized too strongly that inflation which has been called "the meanest thief" falls most heavily on those who have retired on fixed incomes. The late President Eisenhower put it very well in his State of the Union Message when he said, "Inflation is not a Robin Hood taking from the rich to give to the poor. Rather it deals most cruelly with those who can least protect themselves. It strikes hardest at those millions of our citizens whose incomes do not quickly rise with the cost of living. And when prices soar, the pensioner and the widow see their security undermined. . . ."*

An Answer—Or at Least the Model of One. The answer to this problem, these dissidents hold, is to be found in a financial vehicle which invests directly in the economy. Thus, the argument runs, a person who holds 1,000 shares in a company with one million shares owns 1/1,000th of the company. If the company is worth $1 million, the 1,000 shares are worth $1,000. If now because of inflation the com-

* Quoted in George E. Johnson, *Variable Annuities & Variable Life Insurance, Variable Pensions, Investment Annuities, Economic Index Annuities*. Washington, D.C.: The Reprint Co., p. 22.

pany's value increases to $2 million, the investor's shares would be worth $2,000. Admittedly, this $2,000 may not buy him any more groceries than the $1,000 invested originally, but at least his equity would not have eroded.

It would not do of course to invest in the corner laundromat or even in the stock of any *one* major company, for there is always the risk that this individual enterprise might not fare well. But a prudent investor who spreads his investment over a broad spectrum of America's leading industries has every reason to expect to come out standing on his feet, they contend.

What Are the Facts? This model, like so many others that men conjure up, is disarmingly simple. But does it stand up under careful scrutiny? All too often, we have discovered, theory is "all grey, and the golden tree of life is green." How would a broad portfolio of stocks fare in the face of inflation? If it would not provide a perfect hedge against the shrinking dollar in fair weather and foul, would it do better than fixed-dollar investments?

Now when we track stock prices and yields, we find that they tend over the years to compensate for rises in the cost of living. But as the graphs reproduced below show, the correlation is by no means perfect.

The growth in stock values and yields compensated, in most of the years covered by the charts, for the rise in the cost of living. But there were also several periods when this comforting situation failed to be obtained. In 1973, for example, the cost of living posted an 8.8 percent increase, the highest in any single year since 1947, while the Dow-Jones Industrial index fell 16.5 percent. The year 1974 presented an equally adverse picture.

One highly regarded authority, Benjamin Graham, addressed himself to this question in the latest edition of his now classic work which has been called "the Bible of the investment field." "Do not common stocks have a built-in protection against inflation, and are they not almost certain to give a better return over the years than bonds?" he asks.

"On this point, we can be categorical," he writes. "There is no close time connection between inflationary (or deflationary) conditions and the movement of stock earnings and prices. The obvious example is

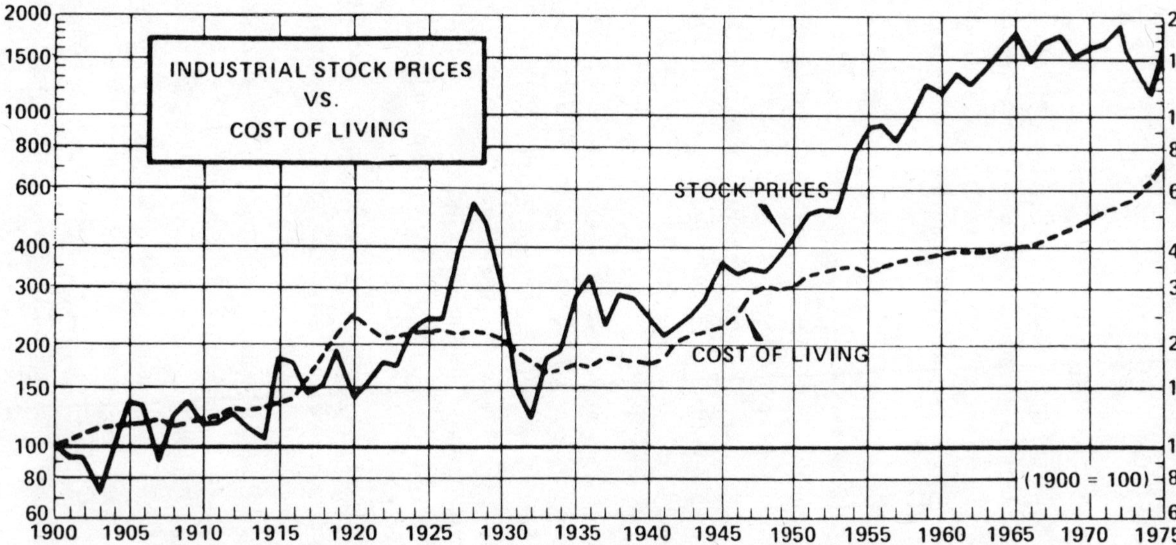

Source: Dow-Jones industrial stock average. Consumers' Price Index, Bureau of Labor Statistics, U.S. Department of Labor. Reprinted from *Investment Companies* 36th edition, Copyright 1975, Warren, Gorham, and Lamont, Inc., 210 South Street, Boston, Mass. 02111. All rights reserved.

the recent period, 1966–70. The rise in the cost of living was 22%, the largest in a five-year period since 1946–50. But both stock earnings and stock prices as a whole have declined since 1965. There are similar contradictions in both directions in the record of previous five-year periods.''*

The recent period has been one which underlined, rather dramatically this lack of correlation between stock market results and inflation. Thus, a major consulting firm in its *Investment Performance Survey* of bank and insurance company commingled funds pointed out that over the 10-year period, 1966–1975, the ''returns experienced in the equity market were disappointing relative to inflation.'' (Quoted in the bulletin published by the S. M. Hyman Company, December 1976 issue.)

It's the Long Pull That Counts. We must remember, however, that when we are dealing with funds for retirement, we are less concerned with five-year periods than with longer time spans—accumulation periods of 30 years or more in many instances, with a payout period of an additional 15 years (assuming the life expectancy for a male age 65, as given in one widely used table). If then *in the long run,* the market promises some hedge against increases in the cost of living, counter trends during shorter periods might be tolerated with equanimity. For even if for a few years, the market fails to follow price increases, or even more perversely, goes down while prices edge upward, the entire life cycle of the retirement plan may still be viable.

Bringing All the Evidence to Bear. It is a reflection of today's acceptance of inflation as a way of life that a most penetrating analysis of this entire question first appeared only a generation ago. The study set out to ''determine whether there is any way to provide a retirement income which would overcome some of the troubles inflicted by inflation.''† To this end, it compared the purchasing power that would have been realized under each of *three* types of annuity.

* Benjamin Graham, *The Intelligent Investor,* 4th Ed. (Revised). New York: Harper & Row Publishers, Inc., 1973, p. 20.

† William C. Greenough, *A New Approach to Retirement Income,* 1964 Fourth Printing. Teachers Insurance and Annuity Association of America.

The first was a conventional annuity, based on fixed-dollar investments. Until recently, this was the only kind of annuity offered by life insurance companies, and still accounts for the bulk of life incomes being paid out by insurance companies under individual retirement plans and under pension and profit-sharing plans, as well as to beneficiaries of life insurance policies. To arrive at rates of return for this type of annuity, Mr. Greenough averaged the yields on investments realized by all life insurance companies active during the periods under scrutiny. The second type of hypothetical annuity studied was a 100 percent common stock fund, derived from the broadest indices of the stock market extant at the time. This second model would be akin to the variable annuity of which we will be hearing more later. Mr. Greenough also calculated the results that would have been achieved under a combination fund, split 50-50 between fixed-dollar and common stock investments. "By combining a unit annuity and the fixed-dollar annuity," Mr. Greenough postulated, "the individual would be choosing a conservative program offering him the best foreseeable prospect for security in his old age regardless of the direction in which the American economy moves."*

Real Dollars vs. Theoretical Ones—The Bottom Line. The incomes that would have been received under these annuities were then related to the cost of living in the particular year. The real purchasing power of the income available to the retired person were thus brought into focus. Let us see how these would have shaped up, comparing the fixed-dollar annuity with the "middle-of-the-road" combination annuity.

In all, 75 individual time units were analyzed. For each time unit the payouts in terms of real purchasing power under the three different annuities were compared. Mr. Greenough tallied the number of occasions in all three periods when the purchasing power of the annuity was less than 90 percent of what it would have been if the price level had remained stable; in other words, when the annuitant would have suffered a loss in purchasing power. Under the fixed annuity, this was the case in 65 out of 75 possible situations. For the combined annuity, investing 50

*Ibid., p. 47.

percent in fixed dollars and 50 percent in common stocks, this occurred only 25 times.

An Even More Surprising Finding. The study also tallied the number of periods under each of these annuities when the retired person would have enjoyed increased purchasing power because of a *decline* in prices. Here one might expect the fixed-dollar annuity to shine. First checked were the number of periods during which the annuities exceeded 110 percent of purchasing power. Under the fixed-dollar annuity (the life insurance variety) *this never occurred in any single period* of the 75 under consideration. The combined annuity (50 percent fixed dollars and 50 percent common stocks) managed to score 16 times.

He then tabulated the number of occasions when the annuities were between 90 and 110 percent of purchasing power. Of the 75 periods under review, the fixed annuity yielded ten such occasions; the combined annuity managed this 34 times.

The fixed annuity's purchasing power was less than 90 percent in over 85 percent of the periods. This was disquieting enough. But even more damning was the fact that in more than half of all possible cases, the purchasing power was *less than two-thirds* of what the retiree might have expected. For the combined annuity, this occurred in only 12 percent of the periods. Furthermore, the fixed annuity returned *less than 50 percent purchasing power* 12 times, while the combined annuity produced so dismal a result only once.

Running the Toughest Course. The accumulation period 1920–1930 followed by an annuity payout for 1930 to 1950 was especially interesting, for in this instance, the individual purchased his stocks at rising prices and began to receive his annuity payments when stock prices had declined precipitously. The period therefore subjects the theory to its severest test. *It is interesting to note that even in this period, the variable annuity exceeded the fixed annuity in all but four of the 20 years.*

Certainly then if the past is taken as any guide to the future, and this is admittedly a big "if," one must opt for a retirement plan that incorporates a variable dollar investment.

No Neutral Territory. Mr. Greenough did not rule out the possibility of declining prices. In common with most economists, however, he believed that our economy carries within itself a built-in inflationary bias, fuelled by heavy expenditures for defense, the tax structure, escalator wage clauses, cost-plus contracts, government subsidies, large-scale expenditures for welfare, Medicare, Medicaid, and so on.*

"At one time the forces of inflation or the forces of deflation seem to be stronger," Mr. Greenough concluded. But planning for retirement is a very long-range process and as a consequence he postulated that transitory shifts in the economy were relatively unimportant. The objective he urged "must be to provide reasonable security for the retired person against inflation." While he admitted that "there seems to be no perfect protection against inflation," he suggested that "retirement security can be substantially enhanced by broadening the scope and diversification of the investment of funds during working years."†

Can we take the experience of the near-century which Mr. Greenough charted so comprehensively as a guide to the future? Economics is not an exact science. Little understood phenomena with which we have never contended before make their appearance for the first time. "No one can deny that the current scene presents a picture very different from what we have been led to believe we understand. Chief among the problems that seem to defy our understanding because the past holds out so little guide is that of inflation. The inflation we now face is different not only in degree but in kind, too, from the inflation of the mid-Sixties; and since it has occurred in every economy of the free world it was fair to assume that there is a new situation.‡

One cannot rule out the possibility that the stock market will continue to slide in the years or decades ahead. Or that as a minimum it will fail to keep pace even loosely with the rise in the cost of living. Or for that matter that prices will not come down. Or that we are not poised on

* It is instructive to note that in 1973, Congress recognized inflation as a fact of our national life, and wrote into the Social Security Act an automatic adjustment factor to compensate for any future increases in the cost of living.

† William C. Greenough, op. cit., p. 8.

‡ These comments were made by Sir Frederick Catherwood, director general of the National Economic Development Council of the United Kingdom.

the edge of a worldwide depression which will uproot the very fabric of our social and economic system.

Insurance for One's Sunset Years. Now if you are convinced that the capitalist system is in its "death throes" and cannot endure for more than a relatively short time, or that in any case, all money is bound to be worthless, then much can be said for following the Biblical injunction "to eat, drink, and be merry." But if you harbor some hope, no matter how tenuous, that the system may just manage to muddle through, you may want to take out some "insurance" for your sunset years.

Gambling with Retirement Funds? It is undeniable that one should eschew as much as possible gambling with funds being accumulated for retirement. But doing nothing to try and hedge against inflation does not avoid gambling. This course merely gambles on the stability of the dollar over extended periods of time. In any long-range planning, one cannot afford to turn one's back on inflation, the insidious eroder of our dollars. Some "insurance" against its worst ravages must be undertaken.

Whether the stock market offers a sound medium for the regular accumulation of retirement funds and how this form of investment may be fitted into our overall financial planning will make up the subject of our next chapter.

9 ⁓ The Stock Market? Really?

It goes without saying that dollars being accumulated for retirement must be surrounded with maximum security. Traditional (fixed-dollar) insurance and annuities do provide maximum safety of principal and a guaranteed rate of return. But as we have seen they afford no security against one of the gravest threats to the retirement program—the steady decline in the dollar's purchasing power which has become a fixture of our economic system. It cannot be emphasized too strongly that over the long pull, even the most modest rate of inflation will make serious inroads into a retirement program. Thus, in only 10 years, a relatively demure inflation rate of only 4 percent will increase the cost of living by 48 percent; 7 percent inflation over this same period will just about double the cost of living, and so on. Needless to say, inflation on the level with which we have become all too familiar in recent years will wreak even greater havoc with the dollar's purchasing power. And all this in a 10-year period, a comparatively brief span compared to the period during which the usual retirement fund is accumulated and then paid out.

As might be expected, projecting inflationary effects over periods that more accurately reflect the average retirement situation produces consequences that are even more chilling. Thus, in a 30-year period a 3 percent annual inflation will increase the cost of living almost 2½ times; at 4 percent, the increase will come to 3¼ times; at 5 percent, it will be 4.3 times; at 6 percent, it will be close to 6 times.

Don't Hide Your Head in the Sand. To concentrate on safety of principal without concern for what the principal will *buy* is to hide one's head in the sand. It is a course which courts financial disaster no less than entrusting one's retirement dollars to the wildest form of speculation.

William C. Greenough's penetrating study, summarized in the preceding chapter, explored the hedge against inflation which might possibly be found in common stocks. He compared the purchasing power of a conventional, fixed-dollar annuity, you will recall, with that of an annuity invested in common stocks. He also checked the results of a "combination" annuity, divided equally between fixed and variable dollars, the latter in common stock. This third type of annuity, combining fixed and variable dollars, he felt, could be looked to for some protection not only against inflation, but against *de*flation as well because of the fixed-dollar investments it included.

The Lesser of Two Evils. The combined annuity did not provide a perfect answer to inflation but it did in the majority of cases stand up much more manfully to the problem, it was demonstrated, at least over a long period.

It would appear then that in this matter, as with most of the larger problems we face in an imperfect world, we must opt for the "lesser of two evils."

If we take the long view at the same time as we do everything possible to minimize the risk in the investments we make, direct participation in the country's economy through the medium of common stocks may hopefully give us some bulwark against the worst ravages of inflation. To paraphrase Winston Churchill's aphorism about democracy, investing in the stock market to hedge against inflation might be the second worst system in the world; the only worse one being all the others.

At the time this is being written, the stock market is toiling mightily to try to recapture the ground it lost in 1973 and 1974, when the Dow-Jones Industrial Stock Index declined 40 percent from its all-time high of 1,020—its worst slide in 33 years. (The other widely consulted stock market index, the Standard and Poor 500 Composite Index dropped from 118 to 68 for a 42 percent decline.) On several occasions, the Dow-Jones index managed to break 1,000 but in each instance it could not sustain the momentum. But even at 1,000, the market is still just about even with its level at the close of 1972. Some analysts were forecasting a "500 market," a development which would reflect a further decline of 18 percent.* Individual investors fled the market in droves. (The New York Stock Exchange in September 1974 estimated that 1.6 million individual investors had gone out of the market.)

The fixed-dollar galaxy, by contrast, is moving ahead quite strongly. The prime rate (the interest rate charged the highest-grade borrowers), while down considerably from its previous highs, still stands over 6.7 percent. Even savings banks, with deposits insured by the Federal Government are *guaranteeing* close to 8 percent.

If ever there was a period in which the market heartlessly moved in the opposite direction from the spiraling cost of living, it would appear to be the present one. How then can one turn one's back on all this disheartening evidence and obdurately invest in common stocks?

No Magic Elixir. To defend this seemingly sottish stand which flies in the face of so much currently fashionable opinion, it might be best to spell out what it is *not*. First and foremost, it must be stated that this program is not based on any forecast of market trends in the coming period. It is in no shape, manner, or form a "system"—for beating the market, or the experts, or the specialists or any section of the investing public. What is being advocated, and this cannot be stressed too strongly, is the setting aside of relatively small sums on a regular basis, *over long periods of time*. And the all-important element in the picture is not the level of stock prices (or yields) at any particular point in time, but precisely the need to continue doggedly on an established course through all the ups and downs of the market. "Time itself, rather than timing, or guessing market action, is the secret of investment success,"

* Market forecasting is apparently a field which democratically permits of the widest variety of opinion. Thus, at the same time as books which offer advice on how to profit from the impending stock market crash make their way past sex manuals to the top of the best seller list, other savants who were heavily bearish until recently are now prophesying recovery and a market rise to a level that will exceed anything seen to date!

"The Dow Jones Industrial Average could well approach the 2,000 level within the next 3 to 4 years . . ." from an advertisement for the Value Line Investment Survey in *New York Times*, March 29, 1975.

is the way one analyst put it.* And it is certainly true for the long-range retirement program.

Insurance—Just in Case. Although we *are* talking about investing in the market, our objective has nothing in common with the killing you are sure you can make as soon as you get the time to really devote yourself to a study of the market. Nor is the program being advocated—the regular deposit (preferably no less frequently than once a month) of a fixed sum—calculated to beguile you from the quest of another Xerox or Avon or whatever glamor stock makes up the content of your favorite daydream. If your sister's college chum and dearest friend is the girl friend of the president of the XYZ Corporation which is certain to become the Polaroid of the 1980s, you should by all means allow nothing to interfere with your becoming a millionaire. Naturally when this happy state comes to pass, the modest little retirement program that is being advocated here will have been rendered unimportant. But just as you take out life insurance, to protect against "dying too soon," although you have no intention of dying prematurely, you should give serious thought to putting a floor under the funds you will have on hand when and if you reach retirement age. You should also *insure* against "living too long."

The program being urged herein is not based on any crystal ball in which the future of the stock market is reflected. And since any single security, no matter how apparently solid, can come a cropper over the years (vide Penn Central as just one example) any plan for investing in common stocks must incorporate diversification over a broad spectrum of America's large corporations. The medium must also permit the investment of relatively modest sums and the reinvestment in full of all dividends and capital gain distributions, no matter how small.

Not All Eggs in One Basket. One natural candidate for this role is the investment trust, of which the mutual fund is the best known example. In almost every mutual fund, the investor's dollar is spread out over a

**Johnson's Investment Company Charts*, Twenty-Sixth Annual Edition, 1974, Buffalo, N.Y.

relatively large number of securities. The law normally limits the amount a fund may invest in any one industry, or any one company. Any and all dividends and capital gain distributions may be reinvested in the entire portfolio. Most funds are also free to move into cash, preferred stocks, bonds, convertibles, and other debentures—all in line with their assessment of the economic climate. Thus, a typical common stock fund which I have selected at random presents the following investment picture:

Common stock	*95.6 percent*
Other Assets cash, notes, and so on	*4.4 percent*

The 95.6 percent invested in common stocks comprises 76 companies distributed among 18 separate industry groups. The fund holds seven stocks in the automotive industry, three in banks and finance, four in building, five in chemicals and drugs, two in communications, two in data processing and office equipment, one in electrical equipment, five in food, two in leisure products, five in machinery and metal fabrication, three in merchandising, two in paper and containers, nine in petroleum, five in railroads, six in steel, two in textiles, two in tobacco, and eleven in utilities.

Furthermore, all the companies represented are substantial, with average assets at almost $1 billion; the smallest among them credited with $128 million. All but one of the companies have been in business over 30 years, 45 over 50 years, and one over 100 years. Over half of the companies have had an unbroken record of dividend payments for over 30 years, with none having paid dividends for less than 18 consecutive years.

You Can't Do It Yourself. To buy just one share of each of the stocks held by this fund would cost over $1,400 at mid-1975 prices. Like most funds, this one accepts investments of as little as $25, although some of its competitors have a $50 minumum.

The investor in a fund is entitled to his allocatable share of all the dividends and capital gains paid by the securities, which the fund holds. Such distributions, no matter how small, may be reinvested for him in the entire portfolio of the fund. Thus, an investor who started a share accumulation account in this fund with $25 would purchase 3.333 shares (at today's price). If the fund declares a quarterly dividend of 6 cents per share, he will be credited with about 20 cents. This sum can be reinvested in the entire portfolio of 76 securities, adding a little over 2/100ths of a share of the fund to his holdings.

A mutual fund, it is clear, is a most practical and well-nigh unique instrument permitting participation in a diversified portfolio of securities. And it can, if a moderate amount of self-discipline is marshalled, hold out some of the thrift-enforcing magnetism of the insurance premium notice. Just as life insurance may provide moral support to those who would "not save otherwise" so the mutual fund can exhort those who would not otherwise invest systematically for their inflation-prone retirement years.

How Good Are the Experts? In addition to diversification and the all-important administrative and bookkeeping services they offer, the funds also place great weight on their expertise in managing their clients' money. Charting a course through the treacherous shoals of the stock market is a highly technical matter, they maintain, which should be left to the professionals. To this end, they employ staffs of economists, researchers, and market analysts to safeguard and enhance the dollars entrusted to their tender care by the investing public.

The fund's effectiveness in managing investments is a subject that evokes much heated, often acrimonious debate. There is a respectable body of opinion which contends that the "think tanks" employed by the funds are an exercise in futility, that all their toil and trouble yield results no better than would be achieved by throwing darts at a stock list.

"The idea that the record of stock market professionals is no better than that of the averages is not new. Academicians such as Irwin Friend of the University of Pennsylvania's Wharton School have long claimed this. So have Professor Milton Friedman of the University of Chicago and Professor Paul S. Samuelson of the Massachusetts Institute of Technology."*

* *New York Times,* Financial Section, April 29, 1973.

The Bankers. Support for this jaundiced view of professional management is widespread and has been buttressed by persuasive evidence. The American Telephone and Telegraph Company in February 1973 took stock of the results achieved by 31 *banks* who had been in charge of managing a portion of the company's $10 billion pension fund. It reported that under the aegis of the banks, the fund had increased in six years by about 8 percent a year, which compared with a 9 percent increase in the Standard and Poor Index of 500 stocks.

The Fund Industry. The mutual fund industry's own figures, the critics point out, lend support to this unflattering view of management expertise. Through its trade association, the Investment Company Institute, the mutual fund industry takes to the pages of leading newspapers and magazines to point to its track record. $10,000 invested in the "average" fund in 1950, it is asserted, would have increased to $103,898 by the end of 1972. This works out to a growth rate of 12 percent a year after adjustment for sales charges, management fees, and other costs. Fairly impressive results, except when viewed against the fact that the Standard & Poor 500 Average grew at an annual rate of 13.2 percent.

The Life Insurance Companies. It is interesting to note that the life insurance companies do not appear to be doing any better with their common stock investments. Reviewing his company's results for 1974, J. Henry Smith, chairman of the board and chief executive officer of the Equitable Life Assurance Society of the United States, the nation's third largest, reported "record gains in insurance sales, premium income and investment return." Mr. Smith admitted, however, that "this was a very difficult year and our common stock performance was adversely affected by the trend of stock market prices toward the end of the year. Our performance for the year, however, *was quite near the popular stock indices,*" he added. (*Journal of Commerce,* February 25, 1975—emphasis not in the original).

But There Are Stars in the Firmament, No? That professional management does not perform better than random selection is a tenet you probably find hard to embrace. For one thing, it outrages a dearly held faith you nurture in your ability to beat the averages if only you could find the time. And in any event, isn't it true that some funds outperform others?

The exhaustive ratings of funds such as are featured by *Forbes,* the giant volume on investment companies published annually by Wiesenberger Services, and the monthly magazine *Fundscope* and its annual guide which runs to some 500 pages, to mention just a few examples, assiduously pore over every twist and turn in the funds' results with the intentness of a physician studying a patient's temperature chart. The records of hundreds of funds are carefully evaluated as to income, growth, charges, changes in portfolio and management policy, and so on. The funds are ranked in order of their performance, and the record is clear. There are indeed substantial differences in their results. Even if it is true that the *average* fund does no better than a random selection would, surely the leading funds outperform the averages.* It would appear elementary then that if one were going into funds, one should certainly choose the best performer. Unfortunately, this seemingly simple prescription is almost impossible to fill. Why is this so?

Chasing Last Year's Miss America. It is obvious that in order to profit from the standout performance of a fund, an investor must know of its superior ability *in advance* of investing in it. Let us say then that

* The question is beset with rather discouraging technicalities. Thus, great interest centered on the very exhaustive study of mutual funds, popularly known as the Wharton School Report (U.S. Government Printing Office, Washington, D.C., 1962). The report yielded such thickets as the following:

"To obtain the corresponding rate of return for all New York Stock Exchange stocks, some weighting for each stock must be specified. Two weighting schemes are available for comparative purposes, one involving equal investment in each of the stocks, the other investing proportional investments (the weights are proportional to the value of the stock outstanding). Equal investment in each of the New York Stock Exchange stocks would have yielded annual rates of return of:

12.4% January 1960 through June 1969
7.0% January 1960 through March 1964
17.8% April 1964 through June 1968

respectively, according to Fischer's combination link relatives. Proportional investments would have yielded annual rates of return of 9.9%, 9.9% and 9.8%."

you were converted to the mutual fund way in 1962. You consulted one of the standard guides to the crowded firmament of the mutual fund industry (the August 1962 issue of *Forbes* Magazine) and found that a little over 100 funds had been in operation for the better part of the eight-year bull market ending on December 31, 1961. And that of these, the Dreyfus Fund outperformed all its common stock competitors. The record showed that $100 invested in Dreyfus at the beginning of the period under scrutiny would have been worth $505. This was indeed an outstanding record, since only five other funds were even as high as $400. You invest in this fund, hopeful that your foresight will be rewarded in the coming period. Twelve months later, you take stock of your investment. The August 15, 1963 issue of *Forbes* reveals that your fund, which had been #1 when you bought it, has now come up with a rather lesser performance for the past 12 months. It is now 48th among its counterparts for the period June 30, 1962 to June 30, 1963.

If At First You Don't Succeed. You philosophically put this down to bad luck and check for the new frontrunner, which you find is American Investors Fund. You switch into this fund and this time your sagacity seems to be rewarded. American Investor Fund's growth for the succeeding year again passes all its rivals. One year later, just to make doubly sure, you have another look at your selection and discover to your chagrin that 120 common stock funds outperformed it; actually only some 58 funds turned in a poorer record for the year. You conclude that it's time to move your dollars into the Over The Counter Securities Fund which beat all its competitors at least among funds which had been around for 10 years.

One year later, your fund has fallen behind 21 others. And so you follow the new champion's siren call—into Channing Special Fund—which a year later comes in 23rd. This time, Enterprise Fund leads and stays out front for a second year. But in what is becoming an all too familiar pattern, it cannot hold its lead for a third year and for the period June 30, 1968 to June 30, 1969, it falls to 40th place. Cowed but still not beaten, you move into the new star, the First Sierra Fund. A year later, its bright promise is somewhat dimmed as it polls a 70th place. ICM Financial Fund takes the lead for the year ending June 30, 1970. On June

30, 1971, this fund is running 165th in a field of 193. You try again, this time with Admiralty Insurance Series which is first for the year but closes with 113 of its competitors ahead of it. . . .

Our tracking of the top performers based itself solely on the annual performance of each of the contendors. Analyses of much greater sophistication can be, and have been, evolved. Funds can be classified as to their "objective"—long-term capital appreciation, high-income yield, stability in fluctuating markets, high volatility, and so on. Furthermore, Dr. Edward Marcus, Professor of Economics at Brooklyn College, has observed, "By different statistical approaches and guidelines, we can come up with different answers showing how well or poorly the average mutual fund has performed."*

Even if a particular fund cannot hold its place as #1 each year, it may still be preferable if it can manage to stay in the upper echelon for more years than its competitors. Studies of this kind abound, some so involved as to tax all but the hardiest souls.

Trying to Hold On to Greased Lightning. The entire question was explored more formally by Eugene Fama of the University of Chicago who compiled yearly rankings for 39 funds over a 10 year period and found virtually no consistency in their performance. Table V shows the yearly ranking for three funds over a period of 10 years.

TABLE V. FUNDS AND THEIR RANKINGS

Year	*Keystone S-4*	*Chemical Fund*	*International Resources*
1	29	1	10
2	1	39	37
3	38	14	39
4	5	27	22
5	3 (tied)	3 (tied)	35
6	8	33	1
7	35	1	37
8	1	27	39
9	1 (tied)	4	1 (tied)
10	36	23	11

* Quoted from an article in the Commercial and Financial Chronicle by *Fundscope,* vol. 14, no. 4, April 1971, p. 10.

It can be seen at a glance that these funds have gone back and forth from the top of the ranking (1) right to the bottom (39).* Prof. J. Peter Williamson of the Amos Tuck Graduate School of Business Administration at Dartmouth did a more comprehensive study of 180 mutual funds. "If you go through and rank mutual funds for any period and then rank them again for a subsequent period, there is little or no correlation between the two periods," Prof. Williamson found. This effectively deflates any claim for management's ability to produce results superior to those of random selection, Prof. Williamson concludes.

Furthermore, even if a pattern of superior performance could be traced for a particular fund, or several funds, the chances are that few will keep the same managers over the protracted periods we are considering. Thus, a financial writer in a leading newspaper recently found that of the 20 leading funds in the latest quarter ending on March 31, 1975, only six had been in business for as long as 10 years, and that "few have been under the same portfolio management for 10 years" (Robert Metz, *New York Times,* April 2, 1975). According to these experts, trying to latch on to the leading fund is like trying to hold on to greased lightning. As a stockbroker of my acquaintance puts it, "The quest to invest in the top mutual fund is chasing last year's Miss America."

Till Death Do Us Part. The results cited above certainly make out a good case for the futility of trying to settle on a fund which will be a consistent frontrunner over the many years that are involved in a retirement plan. Or of trying to stay ahead of the mob by moving in and out of funds as their batting averages fluctuate. Admittedly, this latter course could be pursued without too much loss if the selections were confined to "no-load" funds (to be discussed in a later chapter). But the practice of responding year by year to the current level of a particular fund is poised on very thin ice. It is the direct opposite of the end to be sought in any retirement plan, to wit: to invest regularly in a diversified portfolio of leading stocks *for the long pull,* without getting drawn into the exciting game of trying to outguess the market. This pastime, ap-

* Burton G. Malkiel, *A Random Walk Down Wall Street.* New York: W. W. Norton & Company, Inc., 1973, p. 153.

pealing though it is, is diametrically opposed to the monogamous stance of picking a fund and staying with it until "retirement do us part."

But even if an individual believes he *can* do better than the funds' experts, his enthusiasm should be dampened considerably by the fact that the commissions on transactions of the kind performed by the funds would come to about $900, or some 65 percent of the cost of the securities being bought.

Every effort should be made to look on the retirement program as an insurance policy which calls for regular premiums, *regardless of the state of the economy or the level of the market*. The entire strategy should be relegated to a separate compartment of one's investment life which needs no reconciling with any pet theories on investment.

Your Pet Theories Notwithstanding. If you are a chartist, or a devotee of the "filter system," or the "relative strength system," or the "price-volume system," or the "reading chart system" (for example, "Is the downward penetration of a head-and-shoulders formation a reliable bearish omen?") do not feel that you have to resolve the "controversy" between your special strategy and the aridly unimaginative retirement plan being advocated.* Strange as it may seem, the wisest course, if you are committed to pitting yourself against the stock market, is to go on doing what you think you do best, at the same time as you embark on the unexciting program being advocated here—talking through both sides of your mouth, as it were. The plodding, bullheaded program of "withholding" of a fixed sum every week or month to be sequestered in a diversified portfolio of high-grade stocks in fair weather or foul, in face of the hot tips that float across your horizon should be viewed as your insurance premium against the risk of "living too long."

The mutual fund, we have seen, offers all the necessary ingredients

* These stock market systems and others even more whimsical are very entertainingly discussed in Burton G. Malkiel, *A Random Walk Down Wall Street*. New York: W. W. Norton & Company, Inc., 1973, pp. 112 ff. Here will be found such choice morsels as the "bull markets and bare knees" theory which postulates that the level of stock market prices can be forecast from the hemline of women's dresses. And the investment strategy which bases itself on the belief that the odd-lotter is invariably wrong and that investment success can be assured by buying when this Sad Sack sells and selling what he buys.

of such a program. It provides a variable component as a hedge against inflation plus diversification as a hedge against business failure. In the next chapter, however, we shall see that there is now a newer financial vehicle which incorporates virtually all the benefits of the open investment trust (mutual funds) plus several additional bonuses which may add up to a most exciting retirement package, in your own situation.

10 The Variable Annuity

EARLIER, in Chapter 8, where we discussed the impact of inflation on long-range financial planning, we described the birth pangs of a new arrival on the life insurance horizon—the variable annuity. We found that after the *Sturm und Drang* of its infancy, little energy was expended on its nurture. Almost all of such business as has been written is concentrated in the group field. At the end of 1975, barely 600,000 individuals held such plans.* It is likely, therefore, that you may never have heard of the product and it is practically certain that you have never been solicited in person or even by mail to consider how this modern financial vehicle might fit your situation. The reasons for the variable annuity's obscurity will become apparent later in this chapter.

Annuity Defined. Let us first be clear on what a variable annuity is. The dictionary defines annuity as "an investment which entitles a person to a fixed annual sum for life." The conventional annuity, as well as the life income which a beneficiary may receive from the proceeds of an insurance policy, are in fact such guarantees. The income may be paid monthly, quarterly, semiannually, or annually, but the precise amount of each installment which is guaranteed for life is fixed.

You may recall from our earlier comments that any annuity is the direct *opposite* of life insurance. The insurance mechanism pools the premiums of a large number of individuals to create a fund out of which to pay the beneficiaries of those who die. Those members of the insured group who live long pay for those who die early. Life insurance thus protects against "dying too soon." Contrarywise, the annuity pools the deposits of large numbers to pay each member of the group an income

* *Life Insurance Fact Book,* American Council of Life Insurance 1976, p. 43.

for as long as he lives. Those who live longer are paid from the funds of those who do not. The annuity thus protects against "living too long."

The Same—But Different. The variable annuity embodies this same principle. It too pools the resources of many people to guarantee all an income for life. It differs fundamentally, however, in the nature of the guarantee it extends. Instead of committing itself to a predetermined amount, it promises only to pay a specific *number* of *units* for life. The size of each unit fluctuates, reflecting at each point the value of the underlying investments. As a consequence, the annuity payments received by the annuitant vary from month to month.

It is on this important point that the conventional fixed-dollar and the variable annuity part company. The older annuity, which promises a fixed benefit, must perforce invest its clients' money in fixed-dollar obligations. It basically lends its clients' money. The variable annuity, by contrast, committed as it is to no specific dollar benefit, can go into variable dollars. It invests directly in shares of businesses. The annuitant's fortunes under the latter rise and fall with the investment results achieved by those who are managing his funds.

The variable annuity, like the fixed-dollar variety, can provide an immediate income, or one deferred to begin at a date in the future. It too may be paid for in a single sum or purchased on installments. Like its fixed-dollar ancestor, the variable annuity provides a vehicle through which a participant may share in a broad portfolio of investments made on his behalf. The variable annuity also reinvests all dividends and capital gain distributions in the complete portfolio it maintains for its investors.

You have no doubt begun to detect the strong family resemblance between the variable annuity and the mutual fund which was discussed in the preceding chapter. How do these two financial packages stack up as vehicles in retirement planning?*

* "There is no new thing under the sun," the sage has told us. And while the variable annuity appears to be a revolutionary idea brought about by deep changes in our economic life ("The most modern concept of the 20th century" is the way the Travelers literature dubs the variable annuity), there are examples of similar financial arrangements which date back hundreds of years. Thus, we find records of a survivorship annuity dating back to 1265 in which Robert Newman and his son, Badoin, arranged for a lifetime annuity of

The Principal Surrendered. It needs to be emphasized at the outset that under *any* form of annuity, the participant, in exchange for the life income he is promised, surrenders his capital. Once he has received his first annuity payment, he can no longer recover any of the money he has paid to the company. Some annuities do guarantee a minimum number of payments, if the annuitant does not himself live long enough to receive them, but in all events, he has given up any right to the principal he turns over to the company.

Since surrendering one's principal is an unavoidable consequence of the annuity concept, an individual who reaches retirement with sufficient funds to live comfortably on the income alone will generally prefer to preserve his capital, and leave it to those dear to him, or to some cause which is close to his heart. It is only when the funds he has on hand are not sufficient to keep him in whatever style he fancies for himself that he may be forced to begin invading his capital. This course would expose him to the dread possibility of outliving his resources.

Through the mechanism of the annuity, he can pool his funds with others in a similar situation. Each member of the group will receive a regular income, composed not only of earnings on his capital but also of part of the capital itself. Some will live long enough to receive much more than they invest; others will die before they do. But no member of the group can outlive his income. Because of the "law of large numbers," all are protected against "living too long."

An individual who begins setting aside regular sums toward his eventual retirement has no way of knowing what his situation will be years hence. It may turn out that he will be able to live comfortably at that time without invading his principal, merely by "clipping coupons." In this case he will not be in the market for an annuity. On the other hand, if his resources prove insufficient to produce an income adequate to cover his needs, it may be expedient for him to buy an annuity from some insurance company.

One Important Difference. To get back now to the mutual fund and the variable annuity: An individual who has been accumulating mutual

---

400 Parisian livres. The contract contained a proviso that if the purchasing power of the Parisian pound declined, payment was to be made in the sous of Tournai at the ratio of 50 Tournaise sous to 43 Parisian livres.

funds toward his retirement and finds that he is in fact in the market for an annuity when he reaches retirement age will have to sell his mutual fund shares and apply the proceeds at that time toward the purchase of an annuity from an insurance company.* Such purchase will have to be made at the rates *then* in effect. In light of the improved life expectancy that may eventuate with further advances in medical science, the rates then being charged for annuities may well be substantially higher than those that prevailed when he first embarked on his accumulation program.

By contrast, an individual who initiates the purchase of a variable annuity today is protected against rate increases that may develop in the years that will elapse before he actually begins to receive his annuity income. If the insurance company's rates go up during this time, they will affect only purchasers who come into the covered group after the date of the increase. If, on the other hand, annuity rates are decreased—a situation which could come about if life expectancy were to worsen—one can elect to take the cash accumulated for one's account and apply it to purchase an annuity at the more favorable rates. The variable annuity thus protects the individual against increases in annuity rates, while the mutual fund does not.

It should be pointed out that this protection is not free. There is a charge made for this mortality guarantee. It is nevertheless a plus on the side of the variable annuity.

A Guaranteed "Death Benefit." There is a second element of protection under a variable annuity that the basic mutual fund does not offer. When a mutual fund investor dies, his heirs become entitled to the

* Some mutual funds do offer a "withdrawal" plan under which the shareholder elects to have paid out to him periodically a fixed sum from his holdings. It is hoped that the dividends which the fund will earn will be sufficient to make up the amounts withdrawn, or that if some shares need to be sold in order to reach the desired withdrawal that the growth in the fund's asset value will compensate for the amount of shares sold off. In such event, the retiree will be able to look forward to an income which continues throughout his lifetime. If, however, the hoped-for growth in the share value does not materialize, he may find his equity diminishing, and this at a time when he is no longer productively employed. A program of this kind, it can be seen, is lacking a critical ingredient of every retirement program—the assurance of an income that cannot be outlived.

property. They can convert the property into cash—a mutual fund is always completely liquid—and will receive the net asset value of the shares on the date of the sale. Depending on the direction of the market during the period when the shares were being acquired, this may be more or less than the amount paid by the deceased while he was purchasing the shares.

Under a variable annuity, if the annuitant-investor dies during the accumulation period (before the annuity payout period begins), his heirs are guaranteed a minimum sum that cannot be less than the amount invested prior to the investor's death. To illustrate, assume a 35-year-old investor establishes a deferred variable annuity calling for monthly deposits of $250 which he hopes to make until he retires some 30 years later. He dutifully makes the called-for monthly deposits of $250 for five years (60 payments of $250 each for a total of $15,000) when he is cruelly cut off by death. Because of the charges that were deducted by the insurance company and a decline in the stock market, his shares are worth only $10,000 on the date of his death. His heirs are nevertheless entitled to receive $15,000—the full amount invested by him up to the time of his death.

The second guarantee, the minimum death benefit, will generally be of relatively minor importance, at least after the early years of a retirement program. In any event, as in the case of the first guarantee, the protection against a rise in annuity rates, there is a charge for this mortality guarantee.

Favorable Tax Treatment. A considerably more important plus on the side of the variable annuity arises out of the tax treatment of this form of investment. A mutual fund can (and almost always does) avoid all income taxes on the dividends it receives and the capital gains it realizes from the sale of securities by distributing such to its investors. The individual investor, however, is subject to income taxes on any such dividends and the capital gain distributions whether he takes these in cash or reinvests them in additional shares of the fund.

The purchaser of a variable annuity, on the other hand, does not pay tax on the dividends and capital gains which are realized by the variable annuity company and reinvested for his account. Needless to say, this can loom very significant over a period of years. How much savings will accrue to an individual by virtue of this immunity from taxation will depend of course on his individual tax bracket.

Additionally, when the investor under a variable deferred annuity reaches retirement and wants to begin taking down his monthly annuity payments, he does not have to sell any shares in order to purchase the annuity. By contrast, the investor who has been accumulating his retirement funds in mutual funds will need to sell his shares in order to purchase the annuity. When he effects this sale, he will be subject to tax on the gain in his shares. In addition to protection against rate increases and return of investment in full in the event of death, this difference in tax treatment can add another important plus to the account of the variable annuitant.

What's Wrong with the Picture? As might be expected, the few still weak voices that are sometimes heard praising the variable annuity place great store by the tax savings possible under this relative newcomer to the investment field. And there is no question that it can prove to be an important boon. Now it would be pleasant to be able to report that the situation is as straightforward as it appears to be from the above tally of the pros and cons of the two forms of investment. Unfortunately, as in most such matters, there are shadows that need to be spread on the record, in the interest of an accurate picture.

As indicated above, the individual investing in a variable annuity is not taxed on the capital gains realized for his account by the variable annuity life insurance company. But the insurance company itself *is* subject to taxes of some 30 percent on such capital gains. This tax reduces the amount which the company can credit to the account of its client-annuitants. The mutual fund, which distributes all dividends and capital gains to its investors, we recall, pays no taxes; all dividends and capital gains are passed on to the investor in cash, or reinvested in additional shares, as the shareholder directs. The individual investor must, however, report the distributions and pay the appropriate taxes. It can be seen that in some instances a mutual fund investor may be better off, on this score at any rate, than a holder of a variable annuity. This situation would be obtained if he were in a lower tax bracket than the insurance company, or in those years in which he had investment losses which could offset the capital gains received from the mutual fund.

It is obvious then that on this point no general rule will apply to all individuals. The rate of taxation on capital gains varies from individual to individual. However, this should not pose too thorny a dilemma. The one possible tax *dis*advantage under a variable annuity, we have seen, is that the annuity company is taxed on the capital gains it earns at a 30 percent rate. If this rate is higher than the individual's own rate, he sustains a loss. But even this drawback is almost always certain to be outweighed by the tax savings on ordinary dividends. Such dividends are completely free of taxation. Further savings accrue at the point of retirement when the annuitant does not have to sell his stock and pay taxes on his gain in order to purchase an annuity.

Further Complicating Factors. Weighing these two investment media in the balance is further complicated by the factor of sales charges and, in about half the states, by premium taxes levied on insurance companies. While the majority of mutual funds impose a sales charge (usually about 8 percent of the sums invested), there are scores of established and well-regarded funds that make no such charge. Commonly known as "no-load" funds, they generally redeem as well as sell their shares without any charge. (A listing of such no-load growth funds will be found in Chapter 16.)

The variable annuities sold to individuals are subject to sales charges. These charges are deducted from the amount invested and as a consequence the effective yield of this form of investment is reduced. The attempt to assign points to these competing media is further complicated by the wide diversity of charges imposed by the various annuity companies. Thus, one of the few studies ever done of the load charges imposed on a 10-year investment of $1,000 per annum by 29 variable annuity companies showed percentage charges ranging from 6.7 to 22.2 percent.*

* Mark R. Greene, "Note on Loading Charges for Variable Annuities," *The Journal of Risk and Insurance*, September 1973, p. 475.

Enter Premium Taxes. As if the factor of loadings were not enough to complicate the picture, there is also the matter of premium taxes imposed on insurance companies in about half the states. These taxes range from 1 percent of stipulated payments made by the annuitant-investor to 3 percent. Where levied, these taxes further dilute the tax advantages enjoyed by the variable annuity. There are also enrollment fees charged by some variable annuity carriers, but these are usually one-time costs and do not affect the overall cost too severely. A charge for administration of the funds under their care is also made by variable annuity companies, but these are generally about the equivalent of similar charges made by mutual fund managements, so they will not tip the balance too strongly.

To what extent the tax advantages of a variable annuity will offset the sales charges (and premium taxes where applicable) cannot be determined with any finality except after a study of the individual investor's situation and a "crystal ball" projection of the future investment results. It would appear, however, that if one were to opt for a variable annuity with a low sales charge, he should do better over the years than under a mutual fund accumulation program, all other things being equal (which of course they seldom are). Chapter 16, which rates variable annuities by their loadings, also takes up the question of grading of these charges. There it is shown that the size of the investment contemplated also affects the choice of a "best buy."

Getting Back to Basics. At this point, it is necessary only to reiterate the fundamental consideration which should underly planning for retirement as opposed to investment for building one's future—the need to begin as soon as possible the orderly and systematic setting aside of a fixed sum in a medium which fully invests every dollar in a reasonably wide spread of the securities of American industry; and the importance of a dogged persistence in the program throughout the ups and downs of the market—the euphoria of a bull market and the usually equally unfounded panic selling in bear markets.

Two candidates for the role of retirement planning have been discussed here: the mutual fund and the variable annuity. Either one of these embodies the most important features of this type of retirement planning. Because of the tax picture, the variable annuity, if properly bought, will generally prove more advantageous over long periods of time. It also has a certain "psychological" advantage, in that the daily price fluctuations of this form of investment are not carried in the newspapers. The chances of getting drawn into the tantalizing contest of outguessing the market is therefore lessened, and the chances of carrying through to completion under this type of program is thereby heightened.

As will be shown in Chapter 16, "Retirement Needs: How Much, and from Whom?" connecting up with a superior variable annuity may prove more difficult than purchasing mutual funds. If an investor does find the purchase of a variable annuity surrounded by too many impediments and elects to go the mutual fund way, the overall objectives of a sound retirement program should be adequately served.

11 The "Other" Uses of Life Insurance

WE HAVE NOW analyzed in some depth the two principal risks against which life insurance offers protection—that of "living too long" or "dying too soon." Against the latter hazard, premature death, it has been made clear, we hope, that low-premium Term insurance can be utilized most effectively and economically. As for the accumulation of a retirement fund—protection against the risk of "living too long"—we have found life insurance seriously deficient, offering as it does a very low rate of return even if carried over long periods of time, and severe loss of principal if surrendered in the early years. In addition, like all forms of fixed-dollar investment or savings, the life insurance product fails to hold out any hope of a hedge against the ravages of inflation. For retirement funds, we have seen, some other medium other than the fixed-dollar products offered by life insurance carriers must be brought into play.

In the next chapter, we shall address ourselves to techniques for determining the extent of our need for coverage in these two distinct fields. We shall also set forth the specific policies and products that most effectively and economically meet these objectives. Before we get down to these specifics, however, we must examine some of the remaining areas in which life insurance claims to be useful.

An Ideal Form of Savings? Individuals with no one to protect are frequently urged to buy life insurance because it is an "ideal form of savings." For this worthy goal, some form of endowment policy is recommended, the most popular being the 20-Year Endowment. The policy's advocates may admit that a program of regular savings in a bank would do at least as well as the Endowment policy, but they voice grave doubts about the average person's ability to follow through on such an alternate course. By its very nature, an insurance policy tends to keep the policyholder on the "straight and narrow." It acts as a thrift inducer, they insist. On that happy day when the endowment period is completed, the virtuous policyholder who has been insured during the years is rewarded with a return of all the premiums he paid plus a handsome profit. Thus, as an example, in the Aetna Life Insurance Company (the company which has been our "guinea pig"), a male age 35 can get a $10,000 20-Year Endowment for an annual premium of $431.30. In 20 years, his premiums will total $8,626.00, but he is *guaranteed* a return of $10,000. He has been insured all through the years and now shows a "handsome profit" of $1,374.00. This "handsome profit" is the equivalent of just under 1⅝ percent. And at younger ages, when the premium is lower, even larger gains will ensue at the end of the endowment period. Thus, at age 25, a $10,000 20-Year Endowment policy in the same company will produce a return over cost of $1,662.00 after having provided protection against death during the 20-year period. This represents a better "return" on premiums than is available to the 35-year-old Insured but is still well under 2 percent.

Obviously, these results are much inferior to those that can be realized in any savings bank or savings and loan association. At 6 percent interest, an annual deposit of $431.30 (the premium for the endowment policy purchased by a 35-year-old male) will grow to $16,817.68 in 20 years—some 68 percent better than the cash value of the policy. Current savings bank interest rates which run over 7 percent will of course tip the balance even more substantially against the life insurance savings plan.

Are Bank Managers Smarter? The marked superiority of savings banks returns over those of life insurance carriers is not due to any unique financial sagacity of those who manage bank investments. In the endowment policy, there is a life insurance element. From all we have learned about the life insurance mechanism, it should be quite clear that life insurance *always* costs. Under endowment forms, whose premiums are higher than under a Whole Life policy, the over-payments, the portion of the premium that is not required by the mortality risk, are considerably larger than under the lower premium policy. The reserve accumulates more rapidly; as a consequence, the true insurance protection decreases even more sharply. But there is nevertheless an insurance component in the policy, and for this protection a charge must be made.

All advertising hyperbole to the contrary notwithstanding, there is no such thing as free insurance. The "profit" on the endowment policy is merely another variation on the entirely misleading "net cost" theme which was dissected in Chapter 2—"What Does Term Insurance Really Cost?" As has been demonstrated before, if one is prepared to disregard the power of interest, he can emerge with all manner of nonsense such as "free insurance with handsome profits," the "miracle of cash value insurance," and the like. How well advised it is to accept serious loss of interest for the thrift-inducing discipline of the life insurance premium notice is a very personal matter. It would seem that with tangible alternative savings and investment media, there is little warrant for such a course.

The Early Bird Gets the Worm. Even before the need to protect dependents is in view, young persons, especially young men, are urged to buy life insurance because of the low rate available to them. Premium rates for all forms of insurance, it cannot be gainsaid, increase with advancing years. Isn't it prudent then to make the plunge as soon as possible and thereby enjoy the lower rate in the long years to come?

$10,000 of Whole Life insurance can be purchased by a boy age 15 for an annual premium of $96.30. If this same individual waits to buy until he is 30, the premium will be $150.60. And this premium, over 52 percent higher, will have to be paid every year for life. The argument continues as follows: Assume insurance is carried to age 65 in both instances. The forward-looking young man who buys his insurance at age 15 will be paying an annual premium of $ 96.30 for 50 years—a total of $4,815.00. If he waits until he is 30 before buying, he will pay premiums for only 35 years, it is true, but these will amount to $5,271.00. He will be out of pocket $556.00 more than if he had been carrying insurance from the time he was 15.

This is still another version of the old gambit. It conveniently glosses over the hard fact of "decreasing net amount at risk" which results from the accumulation of a reserve inside (or outside) a policy. This important element is the core of all cash value life insurance, we have seen. If the money which our 15-year-old is urged to pay over in insurance premiums until he really needs insurance—when he is 30—were invested at 6 percent, it would amount to $2,376 by the time he attains age 30. To create an "estate" of $10,000 he needs only $7,624.00 of life insurance, for this sum plus his savings will amount to $10,000. The annual premium for this amount of insurance at age 30 will be $118.38, which, while not as low as $96.30 paid by a 15-year-old, is much closer to it than the $150.60 which is held over the head of a prospect. If we now recalculate the premiums that each would pay until he attains age 65, the 15-year-old purchaser will pay out $4,815, while his counterpart who waited until the need for insurance developed at age 30 will spend $4,143.30. Of course, this same amount of Term insurance can be purchased by the 30-year-old at a rate of some $4.00 per $1,000. If this difference is set aside in a reasonable thrift medium (according to the plan discussed in Chapter 2), the hollowness of buy-early-to-save-money pitch will come into even sharper focus.

Life Insurance as a Tax Savings Device. There is a great deal of talk, much of it regrettably loose, about life insurance as a tax savings device. What are the facts? First, with respect to income taxes, there is in fact a certain tax shelter in cash value life insurance. Briefly, the buildup of cash values in a life insurance policy is not subject to income taxes until the cash value exceeds the premiums paid, and then only when the policyholder surrenders the policy. In other words, while the policyholder is being credited with earnings on his cash values, such yield is generally not subject to income tax except after relatively long periods of time. The Whole Life policy, at any rate, unless it has been carried for many years, produces little or no taxable gain. On higher premium forms, like 20-Payment Life or Endowment policies, the cash value after some years can exceed the premiums paid, but even in those instances, there is some tax benefit.

Uncle Sam Plays Along. The tax shelter in life insurance develops from the fact that the Government, at least with respect to the taxability of cash values, plays along with the "net cost" charade we have dwelt on so repeatedly. It does not separate the portion of the premium going into reserves from that being paid for protection (the mortuary fund), except under certain circumstances in pension plans. The cost of protection is in effect lumped together with the reserves. Understandably, this serves to camouflage the gain actually being earned on the reserves.

This may appear a little difficult to follow. It can be made clear by reviewing the hypothetical case (in Chapter 3) of the individual who responds to an advertisement of a bank plugging its "Programmed Thrift Plan." You will recall that he first undertakes to make regular deposits into a savings account. After the transaction is complete, he goes to a life insurance company (or the life insurance department of the bank where such institutions sell life insurance) and buys a Decreasing Term policy. This policy, which complements his thrift account, decreases at a rate which reflects exactly the growth in his savings account.

The interest credited on his passbook savings is of course subject to income tax. To put him on a par with the owner of a cash value life insurance policy, two special dispensations would have to be made by the Government. First, the depositor would have to be granted the right to defer the payment of income taxes until he actually withdraws his money from the bank. And secondly, when he does withdraw the savings and settles down to compute his taxable gain, he would need to be permitted a deduction from such gain of all premiums he paid on his decreasing Term insurance throughout the years.

You Still Lose Out. No such bonuses extend to a savings bank account, and so the cash value policy scores on this account. In effect, it means that an Insured can buy decreasing Term insurance with tax-sheltered dollars. The problem of course is that in order to take advantage of the tax break, he must tie himself into a cash value policy with all the serious deficiencies of such savings plans. (This tax shelter in cash value life insurance inspired a veritable revolution in the selling of life insurance. It gave rise to the minimum deposit concept which will be discussed in a later chapter of the book.)

"Protecting" Beneficiaries against Themselves. Owners of life insurance are regularly urged to arrange their insurance so that the proceeds which will become payable upon their death are retained by the company and paid out to the beneficiaries in installments, or in the form of a life income. (Some 8.5 percent of the almost $300 billion of policy reserves are being administered in this manner.) All companies offer a number of options in lieu of the single sum payment. The policy proceeds may be held by the company and interest only paid to the beneficiary or beneficiaries. Or, the Insured may direct that the beneficiary receive fixed monthly installments or payments for a stated number of years. Lastly, the companies also offer several varieties of life income options. The highest income is paid under the option which provides a life income to the beneficiary with no minimum guarantee, that is, all payments cease at the beneficiary's death. A second form of this option provides that a minimum number of payments will be made to a second beneficiary if the first dies before having received all the guaranteed payments—60 monthly installments, 120 installments, 240 monthly installments, as the case may be. As might be expected, the size of the payment to be received by the beneficiary varies inversely with the length of the guaranteed period. The policy includes a set of tables which set forth the income under the various forms of life income option, based on the age and sex of the *beneficiary* when the Insured dies, as well as the installments available under the other options.

Within reasonable limits, companies will permit the use of these options in combination. They will also accept instructions from the Insured granting the beneficiary the right to withdraw the principal or stipulated amount of it at stated intervals. Thus, an Insured could direct that at his death the company is to retain the proceeds of the policy and pay the beneficiary interest only on this sum for a number of years. He may also provide that during this time the beneficiary will have the right to withdraw up to a stated amount per year. The proceeds remaining unpaid at the expiration of the period during which interest only is being paid are then to be applied under the life income option with any sums remaining unpaid at the death of the first beneficiary to be paid to a second beneficiary, and so on. These services, which are similar to those provided by trustees, are made available by the insurance company without charge or fees.

The Light-Headed Widow (Sic). Settling policy proceeds under these options is usually recommended as a method of insulating carefully created insurance estates against dissipation by improvident or impractical beneficiaries. Heart-wringing accounts are summoned up of well-meaning but naive widows preyed upon by impecunious relatives or unscrupulous promoters. Forty years ago in a now all but forgotten book a vice-president of the National Life Insurance Company of Vermont addressed himself to this question. "It was once said that 'life insurance paid in one sum vanishes' and that 'ninety percent of all insurance is dissipated in seven years'."* The writer points out that some insurance money is expected to disappear, that "disappearance is not dissipation." He faces up to the stereotype of the simple-minded widow in words that are especially interesting in light of the current women's liberation movement. "The unfair part of the statement under discussion," he continues, "was the insinuation, if not assertion, that this dissipation and waste was the fault of incompetent womenfolk. The time was perhaps when sheltered womanhood might not safely handle substantial sums of money. No one can make that general assertion today. By experience in handling their own property or assisting men in handling theirs, as employee or wife, women have developed an ability to assume the responsibilities of the family and direct its financial affairs with success. Certainly, the investment experience of the male sex in recent years gives it no claim to superior ability."†

How well your beneficiary fits the profile of the crinoline and lace starry-eyed innocent is something you alone can determine. Before making a decision on how to handle your life insurance, it is important to understand that a life insurance company is *not* a trustee. It can hold

* Guy B. Horton, *Making the Best Use of Your Life Insurance,* Montpelier, Vt., 1936, p. 16.

† Ibid., p. 17.

and administer insurance proceeds and pay them out according to your instructions. It cannot, however, exercise any discretion. If your policy stipulates that the beneficiary shall have the right to withdraw $10,000 in any one calendar year, the insurance company cannot decide whether such withdrawal is wise or warranted. Nor, on the other hand, can it increase the amount to be paid out, regardless of how worthy the purpose for which the larger sum is being requested.

Don't Rule with a Dead Hand. Tying up large sums in supplementary contracts (as these arrangements are called) may also prove very costly if interest rates or investment yields increase sharply after the Insured's death. The present period offers a good example of such a situation. If an Insured who died in 1965 had arranged to have his life insurance paid out in installments, his beneficiary would be receiving payments which include interest of some 3½ to 4½ percent, considerably below what could be realized in a savings bank. Beneficiaries under rigidly structured long-term payout periods are also hamstrung in any attempts to make investments that can be looked to for some cushion against inflation.

It is eminently clear that there is no crystal ball in which one can conjure up his family situation as it will turn out many years after he is gone. The attempt to "rule with a dead hand," as the lawyers aptly dub such rigid arrangements, may defeat the very purpose for which the life insurance was originally undertaken. As the previously cited author put it, "It may become more important to send a child to a sanatorium than to send it to college."*

Translating lump sums into monthly installments or life incomes can be very helpful in visualizing our family's needs. But unless there is some overriding consideration, much is to be said for leaving our beneficiaries the flexibility to meet future needs and changes in circumstances that cannot be divined in advance.

In any event, if a life insurance estate is to be set up under the Optional Modes of Settlement it should be done in consultation with an attorney who is experienced in such matters. Life insurance agents all too

*Ibid., pp. 21–22.

often like to play lawyer and sometimes midwife beneficiary arrangements ". . . with holes in the legal structure through which an automobile can pass, and so very many that will prove—as some have proved—unsatisfactory and worse to those whom the policyholder desired to benefit."*

We are now almost ready to tackle the matter of setting up an insurance estate to protect against "dying too soon" and a long-range investment program for retirement protection against "living too long." There remain only a few "extras" that are offered with life insurance policies and a brief review of these is now in order. These will make up the subject of our next chapter.

* Ibid., p. 5.

12 Some Other "Extras"

WITH ONLY A FEW isolated exceptions, all life insurance companies offer as a rider to their regular life policies additional insurance against death by accident. Popularized by the movies and mystery stories as "double indemnity," this added feature proposes to pay, if the Insured dies as the result of an accident, an additional death benefit equal to the face amount of the basic policy. The policyholder who buys double indemnity is actually carrying two separate forms of insurance—a life policy which pays in the event of death from *any* cause and an additional accident policy for death by accident only. Some carriers offer triple indemnity if the Insured is lucky enough to suffer a fatal accident while riding in a common carrier (train, plane, bus, and so on).

An extra premium is charged for this optional feature, although an occasional company includes it in all its policies. I tabulated the premium for double indemnity charged by 72 of the 78 largest companies which account for some 80 percent of the total ordinary life insurance in force in the United States. (Rates for the six other companies were not available.) Although the rate in these companies averages about 98 cents per $1,000, there are some rather wide deviations, ranging from a low of 51 cents to a high to $1.71 (sic!).*

"For a Few Pennies, Mr. Prospect." This feature usually makes its appearance on the scene after the sale of the basic policy has been

* My little research project turned up some interesting if little-noticed data on this frill. As has been noted, companies almost always allow a discount on larger size policies. One carrier tries to recapture part of its largesse by charging more than twice as much for each $1,000 of double indemnity on policies of $100,000 and over as it does for policies between $25,000 and $99,999.

firmed up. "For a few cents extra per $1,000, Mr. Prospect, you can be covered for double indemnity. . . ." Many applicants find this a very attractive proposition, a lot of insurance for an almost 'negligible' premium. And a $25,000 policy somehow feels more like $50,000 of protection, when the double indemnity clause is added. Now from a financial point of view, and this is what insurance is all about, it matters little to your beneficiary whether you die as a result of an accident or succumb to an illness. As a matter of fact, a good case can be made out for the proposition that death by accident will probably put the smallest drain on your estate, avoiding as it often does the heavy medical expenses that attend so many chronic diseases. In any event, what is eminently clear is that the amount of life insurance one needs flows from the gap between his assets and the funds he would leave his beneficiaries. And this in no way depends on whether he is killed in an accident or dies a natural death.

It may seem like only a few pennies, but buying double indemnity on a $25,000 Whole Life policy at age 35 (in the Aetna Life) will add $26.25 to the premium. As against the Whole Life premium of $380.75, this is a relatively small sum but it will buy some $1,800 of life insurance. In other words, for the same premium one can have $25,000 of Whole Life *with* double indemnity or $26,800 of insurance without this feature.

Under Term insurance the situation is much more clear-cut. $25,000 of 5-Year Renewable and Convertible Term (in the Aetna) will develop an annual premium of $107.25 for a male applicant, age 35; adding double indemnity will increase the premium by $26.25. For this sum, over $7,100 of *additional* Term insurance can be purchased. The choice, in other words, is between $25,000 of life insurance *with* double indemnity or $32,100 of life insurance without this rider.

Insurance vs. Gambling. It cannot be emphasized too strongly that the objective in any insurance program is adequate protection at the lowest possible cost. There is no warrant then for gambling in a life insurance program on the manner in which death will occur. What would we make of a policy which promises to pay the face amount in the event of natural death, triple indemnity if the accident is sustained while riding in a common carrier, quadruple indemnity if the common carrier is an airplane in which the Insured is riding as an economy class passenger, quintuple indemnity if he is riding in the first class compartment, sextuple indemnity if the accident occurs on an even numbered day of the month, and so on?

I think we can all agree that a policy of this kind is more a wagering transaction than insurance; it would be more akin to a lottery. It has little in common with a properly planned insurance estate which evolves out of our dependents' needs, not the manner of death.

Waiver of Premium Disability Benefit. In addition to the double indemnity previously discussed, all companies also offer under their basic life policies additional insurance against disability. About 15 percent of the 78 companies tabulated by me, including America's two largest, the Prudential and the Metropolitan, incorporate the coverage into their basic contract, with no specific premium shown for the feature. Rates in companies that make a separate charge for this rider range from a low of 43 cents to a high of 81 cents per $1,000, when purchased with a Whole Life policy by a male applicant, age 35.

The coverage varies somewhat among the carriers, but basically it provides that if the policyholder is totally disabled for a period of six consecutive months (in a number of companies, the period is four months), all premiums under the policy will be waived. Most policies also waive retroactively any premium that was paid after the commencement of disability. In other words, once the Insured has been disabled for six consecutive months, he is no longer required to pay any premiums that will fall due under his policy and he will also receive a refund of any premiums he paid during the first six months of his disability. It is generally stipulated that the disability must commence before the Insured attains age 60, but once disability has begun, premiums are waived even beyond 60.

All rights and benefits to which the Insured would be entitled if he were paying premiums will continue even after premiums are waived. The values under the policy, including any dividends payable under participating contracts continue as though the policyholder were still paying his premiums.

This coverage is actually a disability income policy which undertakes to pay, in the event of the Insured becoming disabled, an annual sum equal to the gross premiums under his policy. Thus, under a $25,000 Whole Life policy issued by the Aetna to a 35-year-old male, the premium, as previously noted, for the basic policy would be $380.75. For an additional premium of $11.25 ($15.00 for a female) the Insured can obtain disability protection that will pay him (or her), if disabled, the $380.75 needed each year to keep this life insurance in force.

As a general rule, isolating the several risks we face will help us devise a more precise answer to the individual exposures. Section III of this book will give exhaustive treatment to the disability question and point the way to an orderly and economical solution of this problem. However, with respects to the disability coverage we are now discussing, there is not available any identical coverage in the usual channels. It is therefore recommended that the disability waiver of premium provision be added to all life insurance policies where such is offered. This added benefit will safeguard the insurance estate, even after the Insured has become disabled, at which time he will naturally have strong reason to continue his life insurance.

Disability Income Provision. The waiver of premium benefit discussed above is not to be confused with a second disability coverage offered by some companies. Under this latter provision, in addition to waiving the premiums on the basic policy, the company will pay the disabled policyholder a stipulated income, usually $10.00 per month for each $1,000 of insurance.

This rider is sold by a relatively small number of companies. As mentioned previously, the entire question of disability is treated in a later section of the book. There the disadvantages of including disability income provisions under a regular life insurance policy will be underlined, and more desirable alternatives to such a course spelled out.

The "Magic of Dividends." Although not an "extra" offered by riders such as double indemnity or the disability benefit, the dividends paid under many life insurance policies are frequently proclaimed as a special bonus—manna from heaven, so to speak. Policyholders join in the celebration, as though the dividends they receive were a tribute to their canniness as investors. After all, they must have done something right to be getting 20, 30, or even 40 percent of their total premium returned to them in the form of dividends. The facts, as is usual with most cases of "something for nothing," are somewhat less exciting, and a closer look serves to dim the luster considerably.

Mutual companies, with negligible exceptions, are required to make annual distribution of any surplus they accumulate, and as a consequence, they distribute dividends, at least after the first or second policy year. The sales allure of dividends is so strong that many stock companies offer "participating" (dividend-paying) policies along with their regular, guaranteed cost (no-dividend) policies. But participating policies, whether issued by mutual companies or by stock companies, are written at higher rates than nonparticipating policies. As a standard text on life insurance puts it, "For the most part, mutual companies issue policies at premium rates higher than those of stock companies, but carrying the right to participate in earnings through dividends which may or may not result in a lower 'net cost' than the stock company."*

Whether a participating policy will produce lower cost than its nonparticipating counterpart is a question hemmed about with so many variables that no straightforward answer is possible. The answer will depend on the companies being compared, the plan of insurance, the age of the policyholder, the size of the policy being purchased, and so on. Even more important is the question of how long the policy will be maintained in force. It would also be necessary to assign a factor for the loss of interest on the extra premium being paid in the early years. Finally, the dividends projected by the company at the time the policy is purchased are merely an estimate, and are not guaranteed. The actual dividends that will be paid over the years will depend on the company's year-by-year mortality experience, earnings, and expenses in each of the years of the policy's life.

This entire question of dividends has been debated heatedly for years, and much ink has been spilled on the pros and cons of the two

* S. S. Huebner and Kenneth Black, Jr. *Life Insurance*. New York: Appleton-Century-Crofts, p. 680.

types of policy. The recent growth of interest in more complete price disclosure to consumers has again brought the question into the center of the arena. But there is apparently no way to resolve the controversy definitively. In the listing of policies that meet our criteria, we shall list both participating and nonparticipating policies. At this time, it is necessary only to remember that the so-called dividends (which some regulatory authorities have tried to have more properly labeled as refunds of premium) are no free bonus conjured up by some special alchemy. There is therefore no reason to pass up a particular policy because it does not pay dividends or on the other hand to limit oneself only to "guaranteed cost" (no-dividend) policies.

From time to time, other "extras" issue forth from the drawing boards of insurance companies' marketing departments, but those discussed above comprise the most popular of the standard additional coverages offered. Now that we have examined and assessed these "specials," we should be in a position to devise a proper program to protect against "living too long or "dying too soon."

13 How Much Life Insurance, and from Whom?

As observed in the opening chapters of this book, the essentially simple life insurance concept is commonly encrusted with goals which it is not designed to accomplish. Its prime function, we have established, is to create "an immediate estate" that is, to close or narrow the gap between our present assets and the funds we want to leave our dependents if we are removed from their midst by death. We have also seen that insurance always costs, all advertising rhetoric to the contrary notwithstanding. It then follows that one has no tangible need for life insurance unless there are persons dependent on him *financially* who would be left in want if he were to die.

If, then, we are in the market for life insurance only to the extent that all our assets (after estate and inheritance taxes) plus any government provisions for dependents would leave a void in our family's needs, it becomes fairly simple to arrive at a reasonable figure for the life insurance we require. This chapter gives several tables to help you lift the question out of the realm of guesswork or haphazard approximation. A few minutes with these tables should help avoid the serious consequences of under-insurance, and the unnecessary expense and possible losses of over-insurance or improper insurance.

Think of Your Estate Needs in Terms of Monthly Income. In deciding the size of the estate you require both in life insurance and other assets, you will do best to visualize the estate in terms of the monthly income it will provide. This approach to the problem will help you avoid the vagueness of thinking in terms of thousands of dollars. To most people $20,000 is a sizable sum, but to a widow with young children, an estate of $20,000 will provide just about $226 a month for 10 years.

When you plot your estate in terms of monthly income, you should, however, take into account the important element of interest on the estate funds. If you neglect the interest factor, an estimate of your needs may be seriously overstated. Thus if you were to figure the amount of money needed to provide $100 a month for 20 years *without* considering the interest on these funds, you might figure $1,200 a year for 20 years and arrive at $24,000 as the required figure. By including an average interest figure, the sum required to provide such a monthly income is cut to $13,764, just a little over half of the previous figure.

To help you arrive at a correct figure for your estate requirements, we have included tables later in this chapter which show at a glance the amount of money needed to provide monthly incomes for different periods of time, when the interest factor is taken into account.

Setting Your Dependents' Needs. Before you consult these tables, begin by drawing up a simple schedule of monthly incomes which your family would require for stated periods. When you have set these monthly incomes, you will deduct any monthly benefits that would be paid to your widow and dependent children under the Social Security Act. These benefits are outlined later in the chapter. After you have deducted any government benefits to which your beneficiaries would be eligible, the income that must still be provided will determine the size of the estate you require. Two simple tables which are included will help you translate these monthly incomes into a single correct figure for your estate. From this figure for the total estate, you will deduct the value of any tangible assets that will accrue to your dependents in the event of your death. What remains after you have deducted the value of these assets will make up the portion of your estate which life insurance must be called on to provide.

In estimating the needs of your dependents, you will as a matter of course take into account the number of dependents, the type of dependency, and the period for which such dependency can be expected to continue under normal circumstances. Thus, dependency may be total or partial. Where a parent is supported in part, only the portion of support contributed by you need be figured. Where the dependent is a child, it is entirely reasonable (if not completely in accord with today's life style) to expect him to assume the burden of supporting himself when he reaches maturity. The present age of the child must therefore be taken into account.

Furthermore, in taking stock of dependency, the wife's earning abilities should be taken into account. The widow without children is obviously in a different position from the woman entrusted with the upbringing of infants or young children. Then again, the older woman presents a different picture in the matter of finding work than the younger woman. Questions of the health of the dependents, their special training, and their ability to earn a living are factors that you alone are in a position to judge and that you should weigh in your estate picture.

In addition to the more usual needs of the family, special health problems may exist in the form of handicapped persons or those requiring unusually large outlay for medical attention. Educational ambitions and the need to "get started" in a business or profession are all legitimate considerations that may be taken into account when figuring the estate required for your individual family situation.

All these factors as well as one's personal preferences make up the inventory of estate needs. They may appear complex, but you will find, if you are prepared to spend a few minutes with the tables that follow, that the computation will present no undue difficulties. And the rewards for this effort may very well be quite high. For on a proper analysis of this question rests the correctness of your entire insurance program. A proper analysis of your needs can make the difference between economical insurance that adequately protects your dependents and inadequate coverage that may leave in hardship the ones you took steps to protect. A correct understanding of your real insurance needs will also help to keep your costs low and avoid burdensome premiums that threaten your entire insurance program with complete breakdown.

Varying Incomes for Different Periods. You begin then by plotting a monthly income to your wife or primary beneficiary for a given period of years. This income may vary considerably, increasing during the height of family dependency, and tapering off or evaporating entirely after a period of years. Decide on the monthly income that your estate should provide for each period of time. If you are head of a family with young children, you will usually wish to provide the largest income during the early years until the children reach school age. The income may then continue on a somewhat reduced basis until the children reach maturity, to be followed by a smaller income to your wife until she reaches 60, and a still smaller income during the balance of her lifetime. If you can manage, you may make provisions for your children's college education. For purposes of illustration, let's assume you are 40 years old and the sole support of a family consisting of your wife, age 39, and two children, ages 10 and 2. You might in such a case plan an income that varies during different periods, something like this:

$1,000 a month for four years, which will bring your youngest child to school age. At this point, your wife might be in a better position to earn some money in part-time work;
$750 a month for the next four years, which will bring the older child to age 18;
$600 a month for the next eight years thereafter, which will bring the younger child to age 18;
$500 a month for the next five years, which will bring your wife to age 60;
$200 a month during your wife's lifetime thereafter.

Deduct Survivors' Benefits under Social Security. After you have decided on the monthly incomes for various periods which you consider essential to the basic support of your family, you can then deduct any survivors' benefits to which your widow and dependent children would be entitled under the terms of the Social Security Act. These benefits, outlined below, can be quite substantial, and should be taken into account in any estimate of your beneficiaries' needs.

What Protection Does Social Security Offer Your Widow? Most people think of the Social Security Act as limited to providing a monthly income to a worker at retirement. What is less commonly known is that the Act also provides certain monthly benefits to survivors of eligible workers *of any age*. These benefits to widows and dependent children are guaranteed payments, paid to the family regardless of its financial condition. There is no obligation on the widow (or widower) and dependent children to prove "need" in order to receive the monthly income to which they are entitled. Although the monthly benefits to any one family group are limited, they can amount to considerable sums. Thus under certain conditions, a widow with dependent children in her care could receive as much as $315,000 by the time her children reach maturity to be followed by an income of $413 for life from the time she reaches age 65, based on 1977 rates. If she lives to age 78, her normal life expectancy, she will receive an additional $64,428, a total of $379,428.

The survivors' benefits which most workers will have earned are usually considerably less than the high figure of $379,428 but in almost every instance, they will provide an important base on which to posit an insurance estate, and must therefore be taken into account.

Is Everyone Eligible for Survivors' Benefits? About 90 percent of the working population of the country is currently insured for some benefits under Social Security. Generally, every individual working for wages and most self-employed persons are covered under the law. A certain minimum number of years in covered employment is necessary, however, in order to become qualified for these benefits.

How Long Must You Be Employed in a Covered Occupation? Survivors' benefits under the Social Security Act fall into two distinct groups. First are the benefits paid to a surviving spouse with children in her (or his) care, payable until the youngest child reaches age 18, or 22 if a full-time student. Second are benefits payable to a surviving spouse who is not caring for any children but is over 60. The employment requirements are different for each group of recipients.

For a mother or father with dependent children (and for the children) benefits are payable if at the time of death the worker was fully or currently insured. (A person is *currently insured* if in the 13-calendar-quarter period ending with the quarter in which he died he had acquired at least six quarters of coverage.) A quarter of coverage is any calendar quarter in which a worker in covered employment was paid $50 or more. A self-employed person acquires a quarter of coverage for each calendar quarter in a taxable year in which he had at least $400 in net earnings from self-employment income. (He must have had at least $400 in net earnings from self-employment in a taxable year before any such net earnings can be counted as self-employment income.) Generally speaking, then, a worker is currently insured if he has worked one and a half years of the last three years in covered employment or self-employment.

For the surviving spouse age 60 or over without dependent children, benefits are payable only if the worker at the time of his death was *fully insured.* To be fully insured at death, a worker generally needs at least one quarter of coverage for each year *since 1950* up to but not including the year of death. This requirement applies to workers born before 1930. Those born in 1930 or later require only one quarter of coverage for each year after they attained age 21. Thus, to qualify in 1976, a worker born in 1933 requires only 21 quarters of coverage, one for each year since he attained age 21 (in 1954). A worker born in 1941 needs only 13 quarters in 1976, since only 13 years have elapsed since 1963, the year after he reached age 21, and so on. However, a minimum of six quarters of coverage is required in all events. On the other hand, once a worker has 40 quarters of coverage, he is *fully insured* thereafter, regardless of his subsequent employment history.

Who Is Eligible for Survivors' Benefits? It is important to understand that the widow (or widower) of a covered worker who is under 60 at the time of the spouse's death can receive survivors' benefits only if at the time of the spouse's death, she (or he) is caring for a child of the deceased worker under the age of 18, or under certain circumstances, if the child is over age 18 and disabled. The surviving spouse and each of the children are entitled to a stipulated monthly income, subject to possible offsets for anyone in the family who earns more than a stated amount in covered employment (to be discussed later). As each child reaches the age of 18, or 22 if a full-time student, the benefit for that child terminates, while the benefits for the parent and any other minor children continue. When the last child reaches the age of 18 the parent's benefit also ceases, under most circumstances to be resumed only when he or she reaches age 60. Disabled spouses between ages 50 and 60 may also qualify.

How Much Will a Widow (or Widower) and Dependent Children Receive? The size of the monthly income that will be paid to the widow and dependent children of a "covered" worker will depend on the average earnings of the worker during his "covered" lifetime, as well as the length of time for which deductions were made from his wages toward his Social Security account. Table VI gives the monthly incomes payable to a surviving spouse with one child under the age of 18, or 22 if a full-time student; for a surviving spouse with two or more children; and for a widow beginning at age 60.

TABLE VI. MONTHLY INCOMES FOR SURVIVING SPOUSE AND DEPENDENTS

Average monthly earnings of deceased worker*	*Surviving spouse with one child*	*Surviving spouse with two or more children*	*Widow at age 60*
$1,275	$866.40	$1,010.70	$413.00
1,175	834.60	973.40	397.80
1,075	800.00	933.20	381.40
1,000	774.20	903.10	369.10
900	736.00	858.50	350.80
800	697.60	813.80	332.50
700	655.60	764.70	312.50
600	593.00	699.40	282.70
500	516.20	631.30	246.10

*Maximum earnings covered under Social Security were lower in past years, and no amounts above the maximum should be considered. Thus some of the higher benefits will not be payable for several years to come.

How Are "Average Monthly Earnings" Arrived At? It should not be assumed that Average Monthly Earnings on which benefits are based (as shown in the first column of Table VI) necessarily reflect all the earnings of the worker in the years prior to his death. Generally, an individual's Average Monthly Earnings are based on his earning after 1950. However, only earnings actually credited to the worker's Social Security account are used in arriving at his Average Monthly Earnings for purposes of establishing benefits. Top limits on the amount of earnings creditable to a Social Security account have been in effect in all the years since 1937, as follows:

$16,500 for 1977 and thereafter.*
15,300 for 1976.
14,100 for 1975.
13,200 for 1974.
10,800 for 1973.
9,000 for 1972.
7,800 for the years 1968 to 1971, inclusive.
6,600 for the years 1966 and 1967.
4,800 for the years 1959 to 1965, inclusive.
4,200 for the years 1955 to 1958, inclusive.
3,600 for the years 1951 to 1954, inclusive.
3,000 for the years 1940 to 1950, inclusive.
3,000 for each employer for the years 1937 to 1939, inclusive.

*The maximum earnings base will be increased automatically to reflect increases in the average salaries paid in the United States.

It can be seen that only a worker who reached age 21 within the past few years and whose earnings prior to his death were equal to or larger than the maximum taxable base in each of those years will have accrued to his account the maximum survivors' benefits. Older workers will accrue lower benefits. Thus, by way of example, the Average Monthly Earning of a worker who was 40 years of age in 1977 and who had been earning the maximum wages creditable to Social Security since he attained age 21 will come to $746. If he died in 1977, leaving a widow and two children, aged 1 and 2, his surviving spouse and children would be entitled to a monthly income of $791.50. If this benefit were paid until each of the children attained age 22 (assuming each is a full-time student until that point) the aggregate monthly benefits the family will receive (subject to such cost-of-living increases as may be enacted in later years) will come to over $192,000. In addition, the widow when she reaches age 60 will become entitled to an income of $323.40 a month for life.

There are several features of the law that may affect the Average Monthly Earnings, but these have been glossed over in the interest of keeping the discussion from becoming too complicated. A precise determination of the benefits is available to any individual without charge. A special inquiry card may be obtained at any local office of the Social Security Administration (Health, Education and Welfare). When forwarded with a few basic facts, this card will bring a reply from the administration offices in Baltimore, Maryland within six to eight weeks. The exact amount of credited Social Security earnings will be set forth.

If the Surviving Spouse or Child Works. It is important to understand that the monthly income payable to a surviving widow or widower and to minor children may be reduced if any of these beneficiaries earns more than stipulated amounts in covered employment. In 1977, the maximum which may be received in any year in wages or self-employment income without loss of benefits is $3,000. For each $2.00 earned above the exempt $3,000, a Social Security recipient will lose $1.00 in benefits. Or looked at another way, if an individual earns more than $3,000 a year, one-half of the excess is charged back against his benefits from Social Security. A beneficiary who is 72 years of age or over is not penalized for outside earnings, there being no limit on the amount he (or she) may receive in wages of self-employment income.

There is another important exception to the limitation on outside earnings. Regardless of how much outside income a beneficiary receives, he will not lose his benefit for any month in which he does not earn more than $250. In certain situations, due to maximums in the law on family benefits, a surviving widow or widower may lose her (or his) monthly benefit for a particular month due to excess earnings, but the monthly income payable to the dependent children may be increased over the sums they were receiving when the mother (or father) was not working. The last point is somewhat technical and it is therefore recommended that when such a situation occurs, the question be pursued at a local Social Security Administration office.

Translate the Monthly Income into a Single Sum Figure. Any survivors' benefits to which your family may be entitled should be deducted from the monthly income schedule you first projected. The balance of income that remains may now be translated into a single sum—the size of the estate you require. Two tables are included to help you arrive at this figure. Table VII shows how much money is required at 6 percent interest to provide an income of $10 a month *for stated periods of years*. Table VIII shows how much money is required to provide an income of $10 a month *during the lifetime of the beneficiary*. You will use Table VIII when you wish to provide an income to be guaranteed as long as your beneficiary lives, instead of merely for a given period of years.

TABLE VII. AMOUNT OF MONEY NEEDED TO PROVIDE MONTHLY INCOME OF $10 FOR:

Years		*Years*		*Years*	
1	$113	11	$ 946	21	$1,412
2	220	12	1,006	22	1,445
3	321	13	1,062	23	1,476
4	416	14	1,154	24	1,504
5	505	15	1,165	25	1,534
6	590	16	1,213	26	1,560
7	670	17	1,257	27	1,585
8	745	18	1,299	28	1,609
9	816	19	1,339	29	1,631
10	883	20	1,376	30	1,652

Table VII will show at a glance the sums necessary to provide incomes for different periods. If you are planning an income that will fluctuate, it will usually be easier to begin with the income for the longer period of time. For example, if it is your intention to provide $1,000 a month for 10 years, followed by a reduced income of $500 for the next five years, you need only consult the table to determine how much money you require for $500 *for the 15 years,* which is $58,250, then add a sum to cover the *extra* $500 a month during the first 10 years of the period, which will require an additional $44,150. Adding these two figures will give you the amount of money required to provide $1,000 a month for 10 years followed by $500 for the next five years—$102,400.

If You Plan an Income for the Lifetime of Your Beneficiary. When an income is to continue throughout the lifetime of the beneficiary, consult Table VIII. This table naturally takes into account the *age of the beneficiary* instead of any fixed period during which income is to be paid. Figures are shown separately for male and female beneficiaries, due to the superior life expectancy of the latter group. For the purpose of simplication, the age of the beneficiary is shown at five-year intervals only, until age 50, for the variations will be relatively minor for the invervening years. From age 50 on, the table gives the values for each age, year by year.

TABLE VIII. AMOUNT OF INCOME NEEDED TO PROVIDE $10 A MONTH DURING LIFETIME

	MALE	FEMALE
Age of beneficiary	*Amount of money needed*	
25	$1,870	$1,921
30	1,822	1,886
35	1,764	1,843
40	1,692	1,791
45	1,605	1,726
50	1,508	1,650
51	1,487	1,633
52	1,466	1,614
53	1,444	1,595
54	1,421	1,575
55	1,397	1,554
56	1,373	1,532
57	1,349	1,510
58	1,323	1,486
59	1,298	1,462
60	1,272	1,436
61	1,245	1,409
62	1,218	1,382
63	1,190	1,353
64	1,162	1,324
65	1,133	1,294
66	1,105	1,263
67	1,077	1,232
68	1,049	1,201
69	1,020	1,169
70	991	1,136

When you consult the table for ages *between* the five-year intervals, you can use the age closest to the one you are interested in. The variations will not be very large, and the figure will be close enough for our present purpose.

If your plans call for an income for a stated period to be followed by an income to continue throughout the lifetime of the beneficiary, it will usually be easier for you to begin with the longest period for which an income is to be provided, the lifetime of the beneficiary, and then add the income for the limited period.

An Example of These Tables in Use. Let's assume that after you have deduced your Social Security survivor's benefits, you still need to provide an additonal $500 a month for the first 10 years, and $250 a month thereafter during the lifetime of your spouse, whose present age is 45. You begin with the income to be provided for the longer period, in this case, your spouse's income for life. To determine any income for life rather than for a fixed number of years, you consult Tables VIII. This table tells you that $1,726 will supply a life income of $10 a month to a female beneficiary age 45. Since the income you are aiming at is $250, you need 25 times this sum—or $43,150. You have now provided for the longer period—the lifetime of your beneficiary—so you now take up the shorter period, the first 10 years.

Since $250 has already been made available for life, you need to add only an additional $250 a month during the first 10 years, which will give an income of $500 during the initial 10-year period. This time you are concerned with an income for a fixed period, so you consult Table VII, which shows $883 as the amount needed to provide $10 a month for 10 years. You therefore multiply this figure by 25 to arrive at the sum which will supply $250 a month—$22,075. Adding these two figures—the amount of the life income and the sum for the 10-year period—gives you the figure needed for the projected estate, $65,225.

In summary form, the calculation appears as follows:

$43,150	to provide $250 a month for life
$22,075	to provide an additional $250 a month for the first 10 years
$65,225	total estate required

A note of caution is in order. In estimating your family's needs after your death, do not fail to take into account such reduction in your surviving spouse's income as would result from being employed, or earning self-employment income (discussed above).

From Total Estate to Life Insurance. Once you have arrived at a dollar figure for your estate requirements, you are ready to deduct the value of all your tangible assets, conservatively appraised, that you may reasonably expect to leave behind. On the credit side of this balance sheet, you will list cash, bonds, stocks, mutual funds (and closed-end investment trusts), real and personal property that can be turned into cash, an interest in a business which is relatively liquid or can be looked to for a continuing income to your dependents, royalties, income from trusts, and so on. You should also check the death benefits, if any, that would be paid to your beneficiaries under a pension or profit-sharing plan at your place of employment. Many of these assets, it is clear, cannot be valued too precisely but, depending on their nature and stability, should be taken in at some conservative estimate of their value. A closely held business is usually more difficult to assess than stock in a major corporation traded on an exchange, and in this matter, one is usually well-advised to consult with one's accountant.

From the final figure for all liquid assets, a sum should be earmarked to cover emergencies and last expenses. A frequently invoked rule of thumb sets a half-year's income and this amount should be considered a basic minimum.

After having credited yourself with all the assets you have on hand any deficiency that remains in your estate must be made up through life insurance.

To Summarize. The steps you took in arriving at a correct figure for your life insurance may be reviewed briefly as follows:

1. Assign minimum monthly incomes to cover the dependency periods of your family.

2. Deduct from these incomes any monthly benefits to which your dependents are entitled under the Social Security Act.

3. Consult the two income tables to see how large a fund is required to make available the monthly incomes you wish to provide.

4. Deduct from this figure the value of tangible assets and property that your family could draw on after your death.

5. Plan a life insurance estate to provide the balance.

The Importance of Keeping Your Life Insurance Up to Date. Since life insurance needs grow out of a family's situation, it is clear that they are not likely to remain static. Responsibilities may increase with the passage of years, or decrease as dependents grow older, become self-supporting in whole or in part, or themselves begin to contribute to the family's exchequer. Even if there are no changes in the family structure, as each of the dependents being provided for grows older, less life insurance will be required to cover the reduced dependency period. Countervailing factors pointing to a need for *increased* insurance are improvements in one's standard of living, shrinkage in the assets on hand, and the impact of inflation which dictates steadily increasing life insurance just to "stand still." A periodic updating of one's financial "map" is therefore in order.

A Word about Group Life Insurance. Some 40 percent of all life insurance in force in the United States is written under group insurance plans, with the total for this form of insurance climbing rapidly on its way to $1 trillion. Employer-employee groups account for almost 90 percent of this amount; the balance is divided among union-sponsored plans, professional societies, trade associations, and savings and investment institutions. Most wage earners are therefore covered under, or have available to them, some group life insurance.

This form of life insurance is generally written at favorable rates, due to economies in underwriting costs, commissions, and other overhead associated with the issuance and collection of individual policies. Additionally, most employer-employee plans are paid for in whole or in part by the employer, thereby further reducing the cost to the covered employee. It is true that the younger employee does not get as much of a "bargain" as his older co-worker due to the fact that the group premium is usually a composite of all the ages in the covered group. But almost always, the cost to the employee is lower than what he would have to pay for comparable coverage.

There is also a specific tax bonus in group life insurance, in that the premium paid by the employer is not considered additional compensation to the employee except on amounts which exceed $50,000. If the employee were buying his life insurance individually and paying for it directly, he would of course have to pay the premium in after-tax dollars. Thus there is a further savings to him, leastwise on the first $50,000 of group insurance.

It would appear elementary to take credit for any group life insurance you have access to when you set the size of your estate. And basically, this is true. Some consideration must be given, however, to the question of the permanence of your present employment. If your present job connection terminates for any reason, your group insurance will come to an end. While you are looking for employment, or if there is no group plan in effect at your new job location, you could close the gap in your insurance "estate" with a Term policy. This would present no problem unless you had become uninsurable. Your only alternative would then be to convert the group life insurance you were covered under at your last place of employment. Such conversion would be made *without evidence of insurability* (regardless of your physical condition or financial or moral standing) within the first 31 days after your employment ceased. But the conversion would have to be made to Whole Life at the rate then in effect for your age in the particular company. The increase in premium over the cost of your group policy could be very precipitous. All in all, the question of how much reliance to place on the group life insurance you now have depends on your estimate of the permanence of your present position, whether you are likely to be making a new connection where group insurance is in force, and such considerations.

The Bottom Line. If, after you have added to your liquid assets the group life insurance on which you can place reliance, there is still a deficiency between this figure and the estate you would leave behind, you are in the market for individual life insurance. Term insurance, which addresses itself only to insuring against death at the lowest possible premium outlay, is indicated, for reasons which we trust have been made amply clear.

It is true that Annual Renewable Term, which follows the mortality curve most closely, meets this need perfectly. However, since this particular policy is not as widely offered as 5-Year Term, or is frequently offered in rather large minimum size policies only, our ratings of "best buys" will be based on 5-Year Term.

The Elusive Question of True Cost. The true cost of life insurance is a regretfully complicated matter which has agitated the consumer movement now for many years. In his testimony before the Subcommittee on Antitrust and Monopoly of the Committee of the Judiciary of the United States Senate conducting an in-depth investigation of the life insurance industry, Stanley C. DuRose, then Commissioner of Insurance of the State of Wisconsin, said, "As evidence of the complexity of the problem, I am attaching Exhibit IV, which shows that, in the last fifty years, no less than 21 different attempts have been made to solve this problem. . . . Numerous people are still working to find a solution."

Most of the difficulties in cost analysis develop out of the cash values of level-premium policies. "Termites" (as advocates of this low-premium, low cash value insurance have ungenerously been characterized) are therefore spared the interminable disputes that bedevil the problem. This is especially true if one concentrates on nonparticipating (no-dividend) contracts such as are sold by stock companies.

In Table IX we are setting down, in order of ascending premium outlay over a 20-year period, the 5-Year Renewable and Convertible Term policies of 14 of the largest stock companies for a male age 35. Female rates are somewhat lower at all ages for life insurance, although the cost for the Waiver of Premium Disability provision is higher. All these policies may be carried at least to age 65. There are some differences among them as to the highest age at which they may be *converted,* and this information is shown. These 14 companies, which make up less than 1 percent of the stock carriers of the country, account for some 20 percent of the total life insurance in all such companies. They therefore present a cross section of the field and provide a measuring rod against which to check the offering of a competing company.

(Also included are three carriers which write participating policies, for reasons to be set forth.)

The figures are based on a $25,000 policy issued to a male age 35, and include the cost of the Waiver of Premium Disability Provision. (This feature was discussed in Chapter 12.) Shown with each company are the states and territories in which it is licensed.

If You Live or Work in Connecticut, Massachusetts, or New York State. Residents of these states or those who work within their borders may purchase a limited amount of life insurance from the savings banks of their state at extremely low rates. Although this insurance is written on a participating (dividend-paying) basis, we have included these carriers with the nonparticipating (guaranteed costs, no-dividend) companies because their gross premiums, that is, *before* any dividends, compare favorably with the premiums charged by nonparticipating companies. The offering of each of the three states is listed separately below. The banks in all three states do not offer lower rates to female applicants, and in this respect, the regular companies listed will be somewhat more competitive.

If You Live or Work in Connecticut • The maximum insurance available is $5,000. The *gross* premium over 20 years for $5,000 of 5-Year Renewable and Convertible Term for a 35-year-old is $971.50. These costs fall within the higher range of the commercial companies listed above. Dividends declared by the banks will of course reduce the outlay.

If You Live or Work in Massachusetts • In this state, $41,000 of 5-Year Renewable and Convertible Term insurance is available. The gross cost over the 20-year period for $25,000 of insurance for a 35-year-old is $3,721.25. Even *before* dividends, this premium is lower than that of all the carriers listed except for the top two.

If You Live or Work in New York State • The maximum amount of insurance sold by the banks in this state is $30,000. The gross cost (before dividends) is lower than that of all the enumerated carriers except one.

TABLE IX. $25,000 RENEWABLE AND CONVERTIBLE 5-YEAR TERM POLICY—MALE, AGE 35. TOTAL COST OVER 20 YEARS, INCLUDING WAIVER OF PREMIUM DISABILITY PROVISION

(Rates for female applicants are set back, that is, they are lower than for males of the same age. The ranking below by cost will remain applicable to both the male and female risks.)

Company	*Total cost*	*Convertible to*	*States and territories in which company is licensed*
Lincoln National Fort Wayne, Ind. 46891	$3,627.50	65	All states except New York. Also in Panama, Canal Zone, Guam, Puerto Rico, Philippines, Virgin Islands, Canadian Federal Government, and Ontario
Continental Assurance Chicago, Ill. 60605	3,714.00	64	All states and Puerto Rico, Guam, Virgin Islands, all provinces of Canada, and Hong Kong

The company's 5-Year Renewable and Convertible Term is more expensive than its Executerm 4/6 which is written for an initial term of *four* years, and renewable every *six* years thereafter. It is this second policy which is shown.

Company	*Total cost*	*Convertible to*	*States and territories in which company is licensed*
Pilot Life Ins. Greensboro, N.C. 27420	3,760.00	60	Ala., Ariz., Ark., Colo., Del., D.C., Fla., Ga., Idaho, Ind., Kan., Ky., La., Md., Miss., Mo., Neb., Nev., N.J., N. Mex., N.C., S.C., Tenn., Tex., Utah, Va., Wash., W. Va., Wyo., Puerto Rico, Virgin Islands, and military installations in foreign countries
Northwestern National Minneapolis, Minn. 55440	3,960.00	65	All states except New York
Aetna Life Ins. Hartford, Conn. 06115	4,010.00	60	All states. Also Guam, Puerto Rico, Virgin Islands, Dominion of Canada and provinces of Alberta, New Brunswick, Newfoundland, Nova Scotia, Ontario, Quebec, and Saskatchewan
Occidental Life of California Los Angeles, Calif. 90015	4,011.25	65	All states except New York. Also all of Canada, Puerto Rico, Hong Kong, Australia, Japan, Great Britain, Guam, and Virgin Islands
Travelers Ins. Hartford, Conn. 06152	4,197.50	65	All states. Also Puerto Rico, Virgin Islands, Bahama Island, Guam, and Canada

Company	*Total cost*	*Conver-tible to*	*States and territories in which company is licensed*
National Life and Accident Nashville, Tenn. 37203	4,303.75	65	Ala., Ark., Calif., Colo., Fla., Ga., Ill., Ind., Iowa, Kan., Ky., La., Md., Mich., Minn., Miss., Mo., Mont., N.C., Neb., Ohio, Okla., Pa., S.C., Tenn., Tex., Va., W.Va., Wis.
California-Western States Sacramento, Calif. 95814	4,312.50	64	Ala., Ariz., Ark., Calif., Colo. Hawaii, Idaho, Ill., Ind., Iowa, Kan., La., Mich., Mo., Okla., Ore., Nev., N.Mex., Mont., Neb., S.D., Tex., Utah, Wash., Wis., Wyo.
Connecticut General Hartford, Conn. 06152	4,312.50	69	All states. Also Puerto Rico, Canada, and provinces of Alberta, Manitoba, Ontario, Quebec, and Saskatchewan
Provident Life & Accident Chattanooga, Tenn. 37402	4,436.25	62	All states except New York. Also in Manitoba, Ontario, Quebec, British Columbia, and Puerto Rico
Life Ins. Co. of Virginia Richmond, Va. 23219	4,886.25	65	Ala., Ariz., Ark., Calif., Del., D.C., Fla., Ga., Ill., Ind., Ky., La., Md., Mass., Mich., Minn., Mo., N.J., N.Mex., N.C., Ohio, Okla., Pa., S.C., S.D., Tenn., Tex., Va., W. Va.
Franklin Life Springfield, Ill. 62713	4,966.25	65	All states except New York. Also Puerto Rico, Virgin Islands, Canada, and military installations in foreign countries
Nationwide Life Columbus, Ohio 43216	5,110.00	60	All states except Wisconsin. Also Puerto Rico and Virgin Islands

It can be seen at a glance that there are substantial differences in cost among the carriers for the same contract. Thus, the difference between the lowest and the highest 20-year outlay in this relatively small sampling is about 40 percent. It is true that the balance will shift on larger amounts of insurance since companies employ different "discounting" methods. Thus, as an example, the National Life and Accident of Nashville, Tennessee charges about 12 percent less for a $50,000 policy of the same kind; on $100,000 and over, the premium is reduced as much as 22 percent at the younger ages, 16 percent at age 55, and so on.

The 20-year period over which the above costs have been projected is of course an arbitrary period. If the insurance were carried from age 35 to age 65, the rankings would change, but as can be noted in Table X, the shift is slight and the rankings tend to remain within the same general range.

TABLE X. $25,000 RENEWABLE AND CONVERTIBLE 5-YEAR TERM POLICY MALE—AGE 35. TOTAL COST TO AGE 65, INCLUDING WAIVER OF PREMIUM DISABILITY

Company	*Total outlay*
Continental Assurance	$ 9,249.50
Lincoln National	9,372.50
Pilot Life	9,520.00
Northwestern National	9,901.25
Occidental Life	10,084.25
California-Western States	10,431.25
Aetna Life	10,467.50
Connecticut General	10,590.00
Travelers Insurance Co.	10,636.25
National Life	10,891.25
Franklin Life	10,907.50
Provident Life & Accident	11,265.00
Life of Virginia	11,603.75
Nationwide Life	11,987.50

If You Live or Work in Connecticut, Massachusetts, or New York State • (See 20-year table for details about these carriers.)

Savings Bank Life Insurance—Connecticut—$2,317.75 ($5,000)
Savings Bank Life Insurance—Massachusetts—9,625.25
Savings Bank Life Insurance—New York State—9,415.00

Not an Exclusive List. We would again stress the fact that the companies ranked above represent only a small fraction of the carriers writing this form of insurance. Any company whose 5-Year Term policy permits of renewal to age 65 and whose conversion options approximate those in the cited policies may be considered. It should be fairly simple to obtain and compare figures for the total premiums to be paid under any such policy with those in our table. If its costs fall within the lower end of our curve, it may be considered acceptable.

Two Term policies may differ in some of their provisions. One may grant a more liberal Waiver of Premium Disability provision or be renewable or convertible to a later age. If their costs are within the same range, one should of course opt for the contract with the more flexible conditions.

Other Acceptable Term Policies. We have used the 5-Year Term policy as our guinea pig. It should be understood, however, that there are other equally effective forms of Term insurance. The 10-Year Renewable policy can be utilized as can policies that renew every three or four years, or policies whose initial term is for one period of years followed by renewals for different time spans.

A more frequently encountered Term policy is the 1-Year or Annual Renewable Term, as it is usually labeled. This policy is usually offered only in minimums of $100,000 although some companies make it available in lesser amounts. If one is in the market for a larger policy, he would be well advised to check the Annual Renewable Term policy against the company's 5-Year Term. All that needs to be done is to total the five annual premiums under the Annual Renewable Term policy and compare them with the five level premiums payable during the same period under the 5-Year Term policy. The policy with the lower gross outlay will of course be the one to buy. A caveat is in order on this score. Unless there is a material savings in cost, one should avoid buying a policy which is issued only in high minimum amounts, as it will not be possible to reduce such a policy below the minimum, if insurance needs decrease.

Decreasing Term Insurance. Companies also offer various forms of *decreasing* Term insurance. The amount of insurance under these policies decreases each year they are maintained in force. As a consequence, the premiums do not increase as they do under all forms of level Term insurance. This form of insurance can be incorporated into a program of protection for dependents since it takes less money each year to provide a stipulated income to a beneficiary as he grows older. In combination with level insurance like 5-Year Term, the decreasing variety can make up an efficient and economical package of protection.

The foregoing discussion of Term costs has confined itself to non-participating (no-dividend) contracts offered by numerous stock insurance companies. A buyer who chooses from among the better of such nonparticipating policies can be satisfied that he has done well.

Participating (Dividend-Paying) Policies. As we pointed out at the outset of this discussion of cost, restricting ourselves to nonparticipating policies bypasses almost all of the complexities that surround this question. However, since over half of the country's life insurance is written by mutual companies, which are required to distribute surplus to their policyholders in what is loosely termed a "dividend," and since many stock companies also offer participating (dividend-paying) policies, a word is in order about this broad field, where "the other half lives," so to speak.

The premiums for participating policies are almost always higher than for nonparticipating policies. Dividends under participating policies do not usually begin until the end of the second or third year. They generally increase over the years, and ultimately serve to reduce the policyholder's outlay to a figure which is lower than he would pay for a nonparticipating policy. Furthermore, it is important to bear in mind that dividends are not guaranteed. Companies project dividends at the point of sale based on their current scale which can and usually does change to reflect the company's actual experience over the years. In order to determine whether the higher-premium participating policy is a better buy it therefore becomes necessary to settle rather arbitrarily on the number of years over which both policies are to be studied and to assume that the carrier's present scale will continue into the future years, unchanged. Finally, there is the all-important question of the interest factor to be assigned to the extra premiums paid out under the participating policy in the early years.

The Interest-Adjusted Method. Recently, great prominence has been given to a method which seeks to take into account the element of interest. Known as the "interest-adjusted method," it has been endorsed by the National Association of Insurance Commissioners and mandated into law in several states. Almost everyone agrees that it permits a better cost evaluation than the traditional net cost analysis which was rather exhaustively treated in the opening chapters of this book. As is common with most reforms, it develops difficulties of its own and must therefore be viewed with rather more awareness of its limitations than some of its more passionate advocates would urge on us.

Even if lacking in complete rigor, the interest-adjusted method does give some insight into relative costs, particularly if employed to compare the same type of policy. In this light, in Table XI we set down the interest-adjusted costs of a 5-Year Renewable and Convertible Term policy issued on the participating basis by 30 companies which account for just under half of the close to $2 trillion of life insurance in force.

The dividends projected by the companies are based on their *present* mortality experience, overhead costs, and investment returns, and are not guaranteed for the future.* The final cost of any policy is therefore almost certain to differ from the estimate made when it is purchased. We have therefore avoided pin-pointing their costs too sharply and have instead bracketed them in three cost groups with a range for each.

TABLE XI. 5-YEAR RENEWABLE AND CONVERTIBLE TERM PARTICIPATING PLAN $25,000 FACE AMOUNT. MALE—AGE 35

	20-YEAR INTEREST-ADJUSTED INDEX
From $160 to $174	*States and territories in which company is licensed*
Bankers Life Co. Des Moines, Iowa 50307	All states. Also Puerto Rico and Canada
Berkshire Life Pittsfield, Mass. 01201	Ala., Alaska, Ark., Colo., Conn., Del., D.C., Fla., Ga., Idaho, Ill., Ind., Kan., Ky., La., Me., Md., Mass., Mich., Minn., Mo., Mont., Neb., N.H., N.J., N.Y., N.C., N.D., Ohio, Okla., Ore., Pa., R.I., S.C., Tenn., Tex., Vt., and Va.

* According to the "catechism" as set forth in insurance text books, at any rate. A company's return on its investments, one might assume, is a fairly specific constant in any given year, but this is apparently a considerable oversimplification. Professor Joseph Belth, whose efforts on behalf of more adequate price disclosure have been touched on before has been waging a one-man crusade to pry loose from some of the larger carriers their formulas for computing dividends which as one company put it "involves very sensitive competitive information." While the subject is fairly complex, it does seem reasonably clear that some companies allocate dividends differently between their older and newer policyholders and that the entire procedure does permit manipulation.

TABLE XI. 5-YEAR RENEWABLE AND CONVERTIBLE TERM PARTICIPATING PLAN $25,000 FACE AMOUNT. MALE—AGE 35 (*continued*)

20-YEAR INTEREST-ADJUSTED INDEX

From $160 to $174	*States and territories in which company is licensed*
Bankers Life Co. Des Moines, Iowa 50307	All states. Also Puerto Rico and Canada
Berkshire Life Pittsfield, Mass. 01201	All states except Ariz., Calif., Hawaii, Iowa, Miss., Nev., N. Mex., S.D., Utah, Wash., W. Va., Wis., Wyo.
Home Life Ins. Co. New York, N.Y. 10007	All states. Also in Puerto Rico
Maccabees Mutual Southfield, Mich. 48075	All states except Alaska, Hawaii, Miss., N.J., N.Y., Vt. Also in Canada and Puerto Rico
Massachusetts Mutual Springfield, Mass. 01111	All states. Also in Puerto Rico
State Mutual Life Worcester, Mass. 01605	All states. Also in Puerto Rico and Canada

From $190 to $199	
Acacia Mutual Life Washington, D.C. 20001	All states except Ala., Alaska, Idaho, Me., Mont., Neb., Nev., N.H., N. Mex., N.Y., N.D., Ohio, S.D., Utah, Vt., Wyo.
American United Life Indianapolis, Ind. 46206	All states except Conn., Me., Mass., N.H., N.Y., R.I., Vt. Also in Ontario
Bankers Life Ins. of Nebraska Lincoln, Neb. 68501	All states except Me., Mass., Nev., N.H., N.Y., N.D., R.I., Vt., and Wis.
National Life Ins. Montpelier, Vt. 05602	All states
New York Life New York, N.Y. 10010	All states. Also in Puerto Rico
Prudential Ins. Newark, N.J. 07101	All states. Also in Virgin Islands, Puerto Rico, Guam, Canada, Hong Kong, and United States military establishments in foreign countries
Shenandoah Life Roanoke, Va. 24010	Alaska, Ark., De., D.C., Fla., Ga., Ind., Ky., Md., Mich., Miss., N.C., N.J., Ohio, Pa., S.C., Tenn., Va., W. Va.
State Farm Life Bloomington, Ill. 61701	All states except Conn., N.Y., and Wis. Also in Canada.

From $175 to $189	*States and territories in which company is licensed*
Confederation Life Toronto 5, Ont.	All states except Ariz., Miss., N.Y. Also in Puerto Rico Also in Canada
Equitable Life New York, N.Y. 10019	All states. Also in Puerto Rico, Virgin Islands, and Canada
John Hancock Mutual Boston, Mass. 02117	All states. Also in Puerto Rico, Virgin Islands, Canada, and U.S. defense installations overseas
Metropolitan Life New York, N.Y. 10010	All states. Also in Puerto Rico, and all provinces of Canada
Mutual Benefit Life Newark, N.J. 07101	All states
Mutual of New York New York, N.Y. 10019	All states. Also Puerto Rico, Virgin Islands, and certain Canadian provinces
New England Mutual Boston, Mass. 02117	All states. Also in Puerto Rico
Phoenix Mutual Life Hartford, Conn. 06115	All states except Hawaii, Miss., S.C., and S.D. Also in Puerto Rico and Canada
Security Benefit Topeka, Kan. 66603	All states except New York. Also in Puerto Rico
Security Mutual Life of New York Binghamton, N.Y. 13902	All states except Alaska, Colo., Hawaii, Idaho, Kan., La., Mont., Neb., Nev., N.Mex., Okla., Ore., Tex., Utah, Wash., and Wyo.
Standard Ins. Co. Portland, Ore. 97204	Alaska, Ariz., Calif., Hawaii, Idaho, Mont., Nev., Ore., Utah, and Wash.
Connecticut Mutual Hartford, Conn. 06105	All states except North Dakota
Continental American Wilmington, Del. 19899	All states
Ohio National Cincinnati, Ohio 45201	All states except Ala., Alaska, Conn., Del., La., Me., Mass., N.H., N.Y., N.C., Okla., R.I., S.C., Vt., Wis.
Penn Mutual Life Philadelphia, Pa. 19172	All states. Also in Alberta, British Columbia, Manitoba, New Brunswick, Nova Scotia, and Ontario
Provident Mutual Philadelphia, Pa. 19101	All states except Alaska, Arkansas, and Idaho
Union Mutual Portland, Me. 04112	All states. Also in Puerto Rico and Canada

If You Live or Work in Connecticut, Massachusetts, or New York State • Very low-cost life insurance in limited amounts is available to individuals who live or work in one of these states. These products were discussed earlier in the chapter at the end of Table IX.

Financed Life Insurance—Back-Handed Term. To complete the listing of Term policies, it is necessary to add a product which seeks to approximate the low outlays for Term insurance through a Whole Life policy. Life insurance, we have seen, comes in two basic forms: Term insurance, which covers only the mortality risk, and all other policies, which combine a savings element with protection. As might be expected, the premiums for Term are considerably lower than for policies which incorporate a savings feature. In the face of an almost continuous inflation, buyers of life insurance, particularly the more sophisticated, and some carriers began to have second thoughts about the conventional life insurance product as an investment medium. These misgivings were intensified by the overall surge in the stock market which carried the Dow-Jones Industrial Stock index to over 1,000 in 1972. (In 1942, the index had closed at 119; by 1952, it stood at 292; the close of 1962 saw it top 650.)

Within the industry, there was so much hand-wringing about the increase in the amount of Term insurance being written, and the consequent loss by insurance companies to competing institutions of their share of America's savings. (The agonizing within the insurance business on this critical question was chronicled in Chapter 8.)

An Inspired Marketing Approach. Almost unnoticed at first, there emerged a method of selling cash value insurance which did not call for the higher cash outlay of such policies. Agents, particularly those who dealt with the more affluent public, laid before their prospects a new approach to the "tried and true" cash value Whole Life policy. The client would buy a regular Whole Life policy and each year borrow the full cash, or more accurately the full loan value. He would take out of pocket only the *difference* between the loan and the required premium. In this way, his outlay would be kept to a minimum.

With an Assist from Uncle Sam. The cash values, growing snugly inside a cash value policy, were already enjoying a heart-warming immunity from income taxes—they were tax sheltered, so to speak. And now, mirabile dictu, when they were borrowed out by the policyholder, the *interest* paid on the loans was tax deductible. All together, it could be shown without too much difficulty, the net cost to anyone in a respectable tax bracket could well be less than the cost of straight Term insurance, being purchased with after-tax dollars.

A House Divided. Even though the policy's cash values were being "stripped" systematically, the policy was a Whole Life policy, and commissions were paid on that basis. As might be expected, the agency force took to the product like duck to water. The steady din or warnings against Term insurance as a sure road to impecunity and an indigent old age were all but stilled. On the company level, there was considerably less unanimity for this new creation. A few carriers tried to hold the line against this form of back-handed Term, but most saw in this new approach a device for attracting large quantities of new business, and an effortless way to lend out money to their own policyholders at 5 or 6 percent, rates which looked very attractive until a few years ago. As more and more companies began to compete for this type of business, special policies and riders were designed to make "minimum deposit" insurance ("mini-dip" as it was affectionately dubbed in the field) even more irresistible.

Better than Ever. First, a special rider was produced which would provide additional Term insurance each year to make up for the reduction in the death benefit that resulted from the increasing loans being made in the policy. Then special policies were brought forth with unusually high first-year cash values (where the older Whole Life policies generally had none) so that the policyholder could get some assistance with the first year's premium from a policy loan. (Some states banned these policies on the grounds that they discriminated against other Whole Life policyholders who were dutifully paying their premiums in the old-fashioned, uninspired way.) Finally, a new option was offered under which dividends could be applied toward the purchase of one-year Term insurance additions, again in an amount sufficient to make up for the loans, and thereby restore the policy's death benefit to its original amount.

Uncle Sam Shows Signs of Pique. As the volume of this business mounted, the Internal Revenue Service became concerned about the tax dollars that were slipping through its fingers in the form of deductions from taxable income for loan interest being taken by "minimum deposit" Insureds. There was talk about making such interest nondeductible. Finally, a compromise was arrived at, to wit: Interest on policy loans purchased "according to a plan which contemplates the systematic direct or indirect borrowing of part or all of the increases in the cash value of the contract would not be deductible" by the taxpayer. But there was a saver. If the policyholder paid four or more of the first seven years' premiums in cash, he could borrow all the rest, and get the benefit of a deduction for all interest. In any event, no limitation applied to policies purchased before August 7, 1963 even if *all* premiums were paid by loan.

Bloodied but Unbowed. While this restriction dulled the high gloss of the new product somewhat, it did not by any means put an end to it. Large amounts of "minimum deposit" insurance continued to be sold without calling the interest deduction into play, or by having the policyholder undertake to pay four of the first seven premiums in cash, and thereby still preserve the tax deduction on the interest. By and large, business could continue more or less as usual.

History Catches Up. The sharp rise in interest rates of the past few years introduced a new element into the picture which was much more damaging. For close to a century, the right to borrow against the cash value of a policy had been a contractual one. Different rates of interest were in effect during various periods, but by 1939, most companies employed a 5 percent rate. This rate was increased in most policies issued after 1969 to 6 percent, except in New York State which clung to the 5 percent figure. These rates were generally in reasonable relationship to the going cost of borrowing money.

The recent surge in interest rates made the guaranteed loan rates of insurance policies a great bargain, and there was a sharp increase in loans made against life contracts. The monies which the companies were required by contract to lend their policyholders at 6 percent (or even 5 percent as the case might be) could have been earning 10 percent or better in the company's regular investments.

To staunch the outflow of money at these depressed interest rates, some action became imperative. In state after state, legislation has been enacted which allow policies to be written with higher interest rates, or with flexible rates of up to 8 percent or 8½ percent. Some such situation is now in effect in over ⅔ of the states.

Where Do We Stand Today? In the face of these developments, where does minimum deposit stand vis-à-vis simple Term insurance? It seems eminently clear that with the interest factor such an important element in the minimum deposit device, an increase in the rate at which the Insured is borrowing money will knock this mutant Term insurance species well out of the box. In states where policies now being issued carry a flexible loan interest rate, the situation is essentially the same, even if the companies are currently lending money at less than the maximum permissible rate. It is only where an interest rate of 6 percent or less is still guaranteed *contractually* that there is any question of choice. Each individual's situation calls for careful analysis. The formula set forth in the Appendix can be employed to make a rigorous comparison of the two approaches.

As a General Rule. In any event, it can be stated as a general rule that a 5-Year Renewable and Convertible Term policy from the lower end of the cost spectrum of such contracts (as set forth earlier in this chapter) will stack up favorably against its minimum deposit competitor, if proper weight is given to the interest on the higher outlay generally called for in the earlier years under most minimum deposit contracts.

For the Already Initiated. For those who have been carrying minimum deposit policies for some time, the question is somewhat more complicated. Shall they now discontinue these contracts and opt for straight Term? This question is covered in the next chapter which takes up the entire situation of those who are not coming into the insurance market for the first time, but would make a transition from existing coverages to low-cost Term. At this point, the important point to be stressed is this: Armed with an understanding of the true function of life insurance—protection against the economic consequences of premature death—every individual can determine his needs in this direction. He will avoid being drawn into a quest for other forms of security which the product cannot give. From the tables in this chapter, it should be quite simple to estimate the extent of his needs for protection, and to channel his premium dollars into the most economical offerings in the field. The "dying too soon" hazard covered, he can now focus on insuring against "living too long." How to most economically make provisions for this contingency will make up the subject of a later chapter, after the discussion on "switching" which follows.

14 The Switch to Term

THOSE COMING INTO the market for life insurance for the first time, or considering increasing the coverage they are now carrying, can use the guidelines previously established to measure their real need for protection and then fill any such need with a policy that measures up to the standards set forth. But what course is to be followed by those who presently own policies of the cash value variety? In now seeking to bring their protection and retirement programs into line with the times, should they forthwith drop all their existing policies and replace them with straight Term insurance?

A Few Caveats. Of all the failings attributed to Term insurance, and they are numerous it will be recalled, none is more consistently harped on than its unsuitability to any but purely "temporary needs." Where a policyholder has wandered onto this allegedly treacherous terrain of Term, he is importuned to get on the solid ground of "permanent protection" (read: cash value life insurance) as soon as it is at all possible, as though he had hold of a hot potato or a highly caustic chemical which could damage sensitive animal tissue.

Zealous consumer advocates who have been converted to the Term insurance gospel, as set forth in this book, often rush to man the opposing barricade, and urge immediate dropping of all cash value policies and their replacement with Term contracts. This course may need to be hedged about with a note of caution; an orderly retreat with one's flank protected may be indicated rather than headlong flight.

First, it should be pointed out that there can be no thought of replacing *any* policy unless the policyholder is insurable, and at standard rates. Any new policy being eyed is to be applied for while the old policy is still in force, some six weeks or so before its anniversary date. All questions asked in the application forms are to be answered accurately and completely, and any other information requested furnished. Only after the new policy is issued, *and the first premium paid,* can the old policy be discontinued.

The Fight to Switch. An individual who decides to replace an existing policy may find that there is more at issue than merely applying for a new contract. Every application for life insurance asks the applicant, and his agent, whether the insurance being applied for is intended to replace an existing policy in the same or any other company. If the answer is in the affirmative, the new company will hold up issuance of any policy until the old company has been put on notice that one of its Insureds is attempting to discontinue his policy. This is calculated to give the old company an opportunity to "conserve" its business. This practice may appear to be merely a compact among members of a "cartel," but it is actually rooted in an attempt to prevent policyholders from acting against their own best interests.

As was pointed out previously, the largest part of the expenses connected with life insurance are incurred at the time the policy is written. A relatively high first-year commission, medical and inspection fees, the expense of writing and issuing the contract and setting it up on the company's books for servicing and collection of the subsequent premiums all make their appearance at the inception of the policy. As a consequence, there is a drain on the policy reserves (and actually on the company's surplus) which can only be recouped in the later years. This drain affects the values that the policyholder can recapture if he drops a policy in its early years.

The inter-company agreement among the carriers which is under discussion was established to give the carrier on the existing policy the opportunity to get the client's ear and point up any drawbacks of the projected switch over which may not have been made entirely clear to him by the agent involved in writing the new policy. If the change is being applied for in the same company, the agent is subject to a schedule of charge backs on any commissions he will receive for the new policy, at least during the early years of the old contract.

The Regulators Take a Hand. In their efforts to protect the members of the insurance-buying public from unscrupulous or badly informed salesmen who would "churn" them into new policies in order to earn a first year's commissions, the Insurance Departments of many states have instituted anti-twisting regulations. The agent who is involved in a replacement is mandated to make a "complete comparison" between the old and the suggested policy. In some states, he is required to complete a rather elaborate form which the new carrier must keep on file for a stated number of years.*

If all the procedures required in replacing are complied with, there is no reason why the desired policy should not be issued. It should be emphasized too that the new policy will be contestible for the first two years, while the old policy may well have passed this possible barrier. But if application for the new policy has been made in complete candor, there is no reason to be overly concerned on this score.

What If You Decide to End It All? Policies that have been in force for less than two years during the lifetime of the Insured may not be called to pay off in the event of his suicide. After the two-year period, no such limitation applies. For this reason, an old policy may well cover the suicide risk which the new policy will not—for the first two years. Suicide is of course a personal matter, and you alone are the best judge of how much this difference in coverage may mean to you. If you're not

* In New York State, a "Notice to Applicants Regarding Replacement of Life Insurance" must be delivered to a prospect considering replacing an existing policy. This notice which states that "As a general rule it is not advantageous to drop or change existing life insurance in favor of new life insurance, whether issued by the same or a different insurance company" sets forth a series of possible disadvantages to an Insured in the act of replacing old policies. It is pointed out that the initial costs of life insurance policies are charged against the cash value increases in the earlier policy years, that the suicide and incontestable clauses begin to run anew in a new policy, that the old policy may contain more favorable provisions than the new policy, and so on.

The regulations do allow that policyholders have the right to replace existing life insurance even if they have indicated in an application that such was not their intention. However, patterns of such action by policyholders of the same agent shall be deemed prima facie evidence of the agent's knowledge that replacement was intended in connection with such transactions, and such patterns of action shall be deemed prima facie evidence of the agent's intent to violate the Regulation governing replacement.

sure, you had best give serious thought to clinging to your present policies.

Lastly, there may be some special features in the existing policy that are not replaceable. Particular attention should be paid to disability income riders that were issued by companies who no longer make such benefits available. For the most part, the income coverage provided under such riders is better carried in separate accident and health policies. The entire question is discussed in Section II of the book (Chapters 18 through 22). However, there may be exceptions to this rule, and such riders or any others that are part of an existing life policy should be checked carefully.*

The Good Old Optional Modes of Settlement. Some older policies may contain guarantees under the Optional Modes of Settlement which are higher than similar provisions in policies being issued today. The Optional Modes of Settlement, you will recall, were discussed in Chapter 11 under "Protecting Beneficiaries against Themselves." There it was pointed out that tying up life proceeds to be paid out to beneficiaries over long periods of time suffers from the disadvantages which all fixed-dollar arrangements reflect. One who is committed to buying life insurance at the pure protection cost and investing the difference in a medium which may provide some cushion against inflation will not be likely to arrange for his insurance to be paid out in installments. He will therefore not be forfeiting anything of practical value when he surrenders an old policy, even if the returns promised to beneficiaries are superior to those which today's policies proffer.

If All the Caveats Have Been Noted. After one has checked out all the caveats enumerated above, and his resolve to buy Term and invest the difference remains unshaken, one last point needs to be checked: Is this the optimum time to make the switch, or is it better done at some later date? To arrive at a proper answer to this question calls for taking into account the loan values under the existing policy. A projection should be made of the net outlay after maximum loans that will be

* An outstanding if almost unique case in point would be the disability income coverage issued until recently in conjunction with its life insurance policies by the Mutual Benefit Life Insurance Company of Newark, N.J.

required to maintain the policy in force for the coming 10-year period. Credit should also be taken for tax savings on the interest payable on the loans. For the individual not schooled in life insurance, this may prove somewhat technical. Request can be made of the company for such projection, including an estimate of any projected dividends under the policy, as based on the company's present scale. The projected net outlays should then be set alongside the cost of Term insurance under consideration for this same period. Weight should be given to the interest factor of all sums expended, and for this purpose, the formula set forth in the Appendix can be utilized.

It may be that for some years at least, carrying the existing insurance on a "minimum deposit" basis will be more economical than taking the plunge into a new Term policy. (This method of carrying a cash value policy without tying up any cash values in the policy was discussed in the last pages of the preceding chapter.)

If You Are Already Carrying Minimum Deposit Insurance. As was pointed out in the discussion of this form of life insurance, all interest on policy loans under policies issued before August 7, 1963 is fully deductible. If you have been carrying such a policy under the minimum deposit umbrella, and you are in a fairly consistent tax bracket, it will probably be more economical for you to continue the contract as is. If you have been "minimum depositing" a policy purchased on or *after* August 7, 1963, which you have "tax qualified" by having paid four of the first seven years' premiums, your tax situation will be the same as that of policyholders who bought before the cut-off date, and your interest will continue deductible. It may therefore be advantageous to continue the protection as is.

If you have been carrying insurance on a minimum deposit basis which is *not* tax qualified, that is, you have *not* been able to deduct interest on the loans, you will need to check the costs over the next period against the straight Term product, along lines already indicated.

If these last suggested steps prove too onerous, and there is no impartial expert that can be called on, you may have to forego the economies that might be realized for the first few years before you make the move to pure protection and some form of variable dollar investment media for your retirement dollars.

15 Variable Life Insurance

CHAPTER 7 recounted in some detail the tremors which shook the life insurance industry in the wake of an accelerating inflation that began to plague the American economy in the 1960s. After considerable soul-searching and much jockeying for position vis-à-vis the state and Federal regulatory bodies, a new product was brought into existence. In what was hailed by its advocates as an historical step forward and damned by its opponents as a dangerous volte face, the industry in this product abandoned the guarantees which had been its stock in trade ever since its birth.

The variable annuity did not address itself to the problem of "dying too soon." It was not life insurance but its opposite—an annuity designed to protect against "living too long." It differed from the traditional annuity in a fundamental way—the amount of the payout was not *fixed,* not guaranteed by the insurer. It varied with the performance of the underlying portfolio on which the annuity was posited.

There was, however, one guarantee in the variable annuity, and this related to the death benefit which was guaranteed never to be less than the amount invested by the annuitant. This might be of some benefit to an annuitant who died soon after he had purchased the annuity and when the value of his account had not yet increased to the point where it recovered the charges deducted at the point of sale. But by and large, the investment risk under this new medium was to be borne by the annuitant.

The Light that Failed. Despite its bright promise, this new type of investment has not made serious inroads into the buying habits of the American public. Although the number of people covered by insurance company variable annuities in 1975 rose by 27 percent (as reported by the American Council of Life Insurance), the estimated premiums paid into the conventional, *fixed* annuities were still about five times as high as those for the newer variable variety.

It is difficult to make any estimate of what the public's response to this new concept in financial planning might have been if it were less ignorant of "what it was all about." Such surveys as have been conducted concluded that there was little familiarity with the product among consumers. Thus of 936 physicians polled in one such survey, 20 percent had never even heard of the product and another 25 percent had heard only of the term.* A second survey basically confirmed the fact that respondents lacked knowledge of the variable annuity.†

The New Look in the Variable Dollar. The variable annuity may have failed to take hold, but the underlying concept of the variable dollar which it sought to champion has emerged in a new and even more sophisticated form—variable *life insurance*. This newcomer goes one step beyond the variable annuity and, like the traditional cash value policy, offers security against both the risk of "living too long" or "dying too soon." The important innovation it introduces is that neither benefit is fixed in amount, although there is a floor under the death benefit, below which it cannot fall. With respect to the cash value, there is no minimum guarantee of any kind. In marked contrast to the familiar cash value policy which spells out the exact amount of cash available to the policyholder throughout the life of the contract, the variable life insurance policy guarantees nothing. The cash value, and any possible increases in the death benefit above the guaranteed minimum, depend entirely on the investment performance of the account the life insurance company maintains for these policies, which is invested primarily in common stocks.

* Robert A. Rentz Jr., "Variable Annuities: Implications of Investor Attitudes to the Insurance Industry," *Journal of the Society of Chartered Life Underwriters,* vol. 26, No. 4, October 1972, pp. 10–17.

† Lee J. Finley and John R. Kerr, "The Management of Innovation: Protection of Equity Products," *Journal of the Society of Chartered Life Underwriters,* vol. 24, No. 2, April 1970, p. 26.

Something New under the Sun? The leading proponent of this new concept in life insurance is the Equitable Life Assurance Society, the third largest in the nation, and it is as yet the only company marketing the product to individuals.* Its wholly owned subsidiary, the Equitable Variable Life Insurance Company is now licensed in nineteen states.† In its sales literature, the company takes pains to distinguish its creation from anything extant in the panoply of financial vehicles. "Before we describe what it is, let's be clear on what it is *not*," reads its brochure on this product, *The Patterns of Life*. "It is *not* a stock purchase plan. It is *not* a mutual fund. And it is *not* a variable annuity. It *is* life insurance." (emphasis in the original)

Variable life insurance is indeed life insurance. Its elements are put together differently from any Term policy with a separate outside investment like a mutual fund or a variable annuity. There are, as a matter of fact, differences in the design of the variable life policies of the several carriers interested in the field. The Equitable Variable Life Insurance Company itself offers an individual a choice of two policies. In each there is a minimum amount of guaranteed death protection. In the Basic Policy, this amount remains constant throughout the life of the contract, and can increase only by virtue of the investment results achieved. In the second plan, the Expanded Policy, for which a higher premium is charged, the guaranteed minimum amount of death protection increases by 3 percent a year until the fifteenth year when it is equal to 150 percent of the initial face amount, and remains constant at that figure thereafter. As mentioned, the actual death benefit in any year under either policy may increase over the guaranteed amount if the investment performance of the account exceeds 3 percent.

Variable life insurance is still only a fledgling, and if it does take hold, more and more companies are sure to get into the act. Refine-

*Like parents of a newborn infant, the company tends to rhapsody. The year 1976, it holds, was not only a *year of historical significance* to the nation, but "also noteworthy in the history of the life insurance industry," for January 13th of that year was the date on which "the first individual life insurance policy ever sold in the United States for the general market was issued by the Equitable Variable Life Insurance Company (EVLICO)" (from the Company's *Separate Account I—Semi-Annual Report,* June 30, 1976).

† Ariz., Calif., Colo., Del., Fla., Kan., Ky., La., Mo., N. Mex., N.Y., N.D., Okla., Ore., Tenn., Utah, Va., Wash., Wyo.

ments of the plan will no doubt be made, and new features introduced. The unit cost of the policy may decrease as the volume of this business mounts, and competition among the carriers may yield further benefits to the consumer.

Different, but How Different? At its present stage of development, how does the new product stack up against a program of straight Term insurance with a separate investment program in some variable dollar medium like the variable annuity or a mutual fund?

First, it should be pointed out that there is, in fact, some advantage in separating the life insurance protection from the retirement fund, for these two needs may not necessarily keep pace. While the death benefit under a variable life policy is variable, and may be a better hedge against inflation, the amount of protection may not continue to be required in an individual situation, as the years go by. Dependents may become self-supporting, additional amounts of life insurance may become available under group policies, or in pension and profit-sharing plans, and so on. Where the two media are separate, the retirement portion of the program may be continued without necessarily continuing the Term insurance in the same amount as when the program was first set up. And since all life insurance costs, as we now know, any savings in premiums that results from cutting back on the life insurance can be put to work to augment the funds being accumulated toward retirement.

On the other hand, the "discipline" element, that is, the forced savings feature, may be stronger with the two elements, protection and investment, packaged together, as they are in the variable life policy. The temptation to divert money from the retirement program to other things may be reduced in such a "combination" program.

A Still Unresolved Problem that Hovers over Variable Life. To date, the income tax status of the death proceeds of a variable life insurance policy has not been ruled on. In the opinion of the companies' learned counsel, such proceeds will not be treated differently from those of the conventional life insurance, which are not subject to income taxes when received by the beneficiary. However, with death and taxes being two of the most certain facts of life, the nature of the taxes that will be imposed is still open at this time.

All in All—Where Do We Stand? To the extent that generalization is possible, there is no warrant for bestowing on variable life insurance a superior status over the Term and separate investment account. Variable life can be accepted into the fold, as an additional tool in plans to face the double exigencies of "living too long" and "dying too soon."

16 Retirement Needs: How Much, and from Whom?

ESTATE NEEDS, we have seen, evolve out of the situation a family would be in if the source of its support were cut off by death *today*. It is a *current* contingency and as such fairly simple to estimate. One's economic situation at retirement is, by contrast, years ahead in the future, and hence difficult to envision with any degree of accuracy. One must nevertheless be concerned about the future, because as someone once said, "we will have to spend the rest of our lives there."

Your Pension under Social Security. Most Americans who reach retirement age will have available to them certain monthly income payments under Social Security. The size of the benefit will depend on the individual's Average Monthly Earnings, as defined in the law. Maximums on the amount of earnings that could be credited toward Average Monthly Earnings were established for all the years since 1937. These have been increased in 12 stages from $3,000 for the years before 1951 to $16,500 for the year 1977. The law also provides that increases in the cost of living will result in an automatic increase in the benefits. It is also more than likely that the base will be further increased in years to come. The income that a worker retiring 20 or 30 years from now will receive is therefore likely to be considerably higher than any projection based on today's formulas. Offsetting such increases is the strong likelihood that the purchasing power of the dollar at that time will have been reduced substantially by inflation.

Estimating the dollar amount of the benefits that will be paid years hence or the real purchasing power of such dollars clearly entails a considerable amount of guesswork. If the current taxable base is projected *without* any increments a worker who is 35 years old in 1977 and has been earning the maximum creditable under Social Security since he began working at 25 will be entitled to a monthly income of a little over $575 when he reaches age 65 in the year 2007.

A conservative course to follow in assigning weight to one's future Social Security benefits is to take them in at their present levels. An estimate of the benefits that can be anticipated at retirement may be obtained at any local office of the Social Security Administration (Health, Education and Welfare). To that figure should be added the amount of retirement benefits that will become available under any private pension and/or profit-sharing plans at one's place of employment.

Whether these elements add up to a retirement income which will accord with one's view of an adequate lifestyle after retirement must be assessed separately by each individual. In view of all the vagaries of the future, however, it would seem eminently prudent for all except the independently wealthy to look to the Social Security system to provide merely a ''floor'' under one's retirement needs, albeit often an important one, and to take early steps to build on this base a program of further insurance against ''living too long.''

Set a Down-to-Earth Figure. The amount to be allocated to this goal should be set at a figure which can be adhered to faithfully, and viewed as a regular obligation to be met like an insurance premium or other demanding responsibilities. Chapter 10 on Retirement, underlined the importance of settling on an investment in a diversified portfolio of high-grade common stocks which permits the regular deposit of comparatively modest sums and the automatic reinvestment of all earnings, no matter how small. Two candidates for this role were analyzed in some depth—the mutual fund and the variable annuity. This chapter will identify the more desirable products in both these fields.

The No-Load Fund. We come first to the field of mutual funds. It will be recalled that in our exploration of this subject, we were unable to locate any pattern of consistently superior performance for any individual fund or funds. In this light, it makes sense to opt for a no-load fund, that is, one which makes no sales charge and imposes no fee on liquidation of shares. (A few of the funds that we have listed do charge a liquidation fee, but only on shares held for six months or less, a factor of no practical significance in our situation.) We have listed only those funds which claim an orientation toward capital appreciation rather that current income, although some eclectically aspire to both goals at the same time (sic!). All of the listed funds allow for reinvestment of dividends. The chart also shows the minimum initial investment and the minimum subsequent investment. Only funds which accept $500 or less as an initial investment and $100 or less subsequently are listed.

Information is given about the fund, its distributor where this is not the fund itself, the minimums accepted for investment, and the states in which the fund is qualified. Table XII lists those no-load funds that have been offering their shares continuously for at least 10 years. Table XIII enumerates funds that are less than 10 years old but have been operating for at least five years.

A Shrinking Violet. Also discussed in Chapter 10 as an alternative vehicle for retirement accumulation was the variable annuity. Since any annuity is based on life expectancies, the variable annuity, like its more traditional ancestor, the fixed-dollar annuity, is marketed by life insurance companies, usually through a wholly owned subsidiary. In sharp contrast to the aggressiveness with which these carriers have promoted their fixed-dollar products, are the essentially flaccid marketing efforts behind the variable annuity. It may therefore take some persistence to actually latch onto a "live" one. In Table XIV are listed some 30 organizations which offer individuals a deferred variable annuity purchasable by periodic payments. As in the case of mutual funds, we eschew any attempt to select star performers, and make a choice solely on the basis of the sales charges imposed.

All the companies impose a sales charge. Generally, the charges scale down with the size of the payment and the total invested. It is therefore not possible to fix too precisely on the annuities with the lowest charges. On the assumption that a funding vehicle for future retirement will call for the deposit of relatively small sums, we have arranged the companies in an order which reflects their sales charges on small purchases.

TABLE XII. FUNDS THAT HAVE BEEN OFFERING THEIR SHARES FOR 10 YEARS OR MORE

Fund	*Distributor, if other than fund*	*Minimum initial investment*	*Minimum subsequent investment*	*States in which qualified*
Amer. Investors 88 Field Pt. Rd. Greenwich, Conn. 06830 203/661-5010		$400	$10	All states except Calif., Mich., Wis.
David L. Babson Three Crown Center 2440 Pershing Rd. Kansas City, Mo. 64108	Jones & Babson (same address) 816/471-5200	$500	$50	All states
Beacon Hill Mutual 75 Federal Street Boston, Mass. 02110 617/482-0795		none	none	D.C., Ariz., Colo., Fla., Me., Md., Mass., Neb., N.J., N.Y., Ohio, Ore., Pa., R.I., S.D., Utah, Vt., Wash., Wyo.
Contrafund, Inc. 35 Congress St. Boston, Mass. 02109 800/225-6190		$500	$50	All states except Iowa, Me., N.C. Licensed in Puerto Rico
Dodge & Cox Balanced 1 Post Street San Francisco, Calif. 94104 415/981-1710		$250	$50	Calif., Hawaii, Nev., Utah
Dodge & Cox Stock Fund (same address as above)		$250	$50	Calif., Hawaii, Nev., Utah

Financial Industrial 1050 S. Broadway Denver, Colo. 80201	Financial Programs P.O. Box 2040 Denver, Colo. 80201 303/777-4071	$250	$25	All states and Puerto Rico
First Multifund of America 32 E. 57 St. New York, N.Y. 10022 212/759-2311		$100		All states
Foursquare Fund 24 Federal St. Boston, Mass. 02110	Eaton & Howard (same address) 617/482-8260	$50	$50	All states except Alaska, Ark., Calif., Hawaii, Ill., Ind., Iowa, Ky., La., Mich., Miss., Mont., Nev., N.D., Ohio, S.C., S.D., Tenn., Tex., Wis.
General Securities 133 So. 7th St. Minneapolis, Minn. 55402	Craig-Hallum Inc. (same address) 612/332-1212	$100	$10	All states except Ky., Mo., N.D., Tex., Wis. Licensed in Puerto Rico
Golconda Investors 505 Park Ave. New York, N.Y. 10022 212/697-0400	Chase Manhattan Bank 14th floor 1 New York Plaza New York, 10015	none	none	Colo., Conn., Del., Md., Mass., N.J., N.Y., Pa., D.C.
Growth Industry Shares 135 S. LaSalle St. Chicago, Ill. 60603 312/346-4830		$200	$25	All states

TABLE XII. FUNDS THAT HAVE BEEN OFFERING THEIR SHARES FOR 10 YEARS OR MORE (*continued*)

Fund	*Distributor, if other than fund*	*Minimum initial investment*	*Minimum subsequent investment*	*States in which qualified*
Heritage Fund, Inc. 200 Josephine St. Denver, Colo. 80206 303/321-7474		$250	$25	Colo. Del., Fla., Md., Mass., Nev., N.M., N.Y., Pa., S.D., Utah
Industry Fund of Amer. 200 Josephine St. Denver, Colo. 80206 303/321-7474		$25	$25	Ariz., Colo., Idaho, Kan. Mont., Neb., Nev., N.M., N.D., Ore., S.D., Utah, Wash., Wyo.
Inverness Growth 1880 Century Pk. E. Los Angeles, Calif. 90067 213/277-1450		$100	$100	Calif., Colo., N.Y.
Ivy Fund, Inc. 28 State St. Boston, Mass. 02109 617/227-4910		$500	$100	All states
Loomis-Sayles Mutual 225 Franklin St. Boston, Mass. 02110	NEL Equity Svces. 501 Boylston St. Boston, Mass. 02117 617/267-6600	$250	$50	All states and Puerto Rico
National Industries 2130 S. Dahlia St.	Industry Savings Plans	$250	$25	All states and Puerto Rico

Denver, Colo. 80222	(same address) 303/756-1501			
Northeast Investors Trust 50 Congress Street Boston, Mass. 02109 617/523-3588		$500	none	All states except Alaska, N.D., Ohio
One Hundred & One Fund 899 Logan Street Denver, Colo. 80203 303/892-1020		$250	$50	All states except Ark., Ill., Ind., Iowa, Me., Mich., Miss., N.H., Ohio, S.C., Wis.
One Hundred Fund (same as above)		$250	$50	Same as above
One William St. Fund 1 William St. New York, N.Y. 10004	Lehman Bros. (same address) 212/269-3700	$250	$50	All states
Pine Street Fund 20 Exchange Pl. New York, N.Y. 10005 212/BO 9-3313		$500	$50	Calif., Conn., Del., Fla., Ill., Ind., Md., Mass., Mich., Mont., N.J., N.Y., Nev., Ohio, Pa., R.I., Tex., Va., D.C.
T. Rowe Price Growth Stock Fund, Inc. 100 E. Pratt St. Baltimore, Md. 21202 301/547-2136		$500	$50	All states and Puerto Rico
Scudder, Stevens & Clark Common Stock 10 PO Square Boston, Mass. 02109	Scudder Fund Distributors, Inc. (same address) 617/482-3990	$500	none	All states and Puerto Rico

TABLE XII. FUNDS THAT HAVE BEEN OFFERING THEIR SHARES FOR 10 YEARS OR MORE (*continued*)

Fund	*Distributor, if other than fund*	*Minimum initial investment*	*Minimum subsequent investment*	*States in which qualified*
Selected American Shares 111 W. Wash. St. Chicago, Ill. 60602 312/630-2762		$200	$50	All states and Puerto Rico
Selected Special Shares (same as above)		$200	$50	All states and Puerto Rico
Steadman American Industry 919 18th St. N.W. Washington, D.C. 20006 202/223-1000		$100	$25	Not listed
Steadman Investment (same as above)		$100	$25	Not listed
Stein Roe & Farnham Balanced Fund 150 S. Wacker Dr. Chicago, Ill. 60606 312/368-7810		$300	$50	All states
Stein Roe & Farnham Capital Oppties. (Same address as above)		$300	$50	All states except Ark., Kan., Utah, W. Va.

Stein Roe & Farnham Stock Fund (same address as above)	$300	$50	All states
20th Century Investors 605 W. 47th Street Kansas City, Mo. 64112 816/531-5575	none	none	All states except Hawaii, Idaho, Ky., N.H., N.C., Wis.
Variable Stock Fund 441 Stuart Street Boston, Mass. 02116 617/261-1900	none	none	Del., Fla., Ga., Md., Mass., Miss., N.J., N.Y., Pa., R.I., Va., W. Va.
Wade Fund, Inc. 5100 Poplar Ave. Memphis, Tenn. 38137 901/682-4613	1 share	1 share	Tenn.

TABLE XIII. FUNDS THAT HAVE BEEN OFFERING THEIR SHARES FOR AT LEAST FIVE YEARS

Fund	*Distributor, if other than fund*	*Minimum initial investment*	*Minimum subsequent investment*	*States in which qualified*
Afuture Fund, Inc. 8 Pennell Rd. Lima, Pa. 19037 215/565-3131		$500	$30	All states, except Alaska, Ark., Conn., Idaho, Kan., Ky., La., Me., Miss., Nev., N.H., N.M., N.D., S.C., S.D., Utah, Vt., Va., Wyo.
Alliance Growth Box 1032, Wall St. New York, N.Y. 10055	AGF Management Co. 115 Broadway, Rm 815 New York, N.Y. 11106 212/BO 9-6363	$100		Del., N.J., N.Y.
Alpha Fund, Inc. 2900 1st Intl. Bank Tower Atlanta, Ga. 30303 404/658-9250		$200	$50	All states except Alaska, Hawaii, Me., Mo., Mont., N.H., Vt.
Americare Growth 601 Sixth Ave. Des Moines, Iowa 50334	Amer. Repub. Equities PO Box AT, 600 5th Ave. Des Moines, Iowa 515/245-6500	$100	$25	Ala., Ariz., Ark., Calif., Colo., Del., Fla., Ga., Idaho, Ill., Iowa, Kan., Ky., Mich., Mo., Mont., Neb., Nev., N.J., N.D., Ohio, Okla., Ore., S.D., Tenn., Wash., Wis., Wyo.

Armstrong Assoc. 3200 First Natl. Bank Bldg. Dallas, Tex. 75202	Schneider, Bernet & Hickman, Inc. (same address) 214/744-5558	$500	$50	Ark., La., Okla., Tex.
Centennial Capital Special Fund	Oppenheimer & Co. 1 New York Plaza New York, N.Y. 10004 212/825-4000	$500	$100	Calif., Colo., Conn., D.C., Ga., Kan., Mich., Minn., Miss., Mo., Nev., N.J., N.Y., Ohio, Pa., R.I., Tex., and Wis.
Churchill Fund, Inc. 1290 E. Oakland Park Blvd. Ft. Lauderdale, Fla. 33308 305/566-5401		none	none	Conn., Fla., N.J., N.Y.
Columbia Growth Fund 621 S.W. Morrison St. Portland, Ore. 97205 503/222-3601		$500	$50	All states
Columbus Fund, Inc. 250 E. Broad St. Columbus, Ohio 43215	Comsec. Inc. 88 E. Broad St. Columbus, Ohio 43215 614/224-0980	$100	$25	All states except Alaska, Conn., Idaho, Kan., Me., Mass., Mo., Minn., Mont., N.H., N.M., N.D., R.I., Tenn., Tex., Utah, Vt., W. Va. Wis., Wyo.

TABLE XIII. FUNDS THAT HAVE BEEN OFFERING THEIR SHARES FOR AT LEAST FIVE YEARS (*continued*)

Fund	*Distributor, if other than fund*	*Minimum initial investment*	*Minimum subsequent investment*	*States in which qualified*
Constellation Growth Fund 20 Exchange Pl. New York, N.Y. 10005	Purcell Graham & Co. 20 Exchange Place New York, N.Y. 10005 212/WH 4-8120	$250		Calif., Conn., Del., D.C., Fla., Ga., Hawaii, Idaho, Ind., Md., Mass., Minn., Miss., Nev., N.J., NY., Ore., Pa., R.I., Utah, Vt.
Doll Fund, Inc. Thackery Lane Mendham, N.J. 07945 201/543-2388		$500	$50	Fla., Md., Mass., Nev., N.J., N.Y. Va.
Eldorado Fund 18158 Westover Southfield, Mich. 48075	Eldorado Fund P.O. Box 1083 Southfield, Mich. 48075	$100	$50	Fla., Mich., N.Y.
F. G. Mutual Fund 4680 Wilshire Blvd. Los Angeles, Calif. 90010 213/931-1961		$100	$25	Ariz., Calif., Ill., Ind., Mich., Minn., Nev., Tex., Wis.
Financial Dynamics 1050 S. Bdwy., Box 2040 Denver, Colo. 80201	Finan Programs, Inc. (same address) 800/525-6148	$250	$25	All states except Iowa, Me., N.H., Ohio Licensed in Puerto Rico

Fund for Mutual Depositors 200 Park Avenue New York, N.Y. 10017 212/973-4705	Through certain mutual savings banks	$200	$50	Alaska, Calif., Conn., Del., Ind., Me., Md., Mass., Minn., N.H., N.J., N.Y., Ore., Pa., Vt., Wash., Wis.
Investment Guidance Investment Plaza Cleveland, Ohio 44114	Roulston & Co. (same address) 216/696-3070	minimum purchase: 10 shares		Ohio
Janus Fund, Inc. 789 Sherman St. Ste. 410 Denver, Colo. 80203 303/572-8808		$500	$100	Ala., Ariz., Ark. Cal., Colo., Del., Fla., Ga., Hawaii, Idaho, Ill., Ind., Iowa, Kan., La., Md., Mass., Miss., Neb., Nev., N.J., N.M., N.Y., Okla., Ore., Pa., Tex., Utah, Wash., Wyo., D.C.
Mates Investment 120 Broadway New York, N.Y. 10005	Shawmut Bank of Boston P.O. Box 4178 Boston, Mass. 02107	$300	$50	Conn., Del., Fla., Ga., Mass., Md., N.J., N.Y., Pa., Tenn., Va.
Nicholas Fund 312 E. Wisc. Ave. Milwaukee, Wis. 53201	First Wsc. Trust Co. P.O. Box 2054 Milwaukee, Wis. 53201	$500	$100	All states except Ala., Idaho, Iowa, Kan., Ky., Me., N.H., N.D., Okla., Vt.
Oceanographic Fund 919 18th St. N.W. Washington, D.C. 20006 202/223-1000		$500	$25	Not listed

TABLE XIII. FUNDS THAT HAVE BEEN OFFERING THEIR SHARES FOR AT LEAST FIVE YEARS (*continued*)

Fund	*Distributor, if other than fund*	*Minimum initial investment*	*Minimum subsequent investment*	*States in which qualified*
Partners Fund, Inc. 522 Fifth Ave New York, N.Y. 10036	Cedar Street Consultants 522 Fifth Ave. New York, N.Y. 10036 212/575-7220	$250		All states except Calif., Wis.
Pro Fund, Inc. Valley Forge, Pa. 19481 215/783-7600		none		All states except Mo.
Selected Opportunity 111 W. Washington St. Chicago, Ill. 60602 312/630-2762		$500	$50	All states except Ark., Me., N.H., Ohio, R.I., Wash. Licensed in Puerto Rico
Smith, Barney Equity 1345 Ave. of Amers. New York, N.Y. 10019	Smith, Barney & Co. (same address) 212/333-7200	$100 or 10 shares	$100 or 10 shares	All states except Alaska, Miss., and N.H.
Spectra Fund 26 Broadway New York, N.Y. 10004 N.Y., 212/483-0030		$500	$50	Alaska, Colo., Conn., Fla., Iowa, Kan., Mass., Mich., Minn., Mo., N.Y. Ore., Pa., Tex., Wash., Wyo.

United Services P.O. Box 2098 Universal City, Tex. 78148 512/658-3562		$250	$50	Not listed
Valley Forge Fund P.O. Box 262 Valley Forge, Pa. 19481 215/MU 8-6839		$300	$100	Conn., Del., Md., Nev., N.J., N.Y., Pa., D.C.
Weingarten Equity 331 Madison Ave. New York, N.Y. 10017	Weingarten, Rosenbaum & Co. (same address) 212/OX 7-9600	$500	$ 50	All states except Ga., Ill., Ind., Iowa, Kan., La., Me., Mich., Minn., Miss., Mo., N.H., N.D., Ohio, Okla., S.C., Tex., Vt., W. Va., Wis., Wyo.
Clarence M. Whipple 2045 Church Rd., P.O. Box 234 Cherry Hill, N.J. 08002	Industrial Valley Bank & Trust Co. Jenkintown, Pa. 19046	$50	none	Conn., Del., Nev., N.J., N.Y., Pa., D.C.

TABLE XIV. COMPANIES OFFERING VARIABLE ANNUITIES

Funding vehicles	*Distributor*	*Subsidiary of*	*States in which licensed*
New England Life Variable Annuity	NEL Equity Services 501 Boylston Street Boston, Mass. 02117	New England Mutual Life Insurance Company	All states and D.C.
Voyager Variable Annuity Fund B	Washington National Equity Company 1630 Chicago Ave. Evanston, Ill. 60201	National Variable Annuity Co. of Florida	All states except New York
Travelers Fund B for variable contracts	Travelers Ins. Co. 1 Tower Square Hartford, Conn. 06115	Travelers Ins. Co.	All states and D.C.
Shenandoah Variable Annuity Fund A	Shenandoah Equity Services, Inc. 2301 Brambleton Ave., S.W. Roanoke, Va. 24015	Shenandoah Life Ins. Co.	Ala., Del., D.C., Fla., Ga., Ind., Ky., Md., Mich., Miss., N.J., N.C., Ohio, Pa., S.C., Tenn., Va., W. Va.
General American Separate Account 2	General American Life Insurance 1501 Locust Street St. Louis, Mo. 63166	General American Life Ins. Co.	All states including D.C., except New York
Paul Revere Variable Annuity Contract Account Fund Service N	Paul Revere Variable Annuity Ins. Co. 18 Chestnut Street Worcester, Mass. 01608	Paul Revere Life Ins. Co.	All states including D.C., except New York

Provident National Assurance Separate Account B	Provident National Assurance Co. Fountain Square Chattanooga, Tenn. 37402	Provident Life and Accident Ins. Co.	All states including D.C.
Jefferson Separate Account A	Jefferson-Pilot Equity Sales, Inc. 101 N. Elm St. Greensboro, N.C. 27401	Jefferson Standard Life Ins. Co.	Ala., Ariz., Ark., Calif., Colo., Del., D.C., Fla., Ga., Idaho, Ind., Kan., Ky., La., Md., Miss., N.J., N.Mex., N.C., Ohio, Okla., Ore. Pa., S.C., Tenn., Tex., Utah, Va., Wash., W. Va., Wyo. and Puerto Rico
Southwestern Life Variable Annuity	Southwestern Management & Reserve 1807 Ross Street Dallas, Tex. 75221	Southwestern Life Ins. P.O. Box 2699 Dallas, Tex. 75221	Ala., Ariz., Ark., Calif., Colo., Fla., Ga., Idaho, Ill., Iowa, Kan., Ky., La., Md., Miss., Mo., N. Mex., N.C., Ohio, Okla., Ore., Pa., S.C., Tenn., Tex., Utah, Va., Wash., W. Va.
CML Variable Annuity Account II	Connecticut Mutual Life 140 Gordon Street Hartford, Conn. 06115	Connecticut Mutual Life Ins.	All states including D.C., except North Carolina
National Life Variable Annuity Account I	Equity Services, Inc. National Life Drive Montpelier, Vt. 05602	National Life of Vermont	All states and D.C.

TABLE XIV. COMPANIES OFFERING VARIABLE ANNUITIES (*continued*)

Funding vehicles	*Distributor*	*Subsidiary of*	*States in which licensed*
CG Variable Annuity Account II		Connecticut General Life Ins. Hartford, Conn. 06152	All states and D.C.
Variable Annuity Life Ins. Co. Separate Account One	Variable Annuity Marketing Co. 2777 Allen Parkway Houston, Tex. 77019	Variable Annuity Life Ins. Co.	All states and D.C.
Prudential's Annuity Plan Account	Prudential Ins. Co. of America Prudential Plaza New York, N.Y. 10019	Prudential Ins. Co. of America	All states and D.C.
MONY Variable Annuity Account A	Mutual Life Ins. Co. of N.Y. 1740 Broadway New York, N.Y. 10019	Mutual Life Ins. Co. of N.Y.	All states and D.C.
Hartford Variable Annuity Life Ins. Co. Separate Account	Hartford Equity Sales Hartford Plaza Hartford, Conn. 06115	Hartford Variable Annuity Life	All states except Maryland and New York
Mutual Benefit Variable Contract Account 3	Mutual Benefit Financial Service Co. 520 Broad Street Newark, N.J. 07101	Mutual Benefit Life Ins. Co.	All states
Life Insurance Co. of N. America	Life Insurance Co. of N. America	Life Ins. Co. of N. America	All states except New Hampshire, New Jersey, and New York

Separate Account A	1600 Arch Street Philadelphia, Pa. 19101		
Equitable Life Assurance Society Separate Account C	Equitable Life Assurance 1285 Avenue of the Americas New York, N.Y. 10019	Equitable Life Assurance Society of the U.S.	All states and D.C.
Lincoln National Variable Annuity Fund B	Lincoln National Life Ins. 1301 S. Harrison Street Fort Wayne, Ind. 46801	Lincoln National Life Insurance Co.	All states except New York
Cal-Western Separate Account Variable Fund C	Calif. Western States Life & Calif. Western Securities Co. 2020 L Street Sacramento, Calif. 95814	Calif. Western States Life Ins. Co.	Ariz., Calif., Colo., Hawaii, Idaho, La., Mont., Nev., N. Mex., Ore., Tex., Utah, Wash. Wyo.
Ohio National Variable Account B	Ohio National Equity Sales Co. 237 William Howard Taft Road Cincinnati, Ohio 45219	Ohio Natl. Life Ins. Co.	Ariz., Ark., Calif., Colo., Del., Fla., Ga., Idaho, Ill., Ind., Iowa, Kan., Ky., Md., Mich., Minn., Miss., Mo., Mont., Neb., Nev., N.J., N. Mex., N.D., Ohio, Ore., Pa., S.D., Tenn., Tex., Utah, Va., Wash., W. Va., Wyo., and D.C.

TABLE XIV. COMPANIES OFFERING VARIABLE ANNUITIES (*continued*)

Funding vehicles	*Distributor*	*Subsidiary of*	*States in which licensed*
Occidental's Separate Account Fund C	Transmamerica Fund Sales 1150 S. Oliver St. Los Angeles, Calif. 90015	Occidental Life Ins.	All states including D.C. except New York
American Variable Annuity Fund	SMA Equities Inc. 440 Lincoln Street Worcester, Mass. 01605	State Mutual Life Assur. of America	All states including D.C. except Ark., Alaska, Del., Hawaii, Idaho, Miss., Mont., Nev., N. Mex., N.D., S.D., Utah, and Wyo.
Franklin Life Variable Annuity Fund B	Franklin Financial Services Franklin Square Springfield, Ill. 62713	Franklin Life Ins. Co.	All states except New York
New York Life Separate Account N	New York Life Variable Contract Corp. 51 Madison Ave. New York, N.Y. 10010	New York Life Ins. Co.	All states and D.C.
Mass. Mutual Variable Annuity Fund 2	Mass. Mutual Life Ins. 1295 State Street Springfield, Mass. 01111	Mass. Mutual Life Ins. Co.	All states

Guardian Variable Account 2	Guardian Life Ins. Co. of Amer., Assoc., 201 Park Avenue S. New York, N.Y. 10003	Guardian Life Ins. Co.	Ala., Ariz., Calif., Colo., Conn., Del., D.C., Fla., Ga., Ill., Ind., La., Mass., Mich., Minn., Mo., Neb., N.H., N.J., N.Y., N.C., Ohio, Okla., Ore., R.I., Tenn., Tex., Utah, Va., Wash., Wis.
IDS Life Variable Annuity Fund A	IDS Life Ins. Co. IDS Tower Minneapolis, Minn. 55402	IDS Life Ins. Co.	All states and D.C.

One last point may be made on the selection. All other things being equal (which they seldom are) there is some possible advantage to a product which is sold in a large number of states, for in the event that a planholder moves he will be in a position to continue to get service from an office in the new state.

In the preceding chapter we touched on another product which has just begun to be marketed—the variable life insurance policy. Although it is now available to individuals from only one company and is still not offered in the majority of the states, it can be considered an acceptable medium for those whose paths it crosses.

To sum up: From the numerous mutual funds and variable annuities listed in this chapter and variable life policies (or other media which offer similar features) an investment vehicle should be decided upon. A program of regular investment of a fixed sum (as a minimum at any rate) should be decided upon. This program should be followed religiously, through all the ups and downs of the business cycle and the fluctuations in the market.

Planning for Security—Not Fun. A program of this kind, it is true, is flat and uninteresting, lacking in the excitement that comes with pitting oneself against the market. Gambling is a deep and abiding passion with a venerable history of over 4,000 years. From the series of prohibitions against it, both secular and religious, which stretch down through the ages, it is clear that it continues to hold a deep place in men's hearts. While "speculation is not identical with gambling" as the Encyclopedia Brittanica puts it, it offers a valuable outlet for this deep-seated mania which is not being expunged by the program being advocated here.

The objective in retirement planning is *insurance*—against finding oneself after retirement with insufficient means to sustain a decent standard of living. And as in all insurance, the important element is certainty. Constancy then is all.

Some Special Groups. In making a selection from among the variable annuity products listed or others that are offered, one should be aware of two factors that may result in reduced sales charges. Most of the companies lower sales charges when the money being invested with them comes out of a life insurance policy in the parent company. Secondly, in almost every instance, charges are reduced, or a separate Fund with lower charges offered as a medium for persons entitled to the benefits of the Self-Employed Individuals Retirement Act of 1962, individuals employed by certain tax-exempt institutions or public school systems, or for monies coming out of certain qualified pension plans. These special categories are discussed in the next chapter.

17 Special Tax Boons for Certain Groups

IF YOU WORK WHERE THERE IS NO PENSION PLAN

Important tax benefits may be enjoyed by persons who are not covered under a qualified corporate pension, profit-sharing or annuity plan, or bond purchase plan. Generally speaking, such individuals may set aside each year up to 15 percent of their gross income, but not more than $1,500 in a qualified retirement account (known as an Individual Retirement Account, or I.R.A.). The entire contribution made by an individual into such an account is deductible for tax purposes. In effect, he is getting an assist in providing for his retirement from the Government. Thus a taxpayer in a 33⅓ percent tax bracket will receive the equivalent of a $1.00 "contribution" for each $2.00 he sets aside. Additionally, all the earnings on these funds are also completely exempt from taxes.

This Ain't Hay! A moment's reflection will show that over the long pull these economies can add up to very substantial sums. To illustrate: Assume a 35-year-old taxpayer is in the 33⅓ percent tax bracket (the rate at which his top dollar is taxed). Although he is eligible for the special tax treatment we are now discussing, he fails to establish the required plan. If he has $1,500 *before* taxes to allocate to a retirement account, he will actually have only $1,000 *after* taxes to deposit therein. All the earnings on these funds will also be taxed—essentially at his normal tax rate. If he continues to make these annual deposits until he reaches age 65, earning 6 percent as he goes along, he will find himself with a nest egg of $58,329.00 at that time.

If He Establishes an Individual Retirement Account. If he sets up an Individual Retirement Account, he can now deposit the full $1,500 each year, since these sums will escape income taxes entirely. Furthermore, all interest on the account (or other yield) will compound tax-free. At age 65, this tax-sheltered fund will amount to $125,703.00 as opposed to the $58,329.00 that would have been available to him without this program. The difference of $67,374.00, it can be seen, serves to more than double his retirement resources.

Bigger and Better Tax Savings. The tax benefits will be even better for individuals in a higher tax bracket, as well as for situations where a rate of interest higher than 6 percent is earned. Thus, for an individual in the same tax bracket who earns 7½ percent annually, the difference would come to over $85,000.00.

What Are Acceptable Vehicles for Such Plans? The Internal Revenue Code spells out the types of "trust or custodial accounts" in which the contributions will qualify for favorable tax treatment. Generally, any corporation or partnership which has demonstrated its ability to act as a fiduciary is acceptable. In this light, most banks, mutual funds, variable annuity, and variable life companies have taken the necessary steps to be qualified as acceptable repositories. If you believe you are eligible to come under this tax umbrella, it should be quite simple to check whether the investment vehicle you are considering is in fact qualified to act in this capacity.

Does This Change the Investment Philosophy? Everything that has been said up to this point on utilizing an investment technique that offers a possible hedge against inflation continues to apply to Individual Retirement Accounts. Most mutual funds and variable annuity and life companies which can qualify as fiduciaries under the law may be considered. One seeking to establish this form of tax-sheltered retirement account can proceed to make selection of the investment vehicle in much the same manner as an individual who is not eligible for an Individual Retirement Account.

The Frosting on the Cake. As mentioned, selection is to be made of a fiduciary which is eligible to act in this field. Many of the sponsors of such funds or variable annuities also operate in the regular, "nonqualified" market. They offer a product to individuals who do not come under this special section of the tax law. Separate accounts are maintained for the two types of investor—the "qualified" and the "nonqualified." Individual Retirement Accounts will receive better rates of return under the separate account utilized in such programs.

No Limit per Family. If a husband and a wife are both eligible to establish Individual Retirement Accounts, each may, subject to the permitted maximum of 15 percent of gross earnings, or $1,500.00 whichever is less, establish an Individual Retirement Account for his (or her) own benefit.

Some Possible Problems. The taxation of distributions from an Individual Retirement Account are somewhat involved, but if the account is maintained to retirement, the participant will generally be in a lower bracket than he was during his working years. Taxpayers who reach age 65 before the close of the taxable year are entitled to double the $750 personal exemption for that year. If married taxpayers both 65 years of age or older file a joint return, their personal exemptions for the year will come to $3,000. These factors will serve to lighten the tax impact of the withdrawals under Individual Retirement Accounts.

There is a requirement that distribution under an Individual Retirement Account must begin not later than when the participant attains age 70½.

If distribution is made to an individual before he is 59½, his income tax is increased by 10 percent of the amount of the distribution which is includible in gross income in the tax year. This type of account should therefore be set up only when there is reasonable expectation that it will be continued. (The penalty does *not* apply, however, if the distribution is attributable to the individual's disability, regardless of his age.)

II. IF YOU ARE SELF-EMPLOYED

Important tax benefits are also available to self-employed individuals who establish approved retirement programs (HR-10 or Keogh

Plans as they are known). While the law states that a qualified trust must be established by an employer for the exclusive benefit of his *employees*, it specifically considers proprietors or partners operating a business or profession as employees for the limited purpose of allowing such individuals to participate in a qualified plan.

There are some special angles to the question of whether certain individuals can qualify. Thus, a clergyman employed by a congregation is not a self-employed person even though his salary is treated for Social Security purposes as self-employment incone. He is considered a "common law" employee and as such, cannot avail himself of an HR-10 Plan. But in the usual trade or business situation, operated by an individual owner or by partners, the eligibility for self-employed plan purposes is clear.

A Common Law Employee May Still Be Able to Qualify. An individual who is employed but earns additional money in self-employment may be in a position to establish a qualified plan based on his self-employment income. Thus, the clergyman whose regular salary from the congregation cannot provide the basis for a self-employment plan may base such a plan on the fees he receives directly from members of his congregation for officiating at baptisms, confirmations, weddings, and so on.

What Contributions Can Be Made to a Qualified Self-Employment Plan? There are fairly involved guidelines for the amount that may be contributed to an HR-10 Plan, but by and large, they limit contributions to 15 percent of the self-employed individual's earned income, or $7,500, whichever is less. As in the case of the Individual Retirement Account discussed at the beginning of this chapter, a qualified HR-10 Plan affords a deduction from gross income of all contributions made, and confers tax-free status on all the earnings realized by the funds. The tax savings, we saw earlier, can amount to a very sizable sum.

But You Can't Pick and Choose. For the one-man business or profession, the Self-Employment Account is virtually all gravy. Where the entity has other people in its employ, each employee who has three or more years of service must be brought into the plan, if it covers any owner-employee. Obviously, a business or profession with employees *other* than owner-employees will have a more involved computation to make in weighing up the benefits of the program for owner-employees. In considering the entire question, it would appear prudent to speak to one's accountant, attorney, or other qualified person before deciding on the course to pursue.

To Be or Not to Be—Incorporated. Many sole proprietors and partnerships face a decision on whether to continue to operate as they do, or to incorporate. In many states, professional men and women can elect to become incorporated as "professional corporations." The question is a many-sided one, and should not be settled solely on the basis of possible tax benefits, although this assuredly can make a serious difference. Incorporation will open the door to installing a qualified pension or profit-sharing plan, or some combination of both. The tax benefits to be realized under such a program may outweigh those of an HR-10 program. Request for a projection of each type of plan should be made of individuals technically equipped to perform such calculations.

While tax considerations are important, they should not provide the sole basis for making a choice in the matter of the structure of the business or profession. There are pluses and minuses on both sides of the equation, and these should be explored carefully with one's counsel and accountant.

III. IF YOU WORK FOR CERTAIN TAX-EXEMPT ORGANIZATIONS

Tax-sheltered annuities are available to employees of public school systems or organizations operated exclusively for religious, charitable, scientific, literary, educational, or safety-testing purposes, or for the prevention of cruelty to animals or children. Organizations of this kind that are wholly owned by a state or local government (other than public schools) are generally not eligible, although the regulations are somewhat complex on this point. Thus, some such organizations may qualify if they are separately organized and are not an integral part of the government, like some state or city hospitals, and so on. The situation of a doctor working for such qualified hospitals depends on whether he is an employee for all purposes such as withholding taxes and Social Security. An individual who believes he may be eligible for a tax-sheltered annuity should make inquiries of his employer to determine whether the organization is one described in Section 510(c) (3) of the Internal Revenue Code.

What Benefits Are Available? An employee of a public school or an organization described in the preceding paragraph can purchase an annuity and exclude the premium for such annuity from his gross income. In other words, much like the Individual Retirement Account which was discussed at the beginning of this chapter, the employee of this type of organization can set aside monies toward his retirement, in this instance, the premiums on an annuity, *before* taxes. And as in the case with I.R.A. and HR-10 situations, the growth in the annuity accumulating over the years before retirement are also free of income taxes. And these savings can loom very large at the end of the line. (See figures under Section I of this chapter—"If You Work Where There Is No Pension Plan.")

How Much Can Be Paid into a Tax-Sheltered Annuity? As in most tax matters, there are some fairly complex rules governing the amount of premium one may deduct from taxable income in any given year. Roughly, 20 percent of the employee's includible compensation may be applied toward the annuity purchase, and deducted. (If the employee takes a reduction in salary to finance the purchase, the maximum deduction will come to 16⅓ percent of his salary before reduction.) Additionally, credit may be taken for past service with the *same* organization (not another organization generally, even if in the same field).

Employees of such organizations as well as those of public schools who expect to continue in the same field of endeavor should give serious thought to the important tax benefits that can accrue to them through the purchase of a tax-sheltered annuity. As in the case of their less fortunate brethren who cannot invoke the benevolence of the Government, the investment medium should be one which offers some hope of being responsive to the inroads that inflation may make into the purchasing power of the dollar over the many years before the annuity payout begins. For this role, a variable of the kind reviewed in Chapter 16 should be considered a strong contender.

An Important Consideration. Most of the insurers in the field offer two separate types of account—one for individuals who have no special status vis-à-vis the tax laws, and a second for "qualified" money, that is, funds coming from a qualified pension or profit-sharing plan, or money being set aside under an Individual Retirement Account, an HR-10 account, or under a tax-sheltered annuity. An employee qualified for a tax-deferred annuity should be sure that the annuity he is buying is one which maintains a special account for "qualified" money.

II

THE RISK OF DISABILITY

18 Assessing the Risk

THE "LIVING TOO LONG" risk covered in previous chapters dealt with the economic consequences of living past retirement. There is, however, another risk that can be subsumed under "living too long"—the threat of a long-term disabling injury or illness that can strike at any time and render us unproductive, economically.

All of us, except the fortunate few who can live by merely clipping coupons or those at the other end of the economic spectrum who are supported by the general taxpayers, are dependent to one degree or another on our continued ability to engage in gainful work. The threat of a disabling injury or illness is therefore one of the most serious financial hazards of modern life. Most disability, it must be remembered, is double-edged in effect. It cuts off the income of the wage earner at the very time when he must assume the burden of onerous medical expenses. Any reserves it may have been possible to accumulate are quickly exhausted; the disabled person becomes entangled in serious debt, or must turn to some form of charity.

The Whole House Comes Tumbling Down. Even if some steps have been taken to take the sting out of catastrophic medical expenses (an important subject to be discussed in the next section of the book), a protracted disability can wreck the most carefully erected financial structure, including one's life insurance as well as any plans for retirement. For all sectors of our economic well-being derive from our ability to produce income in our work or business. It is essential then to properly analyze the disability exposure and take what steps we can to cushion its impact.

First, it is essential to take stock of our situation. Are we entirely dependent on a weekly paycheck for our support or do we have substantial assets which could carry us for a relatively extended period? Are we on "straight salary" or do we have an interest in a business enterprise which could continue to produce income even if we were removed from active participation in it? 'And for how long could such income be expected to continue? If we work for salary or wages, is there a formal salary continuance plan under which we are covered? For how long? Or is there some informal program of this kind on which we can count with some degree of assurance?

Government-Sponsored Protection. After all these possible financial cushions have been tallied, most wage earners will still find a serious gap between the income they can count on during disability and the minimum they require to maintain a decent standard of living. Not all of this deficiency needs to be transferred to a risk-bearing institution through insurance, however. Fortunately almost everyone who works for wages or is self-employed is covered under the Federal Social Security Act against loss of income through disability. Also to be reckoned with is protection against this contingency under some state laws.

First, with respect to injuries arising out of and in the course of our employment: Almost every worker can count on some continuance of wages if he is injured in an occupationally connected accident, and in many states, if he falls victim to an occupational disease. There are wide differences in the extent of the coverage among the various states but, at best, the compensation will fall far short of a minimum standard of living. In any event, since these statutory benefits apply only to disabilities that are work-related, provision must still be made for the larger risk of disability which originates *outside* the place of employment.

Coverage under Social Security. Income benefits during long-term disability, regardless of its origin, have been part of the Federal Social Security system since 1956. Over the years, a series of amendments have so liberalized these benefits that they can be quite significant. We must be clear then on what the Social Security Act does and does not provide in the way of disability income benefits.

Monthly income payments are available to any *covered* worker under 65 who is disabled within the meaning of this term under the law. To be covered, a worker must have a certain minimum employment history. Basically, he must meet two tests. First, he must be *fully insured,* as defined in the Act. Fully insured status requires a minimum number of quarters of coverage, that is, calendar quarters in which he has received wages in covered employment of $50 or more, or a quarter in a year in which he earned $400 in self-employment income. Any worker who has 40 quarters of coverage is *fully insured* for life, even if he spends no further time in employment or self-employment.

An individual who does not have 40 quarters of coverage may nevertheless be fully insured for disability purposes if he has

1. at least six quarters of coverage, *and*
2. at least as many quarters as there are *years* elapsing after 1950, or the year in which he attained age 21, if later. Thus, a worker who becomes disabled in 1977 will be considered fully insured if he has only 26 quarters of coverage, since only 26 years have elapsed since 1950. A worker who attained age 21 in 1962 needs only 14 quarters of coverage in 1977 (one for each year since he attained age 21). If he reached age 21 in 1962, he needs only 10 quarters of coverage in 1977; if he became 21 in 1971 or later, he needs six quarters of coverage, the minimum in all events, and so on.

In addition to being fully insured as outlined above, a disabled worker must have 20 quarters of coverage in the 40-calendar quarter period ending with the quarter in which his disability began. There are special provisions for individuals who become disabled prior to age 31, and for blind persons, but for most workers, the two requirements set forth above—fully insured status and employment for five out of the last ten years before disability—must be met to establish eligibility.

As shown in table XV, the size of the monthly payments depends on the worker's average monthly wage prior to the onset of disability. Maximum family benefits are prescribed in the law, and these are also set forth. There are several factors that can affect the precise amount of benefits, but a fairly reasonable approximation can be arrived at from this table. It should be noted that Social Security disability payments will be reduced if benefits are paid under a Workers' Compensation program based on work-related disabilities.

TABLE XV. EXAMPLES OF MONTHLY CASH DISABILITY BENEFITS (EFFECTIVE JUNE 1976)

	AVERAGE YEARLY EARNINGS AFTER 1950*				
Benefits can be paid to:	*$923 or less*	*$5,000*	*$8,000*	*$10,000*	*$13,000*
A disabled worker	107.90	304.50	427.80	474.00	535.60
A disabled worker and and wife at 62	148.40	418.80	588.30	651.80	736.50
A disabled widow at 50	56.80	152.40	214.00	237.10	267.90
A disabled worker, wife under 65, and one child (Maximum family payment)	161.90	561.90	748.70	829.50	937.20

*The maximum earnings creditable for social security are $3,600 for 1951–54; $4,200 for 1955–58; $4,800 for 1959–65; $6,600 for 1966–67; 17,800 for 1968–71; 19,000 for 1972; $10,800 for 1973; $13,200 for 1974; $14,100 for 1975; $15,300 for 1976; and $16,500 for 1977. The maximum family benefit for a young disabled worker and his or her family in 1977 is $992.10 a month, based on average earnings of $14,700.

As can be seen from Table XV, a worker in the lowest income bracket is entitled to a benefit which is over 77 percent of his average wage prior to his having become disabled. If he has a wife and child who are also eligible for benefits, the family maximum will exceed his average wage by over 26 percent. Although the amount of the benefit increases with the average monthly wage, the *percentage* covered decreases. Thus, for an average wage of $500, the disability benefit is $323, or 65 percent (although the maximum family benefit is still almost 19 percent higher than the average wage). On an average monthly wage of $1,000, the disabled worker's benefit is $485, or 48.5 percent; his family benefit maximum is $849, some 85 percent. It should be noted that these maximums will be payable only in future years, and are applicable only in relatively few situations at present. Actual average earnings for all workers except those who came into the work force only within the last few years will be considerably lower due to the maximums that were creditable to Social Security taxation in past years (see page 144). The spouse of a disabled worker is also entitled to benefits, but only if he (or she) is over 62 or is caring for at least one child under the age of 18 (or a disabled child) who is entitled to a child's benefit.

None of these benefits is subject to income taxes. It is also comforting to note that under an amendment enacted in 1972, disability benefits will be increased automatically to keep abreast of increases in the cost of living as posted by the Consumer Price Index. (An increase of some 5.4 percent in benefits became effective in June 1976 under this provision.) An increase in benefits will also generally be followed by an increase in the taxable wage base. While the percentage of wages covered will differ for workers in different earning brackets, the benefits provided under the Social Act will almost always provide an important base for a disability insurance program.

Some State-Mandated Coverage. In addition to the disability income provisions of Social Security, laws mandating virtually all employers to carry disability income insurance for their workers have been enacted in five states and Puerto Rico. Benefits are required to be provided in these states for all *non*occupationally connected illnesses or injuries.

Income payments begin with the eighth day of disability and are payable for a maximum of 26 weeks in any calendar year. They range from ½ to ⅔ of the worker's average earnings, subject to maximums which vary from state to state, as set forth below:

	Maximum weekly benefits
California	$119 plus $12 for each of the first 20 days of hospital confinement
Hawaii	Subject to maximum payable for unemployment insurance
New Jersey	50 percent of the average weekly wage promulgated by the Commissioner of Labor
New York	$95.00
Puerto Rico	1.21 times the average weekly wage published by the Department of Labor
Rhode Island	$68 plus $3 for each dependent.

Income disability insurance may also be in effect at one's place of employment. As will be shown in the next chapter, group disability insurance is often fairly limited in scope—at least with respects to long-term disabilities. In any event, a tally of the income which we can expect during a period of disability from all of the above sources must first be made. This total can then be offset against the minimum income required to keep afloat during such periods.

To close or at least narrow the gap between these two figures, we must turn to private insurance. But as will be shown, attending only to the *amount* of benefits under a policy may be grasping at the shadow while overlooking the substance.

19 Why the Amount of Coverage Is Only Part of the Story

WITH ONLY A FEW negligible exceptions, disability income policies do not incorporate any savings element in the protection they offer. In return for the dutiful payment of premiums by the Insured the Company undertakes to pay him a stipulated sum in the event he is disabled. At first, this relatively simple agreement appears refreshingly free of the complications that beset life insurance. But as was pointed out over 2,500 years ago by a wise Greek, "Appearances often are deceiving." Strange as it may seem, in disability insurance, we are faced with an array of policies to choose from, even more staggering in number than in life insurance.

The Same—But Different. In life insurance, any $25,000 policy regardless of its type can be expected to pay a beneficiary the same amount as any other $25,000 policy. But one disability income policy providing $500 of monthly income may be liable for no more than $6,000 in any one disability, while a second $500 policy, in the same company, may be called on to pay $180,000, or more. How does this come about?

Policies are written with differing maximum periods during which benefits are payable. One will provide income benefits for a maximum of 12 months in any one disability. Others may cover for 24 months, 60 months, 120 months, to age 65, and so on. Some companies even offer lifetime benefits. To make things even more interesting, there are various combinations like lifetime accident with 15 months sickness; lifetime accident with 30 months sickness; lifetime accident with 60 months sickness; 5-year accident with 5-year sickness; 10-year accident with 10-year sickness; and so on. Further color is added to the crazy quilt by policies which offer all these permutations and combinations *plus* "extended benefits," that is, *one-half* the regular benefits are paid after the full benefit period has been exhausted. Some policies increase the monthly benefits by 10 percent if premiums are paid annually; others reduce the benefits if the disabled policyholder is not continuously confined within doors or if his income in the period preceding the onset of disability had been reduced below what he was earning when he bought the policy, and so on. And finally, not to be outdone by their opposite numbers who merchandise life insurance, the disability people blossom forth with a spate of "extras"—accidental death and dismemberment, hospital benefits, supplemental hospital expense, surgical and medical treatment, accident medical expense, partial disability riders—to mention just a few.

But even leaving these "extras" aside, the basic coverage can be provided in an almost endless number of permutations and combinations. Thus, in a typical company, a 35-year-old male can purchase a policy providing a maximum payout for 15 months in one disability of $400 a month for an annual premium of $91.00. For the same monthly benefits under a lifetime policy, the premium is $239.92, over 2½ times as high. Two policies may offer the same monthly benefit, *and for the same period,* and may still be quite different. This arises out of the "elimination period" which is part of most accident and sickness policies. Under this provision, an initial period of disability must elapse before benefits begin. Frequently, the period differs for accidents and for illnesses. A fairly commonly written policy will pay for disability resulting from an accident from the first day; on illnesses, from the eighth day. The same policy is also offered with waiting periods of 7 days, 14 days, 30 days, 90 days, 180 days, and 365 days. Again, the premium varies substantially with the elimination period. Thus, a 0–7 policy (no elimination on accidents; first seven days of illness) issued to a male age 35 develops a premium of $183.88 for a $400 a month policy, with a 15 months maximum on any single disability. For the same coverage with the first *180 days* eliminated, the premium is $62.56, or about one-third.

A Bewildering Potpourri. These two variables alone—the benefit period maximum and the elimination period—already produce a cornucopia of policies from which a choice must be made. Thus, in a typical company, an applicant is offered over 40 different basic policies, even without giving credit to "extended benefit" riders, and the numerous other "extras" which may be tacked on. These range from a 15-month policy with the first 180 days eliminated to one which will pay benefits for life beginning with the 31st day. The premium for the second policy incidentally is over seven times as high as for the more limited one, for the same individual.

Or, looked at another way, a male age 35 can buy for the same premium any one of the following policies:

1. $270 a month for a maximum of 15 months, 0 elimination on accidents, and eight days on sickness
2. $1,000 a month, for the same period, but with 180 days eliminated
3. $200 a month for life, with the first 30 days eliminated
4. $267 a month for life, with one year elimination.

It is obvious, then, in light of all that has gone before, that in disability insurance, the dollar amount of benefits under a policy tells only part, and often only a small part, of the story. Even with this caveat in mind, there are still two additional elements in disability insurance which must be clarified if one is to thread his way through this heavily mined field.

What Is Disability? First, there is the not inconsiderable question of the nature of the disability that is being covered. In life insurance, the risk being insured against is fairly clear-cut. Modern life-sustaining medical equipment may have brought into being legal questions as to when death actually occurs, but such technicalities aside, the point is reached when all agree that the individual is dead, and his life insurance "matures as a death claim" as the jargon has it. Except for the occasional contest of a claim which is permitted to an insurance company only during the first two years of a policy's existence, there is seldom any question of *coverage*.

In disability insurance, the issue is far more complicated. Is a physician who is prevented by his heart condition from continuing his practice as a gynecologist and obstetrician but who acts as a consultant in sex education and family planning at a hospital disabled within the terms of his disability policy? Does the ability of the Insured to perform some inconsequential, trivial, or incidental duties connected with his usual employment or occupation preclude his recovery under a total disability policy? An Insured suffers a hernia when lifting a water cooler. Does his accident policy exclude coverage because the accident was not produced by *accidental means* but as the natural if unforeseen result of an action in which he had intentionally engaged? Where medical testimony attributes an Insured's cardiac neurosis to a former heart disease, would his disability be due only to imagined ills, a situation excluded under his policy?

If a policy stipulates that coverage will apply only if the Insured is confined within doors and receives visits from a physician, can the company deny benefits if he visits the doctor for treatments, sometimes stops at a store on the way home from the doctor's office and goes out into the yard on occasion to take the exercise which the doctor prescribed? Where an insured farmer is prevented by hypertension from performing any of the physical labor which he had formerly done on his farm, which is now operated by his son who shares the profits with him, is he barred from recovering under a disability policy because he makes some decisions and suggestions from time to time about the operation of the farm? Is an insured who is compelled to give up his undertaking business by hypertrophic arthritis but does light manual work and makes investments for income and profit disabled under his policy? Does a policy which relates total disability to the inability of the Insured to perform the duties pertaining to his occupation require total helplessness on the part of the Insured?

If you think that the above situations are creatures of a fertile imagination, I hasten to assure you that each is cited almost verbatim from an insurance claim which had to be resolved in the courts. And they represent the tiniest part of the accident and health insurance claims that are litigated or brought before the complaint bureaus of the Insurance Departments of the various states. (In the state of New York, by way of one example, in 1973 over 6,000 complaints under accident and health policies were investigated by the state's Insurance Department.)

Whether a particular injury or illness is covered under a disability policy depends not only on the nature of the condition but also on how disability is defined in that policy. And policies differ considerably on this important issue. The more restrictive clauses define "total and permanent disability" as the inability to "engage in any occupation for remuneration or hire" or to "perform any work for compensation or financial value."

"His Occupation" vs. Any Occupation. More liberal policies consider a policyholder disabled if he is "unable to engage in his regular occupation or profession," at least initially. This more bountiful standard is applied for the early years of a disability, usually the first five. If the Insured is prevented by an accident or illness from engaging *in his own occupation or profession,* he is deemed eligible for disability benefits for five years, or the period stipulated. After his disability has continued along these lines for the stated number of years, a somewhat more rigid standard is invoked, and he will continue to receive payments but only if he is unable to engage in any gainful occupation for which he is reasonably fitted, having due regard for his earning ability, his education, training, and experience. There are numerous gradations between these poles, but almost all policies employ some similar language in their insuring clauses.

Insurance Should Insure! It is true that policy language notwithstanding, many courts have held that "total disability" does not require the complete helplessness of the claimant. But since our aim in buying insurance is to minimize uncertainty, not to make case law, we must opt for the policy which embodies the least restrictive coverage.

Disability Protection under Social Security. While we're on the subject of policy terminology, we should clarify the nature of the disability that is covered under the Social Security Act. The disability protection under the Act, which is now available to almost every American person who is gainfully employed or self-employed, it has been pointed out, can be an important ingredient of any disability insurance program. It is therefore important that we understand what is and is not covered under the law. Under Social Security, disability is defined as "any medically determinable physical or mental impairment that can be expected to result in death or has lasted or can be expected to last for a continuous period of not less than 12 months, and that renders an individual unable to engage in any substantial gainful activity." An individual is considered to be under such a disability only if his impairments are of such severity that he is not only unable to do his previous work but cannot, considering his age, education, and work experience, engage in any other kind of substantial gainful work which exists in the national economy, regardless of whether such work exists in the immediate area in which he lives, or whether a specific job vacancy exists for him, or whether he would be hired if he applied for work. In order for work activity to be "substantial," the regulations state, it is not necessary that it be performed on a full-time basis; work activity performed on a part-time basis may also be substantial. It is also immaterial that the work activity of an individual may be less, or less responsible, or less gainful, than that in which he was engaged before the onset of his impairment.

The language of the Act, if literally interpreted, is clearly not overly generous to a finding of disability. Its severity is considerably mitigated, however, by another regulation which provides that medical considerations alone can justify a finding that the individual is under a disability where his impairment meets the duration requirement and is listed in the Appendix to the Social Security Act regulations or the Secretary determines his impairment to be medically the equivalent of an impairment listed in the Appendix.

The Appendix, which the Regulation dryly dubs "lengthy and detailed," runs to over 16 closely printed pages and enumerates hundreds of medical conditions and impairments which alone can justify a finding of disability. A worker who has been disabled by one of the listed conditions for a period of five consecutive months after the month in which his impairment began will become eligible for benefits except when other evidence rebuts a finding of disability, as for example, when he is engaging in substantial gainful activity. In actual practice, then, most serious injuries or medical conditions that have a significantly limiting effect on work-related physical and mental activities, and that continue for five months will qualify a claimant for benefits, unless it is clear that the impairment will not last for at least 12 months, or result in death, or unless the claimant is engaged in substantially gainful work.

In the case of the disability insurance under the Social Security Act, we have obviously little control over the nature of the disability which will be covered. We pay our taxes, as employers and employees, and get what the law offers. It behooves us then all the more when we set out to supplement this protection with other insurance that we select a policy with the broadest insuring clause available. This entire question together with the others which must be answered if we are to make a proper choice of disability insurance will be explored in the next chapter.

Finally, there is one last component of disability insurance that must be understood if we would choose wisely from among the profusion of policies which make up the portfolios of the life companies, the casualty companies, and the specialized accident and health insurers which are in the disability income insurance business.

Policies "Leased" to the Insured. It might appear superfluous to point out that a first requisite of any insurance program is that it provide protection when we need it. And yet, in accident and health insurance, many policies offer little guarantee of this sort. There are numerous policies in force today, or being offered for sale, which may or may not be around in later years when the Insured actually incurs a disability and requires income protection.

This highly undesirable situation can come about under policies whose continuance in force depends entirely *on the company*. One type of contract states explicitly, "The company may cancel this policy at any time by written notice to the insured or mailed to his last address as shown by the records of the company." There is no obligation on the company to explain its reason for canceling, and the policyholder has no recourse against such action, regardless of how faithfully he had paid premiums over the years to maintain his policy.

Only slightly better than a policy of this kind which may be canceled at any time is one which states that "it may be renewed for consecutive periods only with the consent of the company." Some policies of this ilk put it more delicately, employing language along the following lines: "This policy is issued in consideration of the payment of an annual premium of $---- and the payment of a like premium on each anniversary of the register date. . . ." So far, so good. But this rather innocuous statement may be followed by another which reads, "The acceptance of any renewal premium shall be optional with the Company." Under any policy utilizing language of this variety, the company has the option *at the end of each year* to renew or not renew the policy. In effect, the policyholder is in the position each year of an individual making application to the company for the first time. His policy may be only one year old, or may have been renewed for the past 20 years, but the company has the sole and unrestricted option at any renewal date of terminating the coverage. Again as in the case of the cancellable policy described in the preceding paragraph, the policyholder has no recourse against such action. It is of no importance that his original application for the policy was scrupulously accurate in all its statements. The contract is terminated, and the company is not required to adduce any reason for its decision. It has been aptly said that the policyholder does not *own* such insurance but merely holds it on an annual lease which the landlord need not renew at the expiration of any term.

A terminated policyholder can of course try to replace his insurance with another company, but his chances of acceptance are rather poor. As might be expected, the new company will ask in its application whether he has ever received benefits under any other policy, and whether any insurance has ever been declined, canceled, or refused renewal by any other carrier. In addition, most companies are members of a central bureau through which all such information clears. The applicant's history with his previous company will weigh heavily against him.

Pre-Existing Conditions. Even if the policyholder does manage to obtain a new policy (which will probably be written at a higher premium than his old policy), he will generally not be covered for any pre-existing condition. In some cases, the new company may require his agreement to a waiver of coverage on any recurrence of the condition from which he has begun to suffer. But even if no waiver of any specific condition is incorporated in the new policy, the company will not be liable for conditions which originated prior to the inception of its policy, at least until a stated period has elapsed.

It is true that once a claim has arisen under a policy it must be settled in full, up to the policy limit, regardless of whether the policy is cancellable or is renewable only with the company's consent. To this extent, an Insured can count on collecting in full on the *first* claim he presents under his policy. If the policy is of the more liberal variety which can be canceled only at the end of the year, the policyholder is assured of collecting on all claims that arise within the policy year.

The Fatal Flaw. The fatal flaw in either type of policy, however, lies in the fact that one cannot count on having any insurance after these initial periods. Since most chronic illnesses are preceded by temporary disability, there is always the serious risk that the policy will have evaporated before the long-term disability sets in. For even a first relatively mild attack of any disease or condition which threatens to become chronic may convince the company that its Insured is an impaired risk. Furthermore, even if no severe disability appears to threaten, a series of recurring illnesses of short duration may also impel the company to jettison a particular policyholder. The company can actually cancel (or refuse to renew) a policy if it learns of any condition which beclouds its client's health picture, or because of his advancing years which make him a less desirable risk than when he first became insured.

The company's right to cancel or refuse renewal is often defended on the grounds that it provides a safeguard against the "moral hazard" which hovers rather acutely over this class of business. Underwriting this risk, some contend, cannot be handled effectively unless the company is armed with the wherewithal to eliminate those who obtained their insurance by fraud or misstatement and those who present dishonest claims.

These are factors which must be dealt with in the accident and health insurance business. But they do not tell the whole story. While there are no definitive statistics on the number of policies that are terminated for various reasons, it can be stated that accident and sickness policies are canceled or refused renewal *because the Insured has become an impaired risk.* Thus, one authoritative study of this form of insurance cites "five principal causes of cancellation." Two of the reasons given are "impaired physical condition" and "repeated claims for recurrent types of diseases."*

In designing their cancellable and nonrenewable policies, the companies actually take into account their ability to "get off the risk." A leading actuary in the field contrasts this type of policy with those under which the company does *not* have the right to withdraw from the risk midstream. Under the renewable policy, he writes, "It will be impossible to eliminate cases of prolonged sickness and cases of total and permanent disability which it has been possible to avoid heretofore when such disabilities have been preceded by temporary sickness."†

None of the foregoing is calculated to imply that all companies writing this form of insurance will pay only one claim, or that they withdraw from their policies as soon as they have reason to expect a claim. Many companies, prepared to return a reasonable portion of the premiums they collect in the form of claims to their policyholders, try to serve their clients as effectively as is consistent with profitable underwriting. But the significant word here is "profitable." And to you, as an individual arrayed against the odds of a disabling accident or illness which may strike at any time, one question must remain paramount: "Is there any accident and health insurance which can be counted on to provide a regular income when I actually need it, without my being in the situation of the Psalmist who prayed, 'Cast me not off in the time of old age; forsake me not when my strength faileth'?"

Insurance You Can Count On. It is heartening to report that such protection is available. There are policies which guarantee the Insured the right to renew his policy by merely paying the premiums as they fall due, at least through the productive period of life. A "guaranteed renewable" policy, as such contracts are called, would appear to answer

* John M. Laird, "Non-Cancellable Accident and Health Insurance Underwriting Problems," *Proceedings of the Casualty Actuarial Society,* vol. VII, pt. 2, p. 306.

† E. E. Cammack, "Premiums and Reserves on Non-Cancellable Accident and Health Policies," *Proceedings of the Casualty Actuarial Society,* vol. VII, pt. 2, p. 267.

one's needs in this field, but even here a note of caution is indicated. The development of this form of insurance is an interesting object lesson in the wizardry that often distinguishes the marketing departments of insurance companies.

The saga begins with the cancellable policy described above which explicitly grants the company the right to cancel the contract at any time, even in the midst of the term for which the premium has been paid. One creative company hit on the idea of deleting this clause in its entirety. Cancellation of the policy as such was no longer possible. Instead, the insurance would remain in force come what may, until the end of the period for which the premium had been paid. But the company would have the option of accepting or refusing any premium. This was the second type of policy discussed above.

This latter-day "improved" version was first trumpeted as "noncancellable." Not surprisingly, many policyholders who had bought these "noncancellable" policies were deeply disenchanted when they suddenly found themselves without insurance because the company elected not to accept a renewal premium. In the face of growing resentment of such practices, many state Insurance Departments forbade the use of the term "noncancellable" on any policy unless it granted the Insured the sole right to renew his policy until some relatively advanced age. In 1959, the National Association of Insurance Commissioners Report required such renewal privilege to a minimum of age 50 in all policies which would carry the legend or be sold or advertised as "noncancellable."

A Sleeper. The term "noncancellable," hemmed about with this requirement, might now appear synonymous with "guaranteed renewable." But this would be true only for uninitiates in marketing semantics. An unsung mastermind merchandiser came up with a guaranteed renewable policy which complied with the rules by granting the policyholder the option of renewing his policy every year, but with an interesting angle—the company now reserved the right to change the premium at any renewal date for the entire class of Insureds. "The guaranteed renewable, adjustable premium policy is a unique instrument in the array of insurance mechanisms available to the Accident and Sickness insurance industry,'' is the way it was put by one participant in the 10th International Conference for Life Insurance Medicine held in London June 8th to 11th, 1970.* And a unique instrument it was indeed! Whether such a policy should be allowed to strut about as ''noncancellable'' touched off a dispute that went on for some four years. Actuaries in the field raised some interesting questions. ''What is to prevent the Insurer from adopting ''freeze out'' increases in order to effectively nonrenew a troublesome block of business?'' one actuary asked. ''What will prevent the selling of new business at deliberately inadequate rates, with the intention of increasing the cost at renewal, thus provoking dangerous and unfair competition? How effective will the revision mechanism really prove to be in enabling the Insurer to keep business self-sustaining? Will increases merely serve to instigate an assessment spiral?''†

The Great Compromise. The companies themselves were divided on the issue. An executive of two sister companies with a long career in the noncancellable field took a stand for the designation ''adjustable premium renewal policy'' which would appear to describe the policy in a way that the ordinary citizen might understand. But these few dissident voices and those of actuaries, notoriously unimaginative fellows with little ear for the subtleties of merchandising, were silenced in a ''compromise,'' as it was put, ''in order to present a united insurance industry approach.'' The term ''guaranteed renewable'' was to be permitted for a policy where the premiums are subject to change on a class basis.‡

Separate—And Not Equal. So we now have two kinds of guaranteed renewable policies, one of which is also ''noncancellable.'' The difference between them is that the guaranteed renewable but *not* the noncancellable policy allows for increases in premium at any policy anniversary. This is a very crucial factor. It is true that a company seeking to

* R. C. Brackenridge, M.D., M.R.C.P. (Glas.)

† E. P. Barnhart, ''Adjustment of Premiums Under Guaranteed Renewable Policies,'' *Society of Actuaries Transactions,* vol. XII, 1960, p. 474.

‡ Orville F. Graham, vice-president and general counsel of Paul Revere Life of Massachusetts, quoted in *The National Underwriter,* January 9, 1960.

increase its renewal premiums under an accident and health policy for an entire class of Insureds might have to justify its request for the rate rise to the regulatory insurance authorities in its state. But as a standard text in this field put it: "This type of contract does not provide the unconditional guarantee of a noncancellable policy but does provide greater security than the commercial forms."* The question is: Does it provide *sufficient* security? And the answer must be that it does *not*. Although it does permit the Insured the unrestricted right to continue his policy, the absence of a fixed premium may price it out of reach. This could well occur if the company sustained losses under the policy and endeavored to provide for such through a rate increase. The policyholders who were in good physical condition would then go shopping for replacing insurance in other companies. To those in the group who had developed some physical or mental impairment since they first bought their insurance or had made claims over the years, this option would be closed off. They would therefore sweat and strain to pay the higher premiums as long as they could, holding on to their insurance as long as possible. As the "standard" risks departed the company for more benign climes, the loss experience of the remaining group would continue to deteriorate. The company would be compelled to seek successive increases, each of which would drive away more of the policyholders who could manage to obtain any other coverage, and leave only the most impaired risks "hanging on for dear life."

Security that Is Not Secure. A policy of this kind may provide "greater security than the commercial forms" (as the late Prof. Dickerson put it) but if you were one of the less fortunate individuals who could not replace his coverage elsewhere and was therefore paying ever-increasing premiums for a policy (fast streaking away into the astrosphere,) you would hastily agree that this "greater security" was not enough. If insurance is to insure, it cannot be stressed too strongly, it must be on hand when the need for its protection arises. A policy of the kind we have under discussion is therefore seriously defective and should be avoided.

*O. D. Dickerson, Ph.D., C.L.U., C.P.C.U., F.C.A.S., *Health Insurance,* Homewood, Ill.: Richard D. Irwin, Inc., 1968, p. 431.

In the face of the seemingly endless variables that proliferate in the field of income insurance, it is easy to be numbed into hopelessness about the possibility of deciding on a proper insurance program. The situation fortunately is not as dark as it might seem. If we strip away the frills and lay bare certain fundamentals that all insurance is based on, we will find it comparatively simple to come up with a sound and economical insurance program. The chapter that follows addresses itself to the solution of this problem.

20 Getting Back to Basics

If we hold fast to the essentials that *any* insurance program should incorporate, we will find that most of the selling fog that surrounds disability insurance will quickly evaporate. To begin with, all must concede some element of permanence is basic to any insurance, that is, one must be able to count on the policy's being around when and if the need for its protection arises. This is especially important in coverage against long-term disability, since more frequently than not serious illnesses are preceded by temporary conditions. A policy which is not renewable at the Insured's option, we learned, could well cease to be before the long-term disability against which it was bought sets in.

A Sine Qua Non. The only policies which fill the bill on this important score are those that are guaranteed renewable *and* noncancellable, as these terms are now generally used in the insurance business. Because state guidelines on what policies may be so labeled may vary, it is important that any policy you are considering expressly grant you the sole and unrestricted right, by merely paying the premium, to renew year after year, at least until you are 65. There must be no language anywhere which gives the company the right to refuse renewal premiums or requires its acquiescence in the acceptance of any such premium. *Additionally,* and it is important that this be checked carefully too, the policy must be renewable at the *same* premium. No provision is acceptable which allows the company to increase premiums at renewal, even to the entire class of Insureds.

The same standards incidentally are to be applied to any disability policy you may now be carrying. In either case, whether you are applying for a new policy or seeking to determine whether an existing policy is worth continuing, these two points must be checked out. If after you have reviewed your old policy or the literature that blazons forth the virtues of a new policy you are being offered, you are still uncertain or find yourself more confused than ever (a condition which may well prevail), be sure to ask for a statement in writing from the carrier in question. To repeat, you need to be satisfied on two scores:

1. Is the policy renewable at your sole option at least until you are 65?

2. Is the premium which you are asked to pay at inception fixed (that is, one which cannot be changed by the company for any reason)?

Unless the answer to *both* these questions is in the affirmative, you had best pass up the policy, no matter how attractive it might appear. As will be shown in the next chapter, which will discuss the amount of coverage to buy and the companies offering desirable products in this field, eliminating policies which fail to meet these criteria narrows the field considerably.

What Is Disability? We come now to a second important feature of disability insurance. As was mentioned, different policies define disability in varying ways. In the case of the disability covered under the Social Security Act, which was analyzed in some detail in the preceding chapter, there is of course no room for choice. Virtually every gainfully employed or self-employed person comes under the law. One pays the taxes levied on employer or employee, as the case may be, and receives the coverage spelled out in the law. No more and no less.

From Table XV, which set forth the monthly disability benefits for various income brackets, it becomes clear that most individuals, except those who are independently wealthy, will need to supplement their disability coverage under Social Security with some additional insurance from the private sector. At this point, a series of choices opens before the prospective buyer.

One of the more important differences among policies, we observed, was the way in which "disability" is defined. The more restrictive clauses call for "the inability to engage in *any* occupation for remuneration or gain." The more liberal variety consider a policyholder disabled within the terms of the contract and eligible to receive income payments if he is unable to engage in *his* occupation or profession, up to a stated maximum number of years. If he is still disabled at the expiration of that time, it will no longer suffice that he is unable to engage in *his* occupation. He can continue to receive benefits, but only if he is unable to engage in a gainful occupation for which he is reasonably fitted, having due regard for his earning ability from the policy date, his education, training, and experience. The broadest policies employ this "his occupation" terminology without switching over to "any occupation for which he is reasonably fitted. . . ." But these are rather rare; more frequently, they allow a stated number of years on *his* occupation and then go to "any occupation." While the unlimited "his occupation" is preferable, insisting on this type of clause narrows the field of available policies rather sharply. For this reason, we will consider as acceptable any policy which uses the "his occupation" terminology for at least *five* years. But on the importance of a "his occupation" definition for an initial period, we must stand firm. Only policies of this kind qualify for listing in our recommendations.

How Much Is Not Enough. The second feature of disability income insurance previously commented on was the *amount* of insurance in these policies. We found that the dollar amount of monthly benefit payable under a disability income policy gives only a very partial picture of the true coverage. It is essential to take into account the length of time during which these benefits will be paid in any single disability, a feature which we saw can vary from as little as 12 months to as much as 40 years or more (under policies which cover to age 65 or for life). Furthermore, there are important differences among policies as to when these benefits begin; some pay from the first day of the disabling illness or accident, others eliminate an initial period of disability which can range from one week to as much as a full year. (There are even two-year elimination periods.) These two attributes can be combined in an almost endless series of policy forms.

Before we can decide on the proper policy to buy, we must be clear on a basic principle which was touched on in a general way in the life insurance section of the book, and which is basic to *all* insurance. As in the matter of protecting against premature death, we should consider paying out premiums only to cover those risks which cannot be met out of one's own resources. And the greater the potential financial impact of a particular occurrence, the more it calls for being shifted to a risk-bearing institution like an insurance company. It is of little importance that the chances of being struck by such large-scale loss are rare; it is not the *frequency* of the risk but its *potential severity* that must be provided for. This is the principle of the "deductible" familiar to us in other forms of insurance like automobile collision where we retain or self-insure small losses and cover only those which exceed a stated sum.

There is no question that the chances of falling victim to an accident or illness that would disable one for ten years are much more remote than those of short-term illnesses of one or two weeks' duration and that one is much more likely to be away from work for short spans than for a period of years. But while the income loss from a disability of a few months or even a few weeks may be unsettling, it is in no way as catastrophic as a disabling injury or illness that incapacitates one permanently, or for years. And while less frequent, crippling illnesses do stretch on for years, as can be seen from a sampling of the claims records of a company which writes this form of disability insurance:

Nature of illness	*Length of claim (years)*
Epilepsy	26
Poliomyelitis	21
Mental Disorder	21
Bright's Disease	18
Rheumatism and Sciatica	17
Pulmonary Tuberculosis	13
Cerebral Thrombosis	11
Blindness	10
Coronary Thrombosis	9
Spondylitis	9
Cancer	7
Bronchitis & Asthma	4

Long-term disabilities incidentally are not as rare as might be expected; they are not one in a million shots, as is sometimes assumed. Thus, if the term is understood to be any disability which lasts more than six months, as used in a Social Security survey, over six million people between the ages of 18 and 64, who are *not* in institutions, consider themselves "severely disabled"; an additional 5 million said they were occupationally disabled (unable to work full-time or do the same work as before); and 6.6 million had secondary work limitations. This total of close to 18 million in the civilian noninstitutional population between 18 and 64 who are disabled to some degree for over six months is considerably higher than other estimates, but even the most conservative observers arrive at a figure of 3.5 million for the number of persons who are eligible for disability benefits under public or private insurance programs. (These figures must be seen against the fact that the age group under discussion, 18 to 64, comprises only a fraction over half of the total population of the country).*

For the reasons stated above, the first and most important risk to be insured against is the *catastrophic* rather than the more frequent small-scale loss. To this end, we must turn to policies which cover on any single disability for life, or at least to age 65.

Keeping Costs within Control. To further direct our premium dollars to the large-scale loss situations, we must opt for a policy with a relatively extended elimination period, that is, the initial period of disability which must elapse before benefits begin. Premiums for the same policy reduce sharply as the elimination period is increased. Extending the initial, noncovered period of disability under a policy will make it possible to buy larger benefits and for longer benefit periods, thereby fulfilling the proper goal of insurance—to cover the more serious exposures which would be financially shattering.

By way of illustration: Assume $500 can be allocated to the purchase of disability income insurance. For this premium, a 35-year-old male applicant can buy a guaranteed renewable and noncancellable policy providing $1,000 of monthly benefits for a maximum of 30 months in any one disability, payable from the first day on accidents and the eighth day on sicknesses. For the same premium, for a policy with the first 365 days eliminated, he can get $1,550 of monthly income (as opposed to $1,000) payable to age 65 (instead of limited to 30 months).

* The disability statistics are quoted from O. D. Dickerson, *Health Insurance,* 3rd Ed., Homewood, Ill.: Richard D. Irwin, Inc., 1968, pp. 31–33.

Clearly, the first policy could be called on to pay for any number of individual disabilities of a few weeks' or months' duration. But if the policyholder falls victim to a severely crippling illness which disables him for years, his policy would be exhausted after it had paid him for 30 months, when he is 37½ years old. He might well live on for many years, disabled, but without any further insurance protection. And it is precisely this type of loss which spells financial ruin and against which insurance is an absolute necessity.

It would be most comforting of course to be insured against *all* disabilities, short-term as well as the more protracted ones. But in almost every instance, it will quickly become evident that the cost of such all-inclusive coverage is prohibitive. A choice must therefore be made between adequate insurance against extended disability and limited protection on all losses, even those of short duration.

Trying to Outguess the Actuaries. Even if the premiums for such "complete" coverage, that is, against long-term disabilities as well as the less protracted ones, were not out of reach, buying insurance against losses which can be met without too much strain on our own resources is a contest in which the average prospect is rather unevenly matched against the actuaries. "Swapping dollars with the companies," it has been aptly called, and since a portion of the premiums collected by insurers must be consumed in salaries, commissions, profits, and other overhead expenses, the odds are heavily against us poor mortals unschooled in actuarial science. One is reminded of the definition of life insurance by the late cowboy-humorist, Will Rogers. "It's a gamble," he said. "They gamble, you'll live, you gamble, you won't." "If you want to know who's right," he continued dryly, "look at the buildings they're in!"

The next chapter will take up the matter of assessing our need for disability insurance and choosing the most effective and economical policies to cover this important exposure.

21 How Much and from Whom?

TO IMPLEMENT an insurance program covering the economic impact of disability, we must first off determine the absolute minimum monthly income we need to maintain an acceptable standard of living. As offset against this figure, we can credit ourselves with the following:

1. Income from high-grade investments which may reasonably be expected to continue on a long-range basis.

2. Other income from a business whose continuance does not depend on our active participation, or from royalties or other property.

3. Monthly benefits under a salary continuance program in effect at our place of employment. In giving weight to this element, we must of course take into account the question of permanence in our job.

4. Benefits available to us under a *group* disability income insurance plan at our place of employment. Under a majority of these plans, benefits are payable for relatively short periods. For reasons developed in the preceding chapter, we must discount income replacement plans which cover only short-term disabilities. Furthermore, in this matter, as in the case of salary continuance programs, we must assess as carefully as we can the stability of our job situation.

5. The disability benefits which we are entitled to under the Federal Social Security Act. Chapter 15 analyzed the coverage and the level of benefits for the different wage levels. *Important:* If you are covered under a group disability insurance program in connection with your employment, do not assume that both these benefits *and* the Social Security payments will be available. Many group disability programs provide that any monthly income payments to which a claimant might

otherwise be entitled will be reduced by benefits available to him under the Social Security system. It is essential to check on this point.

The difference between the income we can expect to fall heir to from *all* the above sources and the minimum we require in the event of long-term or permanent disability is the area of exposure—the gap which we must endeavor to close by insurance.

Desirable Policies. Table XVI, pages 238–41, lists policies which fulfill the objective of soundly insuring the more severe risks of disabling accident or illness, and at comparatively economical premium rates. Each of the policies is guaranteed renewable to age 65, and also noncancellable (its premium cannot be changed). Most allow for renewal after age 65 by an Insured who is gainfully employed, but at rates which can be reset by the carrier at that time. All (with the exceptions noted) define disability as the inability to engage in the policyholder's *own* occupation for at least the first five years; thereafter as the inability to engage in a gainful occupation for which he is reasonably fitted by his education, training, or experience. (In some cases, the period during which "his occupation" is covered is reduced for occupations which are more hazardous than the company's top classes.)

Rates for disability insurance, as might be expected, are based on the applicant's occupation. The rate shown below in each instance is for the company's best classification under a policy providing $1,000 of monthly income. And, it must be noted, are for males only. The disability insurance situation for females requires separate treatment, and is taken up in Chapter 22.

We must underscore the fact that the list is by no means complete and is not to be seen as ruling out other policies which meet the requirements established at a premium within the range shown. The 19 companies whose policies find their way into our list were culled from a compilation of 113 of the larger companies in this thickly populated field. (The current *Argus Chart of Health Insurance* gives financial information on 1,095 health insurers.) And there are hundreds of others too small for inclusion, as well as numerous private plans and benefit programs operated by fraternals, professional societies, and other associations which may well merit consideration. No policy needs to be ruled out per se if it incorporates the elements we have established and is offered at a rate which approximates those shown in the table. It should also be remembered that rates and coverages are in a constant state of flux, with older policies being amended or withdrawn, and new and "hotter" products streaming off the drawing boards steadily. The listing which glosses over numerous minor differences among the policies is to be taken then as a reference point and used as a bench-mark against which to measure other offerings.

Each policy is listed in order of its annual premium for a male age 35 in the best-rated occupation applying for $1,000 of monthly benefits. At other ages, and for other occupational classes, the balance may shift one way or another, but should remain essentially within the guidelines established.

Those "Cheap" Little Extras. A final word of caution is in order on the buying of any policy, whether it is one which appears on our list or one which is comparable in benefits and premium cost. More likely than not, a prospective buyer will have offered to him a number of "extras" each of which costs only a few dollars—double indemnity for accidents sustained in public conveyances, accidental death and dismemberment, hospital indemnity, partial disability, reduced elimination period if hospital confined, and so on. In this case, as in all forms of insurance, the importance of keeping one's eye "on the ball" must again be stressed.

As has been noted previously, in the hazard we are now discussing, it is the extended or permanent disability which will wipe out or gravely undermine our earning power. Whether they arise from an accident in a public conveyance, or in the bathtub, or from a crippling disease is not the issue. The few dollars for these "extras" which beckon from the wings can be better utilized to increase the amount of coverage in the basic policy payable on *any* accident or sickness.

Let's Not Eliminate the Elimination Period. Even more appealing is the sales pitch which urges reducing the 180-day elimination period being recommended. This extended period before benefits begin, it will be pointed out, will eliminate all but the most unusual conditions. The same policy with a shorter elimination period—30 days for example—

TABLE XVI. COMPANIES OFFERING DISABILITY BENEFITS

Company	States in which licensed	Policy form	Annual premium (180 days eliminated)	Comments
Bankers Life Ins. Co. Des Moines, Iowa 50307	All states including Canada	HH 400	$287.50	Renewable after 65 to 70 at adjustable premium. "His occupation" to age 55, or at least five years.
Monarch Life Ins. Co. Springfield, Mass. 01101	All states except Alaska, Hawaii, S.C.	Sd-70	302.00	Renewable after 65 to age 72 at adjustable rates.
John Hancock Mutual Life Ins. Co. Boston, Mass. 02117	All states including Canada, Puerto Rico and V.I.	P-65 Form 12-73	303.20	Renewable after 65 to age 70 at adjustable premium. Dividends beginning end of third year.
Ohio National Life Ins. Co. Cincinnati, Ohio 45206	All states except Ala., Alaska, Conn., Hawaii, La., Md., Mass., N.H., N.Y., N.C., Okla., R.I., S.C., Vt., Wis.	73-DI-1	304.00	Currently returning 5 percent of premium as "dividend" beginning with end of second year. "His occupation" for 10 years. If Insured employed in occupation other than his own, benefits will be reduced 50 percent of his earnings from that occupation.

Hartford Ins. Group Hartford, Conn. 06115	All states including Puerto Rico and Guam	7807-5	314.00	Renewable after 65 to age 72 at adjustable rates.
Mutual Life Ins. Co. New York, N.Y. 10019	All states including Puerto Rico and V.I.	HI-473	315.00	Only two years, on "his occupation." Renewable after 65 to age 75 at adjustable rates.
Great-West Life Assurance Co. Winnipeg, Canada R3C-3A5	Ariz., Calif., Colo., Conn., D.C., Fla., Ill., Ind., Iowa, Kan., Ky., Md., Mass., Mich., Minn., Mo., N.J., N.D., Ohio, Ore., Pa., S.D., Tex., Va., Wash., W. Va., Wis. and Canada	S702	$317.00	Renewable after 65 to age 70 at adjustable rates.
Prudential Ins. Co. Newark, N.J. 07101	All states including Puerto Rico, V.I., and Canada	SA-DP-72	323.00	If disabled before age 50, benefits payable for life. Only two years on "his occupation."
Connecticut General Life Ins. Co. Hartford, Conn. 06152	All states including Puerto Rico and Canada	H 1180	324.00	Renewable after 65 to age 72 at adjustable rates.
Equitable Life Assurance Society of the U.S. New York, N.Y. 10019	All states including Puerto Rico, V.I., and Canada	DI 114	329.40 (1st year premium $339.40)	

TABLE XVI. COMPANIES OFFERING DISABILITY BENEFITS (*continued*)

Company	*States in which licensed*	*Policy form*	*Annual premium (180 days eliminated)*	*Comments*
Physicians, dentists, osteopaths, and certified public accountants are offered the Professional Disability Income Policy at a lower premium—$312.10 ($322.10 the first year). Policy is similar to the one listed directly above, except that disability is defined as ''total inability'' to engage in ''his occupation'' over the entire benefit period. Furthermore, if disability commences prior to age 50, benefits are payable for life.				
Illinois Mutual Life Ins. Co. Peoria, Ill. 61634	Ala., Ariz., Calif., Fla., Ga., Ill., Ind., Iowa, Ky., Mich., Minn., Mo., Neb., Nev., N.D., Okla., Ohio, Wis., Wyo.	771	334.30	Only two years on ''his occupation.''
Northwestern Mutual Life Ins. Co. Milwaukee, Wis. 53202	All states except Alaska	KKD2	341.40	
Country Life Ins. Co. Bloomington, Ill. 61701	Illinois only	AS-501	$342.90	
Massachusetts Casualty Ins. Co. Boston, Mass. 02109	All states except Alaska, Idaho, Kan., Utah	Series 1000	352.50	Renewable after 65 for life, at adjustable premium.

Aetna Life and Casualty Co. Hartford, Conn. 06115	All states including Puerto Rico, Guam, and Canada	PXN Form 23110	376.00	Benefits payable for life, if disability commences before age 45. Ten year on "his occupation." Includes a Guaranteed Future Increase Option granting the Insured up to age 60, options to increase his coverage at stated option dates without evidence of insurability.
Loyal Protective Life Ins. Co. Boston, Mass. 02215	All states except Ariz., Ark., Colo., Ga., Hawaii, Ky., Miss., Mont., N.C., N.D., S.C., Tenn., Utah, Va., W.Va., Licensed throughout Canada	71-3	379.10	

will cost only a little more and this extra outlay will be quickly recovered in any long-term disability. Thus, the difference between the premium for a $1,000 a month policy with a 30-day elimination period and one which eliminates the first 180 days is only between $100 and $150 per year, depending on the company and the applicant's age at the time of application. It will be argued that if the Insured is disabled for six months or longer *just once,* the policy with the 30-day elimination period will pay him $1,000 for each of the second, third, fourth, and fifth months of his disability—a total of $5,000. Throughout this same period, the policy with the 180-day elimination period, by contrast, would not pay a cent. This $5,000 difference is enough to pay the additional premium on the policy with the shorter elimination period for 33 to 50 years, depending on the particular policy.

If this argument seems irresistible, it should be borne in mind that this additional annual premium (which we are taking at an average of $125) can be used to increase the monthly benefits under the 180-day elimination policy from $1,000 to about $1,350. If the Insured falls victim to an illness or accident that disables him for ten years, he will receive almost $35,000 *more* under the larger policy than under the $1,000 a month contract. In 20 years, this difference would come to some $70,000; if he were totally disabled at 35 and lived to 65, the figure rises to over $100,000, and so on. And this, you will remember, is what disability insurance is supposed to be about.

What about Disability Riders under Life Insurance Policies? As mentioned in Chapter 12, a special rider offering protection against disability is available in all life companies. The optional disability waiver of premium benefit offers protection against disability to the extent of the premium being paid for the underlying life insurance policy. A relatively small number of companies also offer an extra benefit rider which will pay a monthly cash *income* to a disabled policyholder. But few make it available under Term insurance policies.

In any event, where a desirable guaranteed renewable and noncancellable disability income policy is available, it is better to keep this insurance separate from the life insurance protection. For one thing, the amount of disability income available with the life policy is fixed as a percentage of the amount of life insurance being applied for—most usually 1 percent of the face amount, or $10.00 of monthly income for each $1,000 of underlying life insurance. This rigid relationship between the two coverages makes it difficult to respond to each of the exposures with the insurance it requires. Furthermore, the two needs do not necessarily operate in tandem as the years pass. An individual's requirement for life insurance may diminish as his dependents reach maturity but his need for disability insurance may continue unabated. For all these reasons, one is better advised to consider the disability risk separate and apart from the need for life insurance, and to take steps to insure against each of the risks in separate insurance contracts.

As indicated, the rates for the policies recommended in this chapter are for males only. The field of disability income insurance for women has only recently begun to emerge from a near-limbo to which it had been relegated for many years. The entire subject will be treated in the next chapter.

It was observed at the opening of this section on disability insurance, that most disabilities pose a double-edged economic threat. The income of the wage earner is cut off at a time when he is usually called on to meet expenditures for medical, hospital, and surgical care which are often staggering in their impact. A disability insurance program which replaces even a substantial part of the income that would be cut off during disability would still leave a wage warner open to crippling financial losses unless he had provided himself with some reasonably adequate medical reimbursement insurance covering not only himself but also all members of his family who are dependent on him. This entire question will make up the subject of the next section of the book.

22 Disability Insurance: For Women Only

UNTIL FAIRLY RECENTLY, income disability insurance for the female sex was extremely circumscribed and written on a very limited basis, if at all. The companies saw a woman's place in the employment scheme as essentially temporary—a stopover on the way to marriage and motherhood. It was also felt that women were subject to more disabilities than men, and that these were more difficult to monitor, since so much of a woman's activity was conducted within the confines of the home. For many years, then, little if any guaranteed renewable insurance was offered to women, except to the rare individual who had managed to make her way up the executive ladder and appeared irrevocably career-minded.

Even in such cases, the maximum monthly indemnity offered her was lower than what her male counterpart could obtain; benefit periods were shorter and policies often excluded diseases which were "peculiar to the female generative organs," pregnancy, and so on. And premium rates were considerably higher for equivalent benefits, as they still are today.

The Battle of the Sexes. As women entered the labor force in increasing numbers (by 1972, they comprised 38 percent of the labor force and married women made up over 60 percent of the female labor force), it became increasingly clear that the married state was not incompatible with gainful and serious employment. There was some lowering of the barriers against women in the field of guaranteed renewable disability income insurance, but the gap was still quite wide. In the main, the carriers in this field did not seem able to make a real peace with women, even when they were in the professions, continuing to view them as a bit unnatural, out of a woman's "normal" ambience, to to speak, much as Samuel Johnson had felt over 200 years ago when he said, "Sir, a woman preaching is like a dog walking on its hind legs. It is not done well, but you are surprised to find it done at all."

The creeping pace of change began to accelerate with the passage by Congress in 1963 of the Equal Pay Act, followed in the succeeding year by the Civil Rights Act, including Title VII. Finally in 1967, President Lyndon Johnson issued an Executive Order which added sex as a prohibited basis of discrimination to that of race, color, religion, and nationl origin for all federal contracts. And most recently, in 1972, Congress approved the proposed 27th Amendment to the United States Constitution—the Equal Rights Amendment.

These laws and executive orders were soon to be strengthened by the Equal Employment Opportunities Commission which issued guidelines that made it clearly illegal for an employer to discriminate between men and women. These guidelines addressed themselves to questions of sick leave, pension benefits, and other forms of group insurance including disability income programs. Still another agency, the Office of Federal Contract Compliance, set up in 1970 by the Secretary of Labor to administer and enforce the executive orders, further clarified the concept of equality of the sexes in areas of employment and benefits.

While many questions on the treatment of the sexes for insurance remain to be resolved, in most jurisdictions companies are making available to women essentially the disability income policies that they offer to men. Although the justification for a differential in rates is currently being re-examined, all companies are still charging a higher premium for the policies sold to women, believing that such practice can be substantiated by a credible body of statistics.*

*In 1974, several women filed a lawsuit against the Superintendent of Insurance in New York, requesting certain declaratory and injunctive relief to eliminate alleged sex discrimination in both the underwriting and rating of disability income insurance. In May of the following year, the Insurance Department issued a call for the available disability income experience from 26 leading companies licensed to write this coverage in New York. One of the objectives of the study, inter alia, was to determine if sex is a factor in the cost of disability insurance. The Department's questionnaire to the participating carriers yielded data encompassing over 57,000 female claims. This body of statistics was "clearly the

TABLE XVII. COMPANIES OFFERING DISABILITY INSURANCE—FEMALES

Company	*States in which licensed*	*Policy form*	*Annual premium (180 days eliminated)*	*Comments*
Bankers Life and Casualty Co. Des Moines, Iowa 50307	All states including Canada	HH400	$461.90	Renewable beyond 65, if gainfully employed, at adjusted rates.
Massachusetts Casualty Ins. Co. Boston, Mass. 02109	All states except Alaska, Idaho, Kan., Utah	Series 1000	494.10	Renewable beyond 65, if gainfully employed, at adjusted rates.
John Hancock Mutual Life Ins. Co. Boston, Mass. 02117	All states including Puerto Rico, Virgin Islands, and Canada	P-65 PH-12-73	494.40	Renewable beyond 65, to age 70, if gainfully employed, at adjusted rates.
Equitable Life Assurance Society of the U.S. New York, N.Y. 10019	All states including Puerto Rico, Virgin Islands, and Canada	DI114	522.50 (532.50 1st year)	
Physicians, dentists, osteopaths, and certified public accountants are offered a lower rate if engaged in the full-time practice of their profession.				
Illinois Mutual Life Ins. Co. Peoria, Ill. 61634	Ala., Ariz., Colo., Fla., Ga., Ill., Ind., Iowa, Kan., Mich., Minn., Mo., Neb., Nev., N.D., Okla., Ohio, Wis., Wyo.	771	534.88	Only two years on "her occupation."

Mutual Life Ins. Co. of N.Y. New York, N.Y. 10019	All states including Puerto Rico and Virgin Islands	HI473	540.00	Only two years on "her occupation." Renewable beyond 65, if gainfully employed, at adjustable rates.
Prudential Ins. Co. Newark, N.J. 07101	All states including Puerto Rico, Virgin Islands, and Canada	SA-DP-72	595.00	Benefits payable for life if disabled before age 50. Only two years on "her occupation." Renewable beyond 65, if gainfully employed, to age 72, at adjustable rates.
Monarch Life Ins. Co. Springfield, Mass. 01101	All states except Ala., Alaska, Hawaii, S.C.	SD-70	661.00	Renewable beyond 65, if gainfully employed, to age 72, at adjustable rates.

Table XVII, pages 246–47, lists disability income policies which meet all the requirements set forth for males in the preceding chapter. All are guaranteed renewable and noncancellable until at least age 65, provide benefits in any covered disability to age 65, and define disability as the inability to engage in *her own occupation* for at least the first five years before requiring inability to engage in any occupation for which the Insured is reasonably fitted by her education, training, or experience.

Policies are shown in the order of the annual premium for $1,000 of monthly benefits. As was noted in Chapter 21, setting forth rates for males, the list is not to be considered exclusive. It was culled from a standard compilation which analyzes only 113 of the larger companies in the field. Any policy which satisfies the basic requirements set forth and is within the price range indicated may be considered acceptable. Rates shown are for an applicant age 35 in the best-rated occupational classification. They will vary of course for other ages and for persons in occupations which are higher rated.

Except for the listing of the policies in this chapter, the entire discussion of disability insurance in this section beginning with Chapter 18 is to be considered applicable to the disability coverage for women.

As was mentioned previously, disability almost always produced a two-pronged loss—the income of the wage earner is cut off at the very time when onerous medical expenses pile up. Insurance against the potentially crippling impact of medical expenditures must be provided in almost every instance, and this form of insurance is discussed in the next section of the book.

---

largest and most representative set of data on non-government loss of time disability policies ever compiled." Among the many interesting findings, the study showed that women show higher claim costs than men in all age groups below the age group 60–69. This was true for accident *and* sickness insurance; in accident only insurance, the female claim rate showed more mixed results, with lower costs for the age group 20–29, but increasing with age. While there are several complicating factors in attempts to relate the experience under Social Security to that of private carriers, the report concludes that "A review of social security disability benefit experience exhibits a pattern of claim costs that is not inconsistent with those derived from commercial disability insurance experience." (All quotes and figures from the 1975 *Annual Report of the Superintendent of Insurance of New York State*).

III

MEDICAL EXPENSE INSURANCE

23 Assessing the Risk

THE OVERWHELMING majority of Americans believe that the medical care system of the country is poised on the edge of a precipice. And yet paradoxically opinion surveys suggest that while they agree there is a profound medical crisis, they don't regard it as affecting them. "Three-quarters to four-fifths of the population, depending on the survey and the questions asked, are satisfied with the care they receive and their doctors—despite misgivings about the 'system'."*

Opinion surveys, particularly on subjects as emotional as health, frequently elicit contradictory findings, depending on the "slant" of the poll. Nevertheless in this matter, I don't think there is much dispute on the existence of a broadly based consensus which is convinced that the medical care problem is "out of hand" and that only some form of massive intervention by the Government can keep the edifice from crashing down around our ears.

This Is Not Exactly New. Partisans of national health insurance are not exactly newcomers on the scene. Some form of universal health insurance or as a minimum a thoroughgoing revamping of the system of delivering health care has been advocated with varying degrees of urgency for close to 70 years. Concern about this problem has now escalated to the point where it encompasses virtually every sector of public opinion. Thus, in 1970, the usually conservative editors of *Fortune* situated American medicine "on the brink of chaos."

* Theodore R. Marmor, "Rethinking National Health Insurance," *The Public Interest*, Number 46, Winter 1977, p. 74.

What Ails American Medicine? There are profound disagreements on the nature of the illness or illnesses that plague the American medical system. And as a result, there is wide divergence on the prescription to be written for the patient, even though all are in basic agreement on the need for a solution on a national scale. The pervasiveness of public anxiety on this complex question has found expression in the national legislature where in the 94th Congress alone no less than eighteen separate bills were introduced. Each proposed its own version of national health insurance, reflecting beneath its rhetoric, in most cases, the concerns of a particular interest group—the doctors, hospitals, private insurers—or of some sector of the public—organized workers, the unorganized middle class, employers, trade unions, and so on.

Where Do We Go from Here? What will emerge out of the interplay of forces is of course impossible to forecast. The program that does evolve will probably involve a gradual "phasing in" of coverage against catastrophic medical expenses. The insurance industry may well continue to have a role in the system with the Government setting minimum standards to be met. Financial assistance in the form of tax relief, direct grants, or reduced costs will probably be provided for those in lower income brackets, the senior citizen population, and possibly children. Some form of sliding scale is likely with a larger percentage of medical expenses covered for the citizen in a lower income bracket than for his more affluent neighbor. But in one way or another, the aim will be to lift from the shoulders of any individual or family group the crushing impact of large-scale medical costs. (It has been pointed out that the United States is the only industrialized country where medical expenses threaten relatively solid citizens with bankruptcy.)

Until that happy time comes to pass, it is essential that one take steps to provide some cushion against the more serious burdens of medical services. The guidelines to be followed in charting such a course can be employed in putting insurance dollars to work most effectively not only at this time, before the enactment of any universal health insurance scheme, but in picking among the alternatives that such a government-sponsored program may permit as well.

How Much Coverage? The rise in the cost of medical care expenditures has been very dramatic in the recent period.* "Adjusted for inflation, the share of GNP for medical care has increased more than 80 percent over the past quarter century.† In 1975 alone, costs soared some 14 percent. The Government's Department of Health, Education and Welfare estimates an increase in medical costs by 1980 of an additional 40 percent.

In this light, millions of Americans have taken steps to shift some of the financial burden to a risk-bearing institution—an insurance company, prepaid health plan, health maintenance organization, or service-type hospital plan. The number of persons covered under policies designed to insure against the more serious illnesses or accidents, Major Medical Expense, as it is known, has more than doubled in the past 10 years. At the end of 1973, according to the Health Insurance Institute, close to 88 million persons were carrying some form of Major Medical Insurance. We shall see later that this designation is sometimes used rather loosely, and may cover more than the policy itself covers.

The Basic Principle Underlying Major Medical Expense Insurance. A Major Medical Expense policy is drawn to have the Insured retain some initial amount of the risk, with the insurance company picking up only after this "threshold" has been reached. To this end, these policies incorporate a "deductible," that is, a fixed amount of initial expenditures which is *not* insured. This accords with a sound principle in insurance, to wit: that one should absorb or assume as much of any loss as is feasible and insure only any excess over this retained amount. Insurance on amounts below this figure is "trading dollars with the company." Since the premiums for any form of insurance must include expenses of underwriting, commissions and other acquisition costs, taxes, claims adjustment and a profit to the carrier, this course, it has been shown, is economically unsound. And furthermore, since most of us

* It is frequently asserted that the increase in expenditures for medical care has outstripped the other seven elements that make up the Consumer Price Index. This is not exactly true, since food costs led the pack, but the medical care factor has run far ahead of the overall rise in the index— 72 percent for medical expenses to 59 percent for all other items.

† Theodore Marmor, op. cit.

have only a limited amount of dollars to spend, insuring the small losses often means foregoing protection against the jumbo loss, which is what insurance is supposed to be about, as we have seen.

Admittedly, the small loss is more likely to strike than the larger one. But it is not frequency that calls for insurance but possible severity, and it is this catastrophe which Major Medical insurance is designed to cover (or was originally conceived of as covering).

How the Major Medical policy leaves the Insured to assume a portion of the loss will be discussed in the next chapter where the various offerings in this field will be analyzed. What is necessary, however, is first to decide on some figure for medical care which can be absorbed without our annual budget. If our medical costs in any given year do not exceed this figure, we will be able to assume them along with other items in our living costs. There is no more reason to be insuring these budgetable medical expenses than to buy insurance to compensate us for our spending on food. It is only when we are struck by an unusually severe illness or accident and expenses run far ahead of what we are prepared for that we need insurance to fall back on.

With some reasonable figure for our annual outlay for medical care in mind, we can not address ourselves to putting premium dollars to work in the most effective way. This subject is discussed in the next chapter.

24 How Much and from Whom?

In the preceding chapter we saw how a special form of insurance was introduced to afford protection against the unexpected, catastrophic expenses of serious accidents and severe or protracted illnesses. Under these policies, the Insured would retain for payment by himself the ordinary medical costs which could be met out of his normal budget; the insurance would become involved only when a medical problem developed which resulted in extraordinary, "catastrophe" expenditure.

First, a stated dollar amount is set forth in the policy as a deductible. The Insured has no claim against the company for reimbursement of any medical expenditures which fall within this deductible amount. Later we will see that there are other provisions of the deductible clause which need to be taken into account before assigning proper place to this provision in any insurance against major expenses.

The Coinsurance Clause. At this point, we must understand a *second* feature of Major Medical policies which affects the amount of "self-insured" (not covered) expenses. Known as the Coinsurance Clause, it provides that even after the deductible has been satisfied, the company will pay only a stipulated percentage of covered expenses, usually 80 percent, although there are policies which employ a 75 percent coinsurance clause. These clauses limit the Company's share in any claim paid to the percentage stated. Thus, if a policy contains a $500 deductible and an 80 percent coinsurance clause, it will pay nothing on the first $500 expended by the Insured, and then 80 percent of any sums above this deductible. Under a clause of this kind, it can be seen, the Insured may still be called on to expend a sizable sum in the event of a serious or chronic illness. Thus assume his total medical, hospital, and surgical expenses in a particular condition come to $35,000, a far from unusual situation in today's medical world. Under a policy of the kind we are now discussing, settlement would be made as follows: The Insured would bear the first $500 of covered expenses, the amount of the deductible; of the remaining $34,500, the policyholder would be paid 80 percent, or $27,600. The Insured's out-of-pocket costs would be $7,400. In a $50,000 loss, an Insured's share would come to $9,900. To protect against such heavy expenditures, Major Medical coinsurance clauses usually cut out after the Insured has paid a certain amount of the loss. A typical policy provision stipulates that the company will pay 80 percent of the first $5,000 of covered expenses in excess of the deductible, and *100* percent of any amounts above this figure. Some policies cut out after $2,000; others provide that the company will pay 80 percent of the first $2,000, 90 percent of the next $3,000, and 100 percent of any excess. There are various permutations of the cut-off amounts, but the basic principle remains the same. The policy establishes a maximum contribution that can be required of the policyholder in any one medical situation, after which the Company pays all. A ceiling on the amount of expenses which an Insured has to meet is thereby established.

The Same—But Different. Both the deductible and the coinsurance clauses need to be taken into account in arriving at the amount of self-retained expenses under a particular policy. One other, frequently overlooked aspect of the deductible needs to be attended to—the period of time during which the deductible must be accumulated, or "satisfied." All policies contain some dollar deductible but they can differ very fundamentally on the period during which these expenses must be incurred. Two policies may each contain a $500 deductible, but the first provide that the deductible expenses be incurred during a 90-day period while the second extends the accumulation period to a full year. Although the dollar amount of the deductible is the same in both policies, the effect of the clause can prove to be quite dissimilar. For under the first clause, with the 90-day accumulation feature, a policyholder could pay out as much as $166 every month without ever "satisfying" the deductible. A situation of this kind may not be common, but could arise for an individual who is under treatment for a chronic condition which requires continuous therapy outside of a hospital. The policyholder under the second contract with a full year accumulation period would have some $1,500 of covered expenses in a similar situation.

The longer accumulation period affords broader coverage, it is obvious. But the policy with the shorter accumulation period need not necessarily be avoided on this score. It is important, however, to understand the application of this frequently overlooked aspect of the deductible clause. For only then can one correctly project the maximum amount of noninsured expenses that can accrue under a particular policy in a given period of time.

Watch Out for the Sleepers. Major Medical insurance first appeared to meet the problem of burdensome medical expenses, *regardless of their nature*. A maximum limit was written into the policy, either for any single claim or for all claims payable during the lifetime of the Insured. But if this figure were high enough, there was every reason to expect that any medical expenses that developed could be met without too much concern. As the cost of medical services and particularly hospital charges began to spiral, the companies found themselves facing what appeared to be an open-ended liability. Built-in limits on certain classes of medical charges began to be incorporated. Thus, most Major Medical policies written today provide that the maximum covered charge for room and board in a hospital be limited to that hospital's charge for *semi*-private accommodations. Even under a clause of this type, an insurance company is locked into any increase the hospital may make in its daily rates. Many companies go even further and limit the covered charge for hospital accommodation to a flat dollar amount—$50, $100, or $150. Some carriers offer the policyholder a choice of several flat dollar figures, with $150 per day the usual maximum.

Horse-and-Buggy Policies. Many policies are still being renewed from earlier days with even lower daily limits on hospital care, like $30. With the charge for semi-private hospital accomodations in many large cities topping $200, a policy with a $30 daily limit has reversed the roles of company and Insured. The company is assuming the minor portion of the hospital expenses; the Insured has taken over the major one.

There are other "inside limits" which are commonly found in Major Medical policies. Virtually every policy places a limit on treatment for mental and nervous disorders treated outside of a hospital. Another frequently encountered "inside limit" is a surgery schedule enumerating the various procedures to which flesh is heir and stipulating the maximum payable for each procedure. Any policy being considered or being maintained must be checked for its coverage as to these or other "inside limits." For only then can one have a clear picture of the contract's coverage, and the amount being retained as "self-covered" expenses of a potential medical bill.

Even more serious than the inadequate "inside limits" which may still be found in many old policies are the original maximums, or top limits, in these policies. $25,000 seemed only a few years ago to promise security against virtually all medical conditions which one could expect to encounter in the foreseeable future. The steep inflation of medical expenses plus the spread of new forms of surgery like open heart procedures, kidney dialysis, sophisticated life-sustaining machinery, advanced cancer treatments, and the like have rendered such limits dangerously inadequate.

Everybody's Doing It. As the price of medical, surgical, and hospital care continues to zoom upward, with no apparent end in sight, practically everyone with the possible exception of the very wealthy has reason for genuine concern. And virtually every American has taken steps to try and transfer some of the burden to a risk-bearing institution or prepaid health or hospital plan. By the end of 1974, over 171 million persons had some form of hospital expense insurance (according to the Institute of Health Insurance). This figure accounts for 9 out of 10 persons in the under 65 age group plus about half of the over-65 population who carry insurance to supplement their coverage under Medicare. There is some duplication in these figures due to some persons being covered under more than one plan, but even if this factor is discounted, it is clear that almost everyone above the poverty level is covered against hospital expenses to some extent.

Additionally, since hospital policies may still leave sizable amounts of medical expenses uncovered, over 91 million persons have covered themselves under some form of Major Medical insurance. There is no way to ascertain the extent of the coverage under these medical policies, since as was mentioned earlier the term "Major Medical" is applied rather loosely to a variety of policies. But there is no question that millions of people are covered under both a hospital policy and some form of Major Medical insurance. Many carriers, particularly in the group field, will write Major Medical only when there is an underlying Blue Cross policy in force ("over the Blues," as it is called). In such cases, the Major Medical policy is written with a "corridor deductible," for example, $100. This is a no-man's land, so to speak, the amount which is payable under neither of the two coverages.

Are You Overdoing It? An individual carrying both policies along the lines discussed above is covered against virtually all medical expenses (subject to a few states exclusions and the "inside limits") except for the truly catastrophic which exceed the maximum in his Major Medical coverage. The maximum that he can be called on to pay out during the year (if the deductible allows him a one-year accumulation period) is $100 plus the percentage of contribution he is required to make under his Major Medical policy, by virtue of the coinsurance clause, provided his total bill mercifully stays within the policy maximum.

To illustrate, assume an individual or family is covered under two policies—a standard Blue Cross policy and a Major Medical. His obligation to the hospital is picked up by Blue Cross, subject to its provisions. Excess costs incurred by him in the hospital or out are covered under the Major Medical. After he has absorbed $100 of these expenses (the amount of the deductible), the policy covers 80 percent of the first $2,000, and 100 percent thereafter. Except for the expenditures which are specifically excluded or limited, like private room charges in excess of the semi-private room rate, the maximum that he may be called on to shell out of pocket will be $100 (the deductible) plus 20 percent of the first $2,000, above the deductible, or $400—a total of $500.

With this one important proviso in mind, and an important one it may prove to be, this is fairly comprehensive coverage. Does it perhaps cover more than is necessary at least of the lower dollar cost? Should one assume a larger portion of these anticipated medical expenses? If so, what economies in premium outlay can be realized? The following hypothetical case is cited to give one some frame of reference.

Assume a family unit in New York City consisting of a father, age 35, a mother, age 32, and two children. A comprehensive health insurance policy covering basic hospital and Major Medical costs with a $100 deductible will develop a premium of approximately $1,200 a year. A Major Medical policy with a $1,000 deductible will run a little over $250. With a $10,000 deductible, the annual cost is reduced to about $70, and so on. Annual savings of this size can add up over the years, it can be seen.

Your Own Situation Must Control. Naturally, your own economic situation will dictate the proper balance to be struck between the insured and *un*insured. What needs to be stressed here, as it has been before, is that the risk which demands insurance is the one which an individual cannot meet out of his own resources without strain. "Trading dollars with the company" on smaller, less serious losses is a losing game, since only a portion of the premiums paid over to insurance companies can come back in the form of claims, if the companies are to stay in business.

This question is of more than academic interest, at least to those of us who do not have unlimited sums to spend in insurance premiums. (Those with unlimited resources do not generally need any insurance.) Trying to carry insurance on *all* potential losses, large and small, being "fully covered," may give one a psychological sense of security, but it usually entails cutting down somewhere. And if it involves reducing the amount of protection carried on the top limits of exposure, it does violence to the basic function of insurance—protection against the catastrophic.

If a Choice Has to Be Made. Hospital expenses can be very onerous, and it is understandable that most persons will seek some coverage against these costs. Hospitalization insurance has become so widespread, we saw at the opening of this chapter, that almost everyone is covered in one way or another. By contrast, only about half as many persons carry any Major Medical insurance. Now if one must make a choice between a hospital expense policy alone and Major Medical insurance, the latter merits serious consideration as the one to carry, if such can be properly drawn to cover all medical expenses above an amount which has been accepted as within the range of tolerance. Or as a minimum, where only a hospital policy is being carried, immediate steps should be taken to purchase some Major Medical expense policy, even if with a very high deductible to keep the premium costs down.

The Harsh Reality. The preceding advice is unfortunately of limited utility for those who come into the market for Major Medical insurance on an *individual* (nongroup) basis. This is due to the paucity of adequate Major Medical insurance for individuals. Of the health insurers listed in a widely used compendium on health insurance, 26 offer a policy which can be termed Major Medical in any sense of the word. Only two provide an amount of coverage which is viable in the face of today's medical costs and one of these two incorporates an "inside limit" which can prove unsatisfactory if hospital costs continue to mount, as they are likely to do. More of this later, after a word about group policies which account for some 90 percent of all persons covered by Major Medical policies and where truly adequate coverage may be available.

Safety in Numbers. As stated, the phenomenal spread in Major Medical insurance has occurred primarily in the group field. The coverage under these policies is almost always much broader than what the same companies offer to individual purchasers. Since much of these group policies are "tailor-made," it is difficult to generalize on the protection they afford.

As a guide to minimum standards to be looked for in group policies that may be available to one on his job, professional association, or other organization, and to a policy one may now be carrying as well as to new coverages that may soon emerge in answer to governmental action, we are setting down the basic elements that should be looked for in any policy which promises security against the catastrophic, and thereby deserves the name of Major Medical.

The Nitty Gritty. 1. Ideally, the policy should set no maximum on the amount it will pay out, either on any individual claim, or during the policyholder's lifetime. Some group policies are now being written in this way. Only one carrier offers such insurance to individuals, as will be shown later. In the real world, compromise is inevitable, and one may have to settle for something less than the ideal. Any policy that will pay not less than $40,000 on any single claim, or at least $100,000 throughout the lifetime of its Insured might be considered acceptable, at least as most medical costs shape up today, and in face of the circumscribed products available in the commercial carriers.

2. There should be no dollar limitation on reimbursement for hospital room and board, other than a restriction to the cost of the hospital's semi-private room charge.

3. Preferably, the policy should be free of any limitation on surgeons' fees other than a provision that covered expenses will not exceed the usual charges made for comparable surgery in the locality where the operation is performed.

4. The coinsurance clause should cut out after a stated amount of medical expenses has been incurred. Without such cut out, the Insured's liability for expenses, though limited to a percentage, can still prove crippling. At what point the cut out should come into play will depend on the individual's financial picture.

These four conditions should be checked into very carefully, and wherever possible should be part of any coverage.

The Bottom Line. In addition, it is advisable to check the policy's language on "pre-existing conditions." Individually issued (nongroup) policies will not cover medical expenses incurred for conditions which exist when the policy is applied for. However, many will provide that such conditions will come within the coverage after the Insured goes without treatment for a stated period, usually 90 days, and in all events, after the policy has been in force for one year. A provision of this kind can avoid considerable hassles, and is much to be desired.

Where group insurance is available, it will almost always be most advantageous to one seeking Major Medical insurance. Coverage is usually broader, and costs are lower. In employer-employee groups, part or all of the premium is usually assumed by the employer, and the coverage thereby made even more attractive. One is well-advised, however, to check that the group policy does in fact meet the minimum criteria which have been indicated before concluding that no further steps need be taken to supplement the group coverage.

With respect to cost, meaningful cost comparisons are all but impossible under group policies whose rates depend on the composition of the group as well as under individual contracts which differ from one another in so many ways. In either instance, going-in costs mean very little. The premium quoted when the policy is purchased tells very little about its costs in later years, for the company reserves the right to modify the premium on any anniversary. Below we list several Major Medical policies offered by several of the larger carriers to individuals and families. The meager list is not to be considered as preempting the field in any way, and consideration should be given to any policy which meets the requirements already established. Merely as a frame of reference, we show alongside each of the policies, the annual premium for a family of four consisting of a father age 35, a mother age 32, and two children, stressing again that the premiums shown are only the going-in rates.

Cost comparisons in the field of medical insurance are beset by difficulties even larger than in life insurance or disability income protection. For here one must choose from basically different approaches to the problem—individual insurance, group plans, prepaid expense coverage like Blue Cross and Blue Shield, plans offering all-inclusive medical services such as are operated by industries, trade unions, or by doctors in group practice, health maintenance organizations, and so on. Further complexity is introduced by the different rating techniques used in the field. Thus, some carriers structure their rate schedule to increase automatically in five-year age brackets; others base the annual premium on the age of the Insured when he is first insured; in some, the rate increases automatically with the Insured's attained age. Some carriers impose a flat charge for children, regardless of their number, while others impose a premium for each youngster.

The discount range for the various deductibles varies from company to company, as well as the amount of the deductible, and the period allowed for its accumulation. Contracts also differ in their application of the coinsurance clause, the length of the benefit period, and so on. Many companies limit the total deductibles that will apply if two or more family members have claims within the same year.

There are also significant differences in the maximums payable under policies both as to their dollar amount, and as to their application. One policy's maximum applies to all claims made by the Insured during his lifetime; a second relates to each separate illness or accident for which the policyholder makes a claim.

Some Individual Policies—The Best That Are Around. Only one Major Medical policy sold to individuals has come to our attention which satisfies all the basic requirements of this form of insurance. The nation's largest insurer, the Prudential, which is licensed in all states, the District of Columbia, and Canada, offers a policy with an *unlimited* maximum benefit. Except for the limitation on expenses for the treatment of mental illness and functional nervous disorders, the policy pays 80 percent of virtually all medical expenses after its $100 deductible has been satisfied, in a 12-month period. Covered expenses for hospital accommodations are limited to those made by the hospital for semi-private room, but there are no maximums on surgeons' fees, or related expenses like anesthetics (which many policies limit).

For the most part, this policy will render it unnecessary to maintain a separate hospital policy. The company actually offers another version of the contract for a higher premium which pays the first $5,000 of hospital costs without deductible and without coinsurance.

Rates vary with the territory in which the Insured lives. Thus, in Illinois, as an example, the premium for the prototype family described would range from $650 in the lowest rated area to over $900 in the highest. In terms of cost, the policy should prove especially attractive at younger ages when compared with Blue Cross and a separate Major Medical Policy. Before going on to other policies in the field, we would reiterate the fact that the premiums quoted above are current; there is little reason to doubt that they will be increased every year as the costs of medical attention continue to mount.

Next in line with a high, if not unlimited maximum, is the Multi-

Medical policy offered by the Lumbermen's Mutual Casualty Company of Long Grove, Illinois 60049, which is licensed in all states, the District of Columbia, and Canada. The policy will pay up to $250,000 in any one covered injury or sickness. A choice of deductibles is offered—ranging from$1,000 to $25,000 and of the maximum daily hospital benefit, beginning with $50 per day. The maximum is $150 per day, which as we pointed out previously can prove to be a serious defect if hospital costs continue their present upward trend.

The annual premium for the policy varies with the domicile of the Insured. For our model family, in New York City, the annual premium with $1,000 deductible and $150 maximum daily hospital benefit comes to $478.01; in the balance of the state, the annual premium is $382.46. These premiums are constructed on a step-rate basis; they increase automatically as the Insured's age reaches the next five-year age bracket. In addition, the company reserves the right to revise all rates for the entire class of Insureds.

Another policy which offers a $250,000 maximum is issued by the Woodmen Accident and Life Company, Lincoln, Neb. 68508. This company is licensed in Ark., Ariz., Calif., Colo., Hawaii, Idaho, Ill., Ind., Iowa, Kan., Ky., Mich., Minn., Mo., Mont., Neb., Nev., N. Mex., N.D., Ohio, Okla., Ore., S.D., Tex., Utah, Wash., W. Va., Wis., Wyo. The maximum daily hospital room benefit is $90.00.

Beneficial National Insurance Company, 2 Park Ave., New York, N.Y. 10016, is licensed in all states and the District of Columbia. The company offers a Major Medical policy which will pay up to $100,000 for each covered accident or illness. The policy is rife with "inside limits"—a surgery schedule, a limit on private nursing care, on doctors' visits, and so on. The daily hospital rate maximum available is $200 per day; the maximum surgery schedule is $5,000, but this is available only in a $2,500 deductible policy. At present levels, these last limitations would not loom too significant but there is no protection against increases in these costs such as are more than likely to develop.

For our hypothetical family of four, this policy with a $2,500 deductible, a $5,000 surgery schedule, and a $200 maximum daily hospital benefit will develop a going-in rate of $301.52, which rises as the Insured attains the next higher five-year bracket.

Connecticut General Life Ins. Co., Hartford, Conn. 06152 is licensed in all states, the District of Columbia, and Puerto Rico. Policy Form H-2200 will pay up to $100,000 for each covered accident or illness. Policy contains several circumscribing "inside limits" which vary with the amount of the deductible—the higher the deductible, the higher the amounts for these two benefits. Under a policy with a $1,500 deductible, a room and board rate of $115 and surgical maximum of $2,100 are available. These are the highest offered, and even by today's standards are quite low.

Country Life Insurance Co., Bloomington, Ill. 61701 is licensed only in Illinois. The policy maximum is $50,000 on any one accident or sickness. A deductible of $1,000 to $2,000 is offered. With the higher deductible, the daily hospital rate is $60.

Educators Mutual Life Ins. Co., Lancaster, Pa. 17604 is licensed in Ala., Conn., Del., Fla., Ga., Ky., Md., Mich., N.J., N.C., Ohio, Pa., S.C., Tenn., Va., W.Va., and the District of Columbia. The policy contains a $50,000 maximum benefit; top limit available on room and board is $100 per day.

Appendix

IN CHAPTER 2 Table II was set forth which compared a $25,000 Whole Life policy purchased by a male age 40 with an equivalent estate created by purchasing Term insurance and accumulating the annual savings in premiums at 6 percent. It was pointed out that the separate savings fund would be subject to income tax where the cash value of the Whole Life policy was free of such impost. To reflect the effect of such taxation on the results, we have set down below a similar combination Term and separate savings program, accumulated by an individual in a 33 percent tax bracket. The 6 percent interest would be reduced to 4 percent net after taxes, and this his lower interest rate is used in the table.

TERM INSURANCE AND SEPARATE SAVINGS FUND ACCUMULATED AT 4 PERCENT

Year	*B/F fund*	*Prem rate*	*Amt of insurance*	*Premium*	*Premium savings*	*Savings fund*	*Total estate*
1	0.00	4.99	24,666.34	138.09	333.66	333.66	25,000.00
2	333.66	4.99	24,317.58	136.34	335.41	682.42	25,000.00
3	682.42	4.99	23,953.06	134.53	337.22	1,046.94	25,000.00
4	1,046.94	4.99	23,572.06	132.62	339.13	1,427.94	25,000.00
5	1,427.94	4.99	23,173.83	130.64	341.11	1,826.17	25,000.00
6	1,826.17	7.33	22,811.24	182.21	289.54	2,188.76	25,000.00
7	2,188.76	7.33	22,431.36	179.42	292.33	2,568.64	25,000.00
8	2,568.64	7.33	22,033.37	176.50	295.25	2,966.63	25,000.00
9	2,966.63	7.33	21,616.40	173.45	298.30	3,383.60	25,000.00
10	3,383.60	7.33	21,179.55	170.25	301.50	3,820.45	25,000.00
11	3,820.45	11.52	20,809.71	254.73	217.02	4,190.29	25,000.00
12	4,190.29	11.52	20,420.60	250.25	221.50	4,579.40	25,000.00
13	4,579.40	11.52	20,011.20	245.53	226.22	4,988.80	25,000.00
14	4,988.80	11.52	19,580.47	240.57	231.18	5,419.53	25,000.00
15	5,419.53	11.52	19,127.28	235.35	236.40	5,872.72	25,000.00

TERM INSURANCE AND SEPARATE SAVINGS FUND ACCUMULATED AT 4 PERCENT (*continued*)

Year	*B/F fund*	*Prem rate*	*Amt of insurance*	*Premium*	*Premium savings*	*Savings fund*	*Total estate*
16	5,872.72	19.90	18,809.94	389.32	82.43	6,190.06	25,000.00
17	6,190.06	19.90	18,473.20	382.62	89.13	6,526.80	25,000.00
18	6,526.80	19.90	18,115.89	375.51	96.24	6,884.11	25,000.00
19	6,884.11	19.90	17,736.74	367.96	103.79	7,263.26	25,000.00
20	7,263.26	19.90	17,334.41	359.95	111.80	7,665.59	25,000.00
21	7,972.21						

The formula for developing the figures for an interest rate is as follows:

$$X_n = \frac{C - P + 15 - (1 + r)\, I_{n-1}}{1 - p_n}$$

where:

$C = \$25{,}000$
$P = \$471.75$
r = rate of interest
I = fund at beginning of year

Index